# God in the Midst of the Events
# that Shook Quebec

## Autobiography of Ernest Keefe

# God in the Midst of the Events that Shook Quebec

## Autobiography of Ernest Keefe

By Ernest Keefe

**Éditions SEMBEQ** / Collection « Notre histoire »
9780, rue Sherbrooke Est, Montréal, QC  H1L 6N6
editions@sembeq.qc.ca

**God in the Midst of the Events
that Shook Quebec**

Thanks to contributors
Betty, my beloved wife who did a great amount
of work when she was still with us

**Editing**
Julien Laramée
Allan and Mary Macleod

**Revision**
Mrs. Margaret Hodgson
Doug Porter
Matthew Civico

**Translation**
Marianne Petit-Clerc

**Typing**
Marianne Bouliane
Emily Cotnoir
Corey Ann D'Aoust
Lucie Lapointe
Francine Paquet

**Cover design and layout**
Aristide Therrien / AGS SEMBEQ

ISBN 978-2-923614-39-7

Legal deposit - Bibliothèque nationale du Québec, 2017
Legal deposit - Bibliothèque nationale du Canada, 2017

© Published in november 2017 by :

**Éditions SEMBEQ** / Collection « Notre histoire »
9780 rue Sherbrooke Est, Montréal QC CANADA H1L 6N6

Printed in Quebec

Ernest Keefe & Betty Keefe
In memoriam

# FOREWORD

Ernest Keefe was a pioneer, as was my father. The two men planted Churches in the same year, in 1956: my father in Verdun and Mr. Keefe in Danville-Asbestos.

I had the privilege of having Ernest Keefe as my pastor at Église Baptiste Évangélique Centrale on St.Urbain Street in Montréal. He was a good shepherd. He would preach expositional messages, meaty and compassionate. Often, I saw him tearing up when talking about the salvation of Québécois! In order to better reach them, he led a Church move out of an ethnic neighborhood of central Montréal to the more French Canadian district of Rosemont.

It was in the seventies. We were in Revival! God was graciously visiting Quebec. There were many, many conversions, especially among students! Our Seminary, SEMBEQ, was just starting up and I took the first programmed course on Inductive Bible Study based on the Gospel of Marc. Mr. Keefe (I never could bring myself to call him Ernie) was the tutor. He was an excellent pedagogue with a keen sense of exegesis and theology. He gave me a craving to do serious study in the Word of God.

My wife Sharon and I heard God calling us into pastoral ministry. In 1974, we left for four years of Bible training in France. After our first year at the Faculté in Vaux-sur-Seine, we returned to Quebec to participate in a student outreach with Mr. Keefe going door-to-door. He was a super-evangelist. We joked that he had a rubber shoe to keep front doors open as he shared the Gospel. What a model of perseverance and devotion to win souls he was!

When we finished our studies, we returned to Quebec in 1978 thinking we would take a small Church such as the one in Verdun. But Mr. Keefe, his Council and the Church invited us to serve in the mother Church. He became my coach for a year then he left the ministry in my hands and went to do graduate study at Grand Rapids in Michigan. He was a good coach and entrusted me with the youth pastorate then lead pastorate. I learned valuable lessons in member care, Church organization and especially the faithful and persistent passion for the visiting program on Tuesday evenings.

This book will be useful for a complete bird's eye view of more than a half century of God's work among the Québécois. It is well woven like a three stranded cord. The first strand is historical. Ernie Keefe has done a monumental amount of research! He recounts with drama and detail and pithy personal illustrations the beginnings of the Fellowship Baptist Churches in Francophone Canada on the backdrop of the Duplessis era and the Quiet Revolution, then the Revival of the Seventies and into the Church planting efforts in all the main parts of the Province. It is a must read record of God's hand in Quebec. Second strand: apologetics. Mr. Keefe painstakingly explains the Biblical rationale for the Evangelical Baptist position when facing a great number of Roman Catholic practices and beliefs. And the third strand is autobiographical. We learn, with insightful personal and family stories how the author hung up his skates, leaving his passion to enter the major hockey leagues, how he was converted, transferring his confidence fully in Christ's finished work, how he met Betty and their journey not to Africa, but to Quebec Church planting. We see God truly using the Keefes, and others to transform cities and indeed a society.

Now I'm seventy. But I'm still following the example of my mentor. He was the untiring servant of God in Asbestos, Trois-Rivières, Rosemont, Repentigny, Vaudreuil, Longueuil and many other Churches instilling a stable direction and a vision to extend the Kingdom of God in Quebec. By the grace of God, Sharon and I served in the pastorate at Rosemont for 35 years, then three years launching the Church in Saint-Léonard and now helping with Evangelism in Rivière-des-Prairies while making new disciples for Christ in Ville d'Anjou. The example of Ernie and Betty Keefe is worthy to be followed. This book is an inspiration for me and for a whole new generation of workers, evangelists, pastors and Church planters who will serve the Great Shepherd in this province which is still an immense mission field!

*René Frey Pastor, Evangelist*

# Contents

Foreword ................................................................. 7

Introduction .......................................................... 11

Chapter 1
Hockey or Missions ............................................. 13

Chapter 2
God Calls His Team For Quebec .......................... 55

Chapter 3
Asbestos on Fire .................................................. 87

Chapter 4
The Catholic Church Goes on the Defensive at Asbestos ..... 129

Chapter 5
The Church under Attack from Within .................. 147

Chapter 6
School Daze for French Protestants ..................... 179

Chapter 7
Name Calling And The Results ............................. 229

Chapter 8
The Quiet Revolution – 1960 to 1970 ................... 277

Conclusion ......................................................... 319

Appendix A ........................................................ 323

Appendix B ........................................................ 325

Appendix C ........................................................ 331

# INTRODUCTION

In 1955, Wilson Ewin and I were returning from a trip to New Brunswick, pulling a trailer that Wilson had lent to missionaries, and we drew over to the side of the road to let the motor cool down. There was a lookout there on the highway about five miles from the city of Asbestos, from which I could see the city, with the open pit mine and the piles of rock beside it. It was a good-sized town with a population of about fifteen thousand, along with the neighboring town of Danville. We had driven five hundred kilometers in Quebec without seeing a single evangelical church, and here would be a good place to start one, halfway between Victoriaville and Sherbrooke. Right there I had the impression that this was where God wanted me to go. Shortly after, we started to work in Asbestos.

Our presence in Quebec was like David facing Goliath. A handful of missionaries were facing the giant. Opposition took many forms. The Asbestos newspaper once wrote that if a woman received a door-to-door visitation from the Baptist pastor, she should run into the street and call the police. As we shared the gospel message and teachings of the Bible, priests saw their parishioners' faith being shaken. People noticed that the Protestants lived the Christian life in a different way. Pastors could get married, each and every one could read the Bible for himself, and they understood they could have the assurance of eternal life. For three hundred years, the people of Quebec were denied the reading of the Bible. Our goal was to start a church and then let Quebeckers assume the leadership.

It was hard to start a day of visitation. It was like breaking the ice. Once I broke the ice and made a first visit, I was all right for the day. I even sometimes was late getting home for supper, talking to people about the Bible. But the next day, I noticed the ice had frozen again. I still had to break it. I had bought a nice black coat, a hat that businessmen wore in those days, and a nice leather briefcase. This helped me to be well received in homes. I didn't think I was important, but in a sense I really was, because I was bringing a wonderful message that could change lives.

What happened was a movement from God and from the Holy Spirit in the hearts of people. As a young English-speaking pastor, having studied French for only one year, I did not have much influence. But I realized that in Asbestos people were eagerly expecting my visit, curious to know what I had to say. Some people started to believe. As the new believers began sharing their faith, the city of Asbestos became on fire. Some people said it turned upside down. It was mostly the testimony of these new believers in their surroundings that made the impact.

That is how sixty years of trials and triumphs began, serving God and sharing the gospel in the province of Quebec. This book will tell of wonderful adventures in the midst of deep social changes that would transform a society forever.

# Chapter 1

# *Hockey or Missions*

## Early Influences

It was the pre-television era and I, at a very young age, joined my dad, and sometimes my elder brothers, around the mantel radio to hear the play-by-play commentary of a Toronto Maple Leafs hockey game. It was when Foster Hewitt called the games, and colorful King Clancy entertained the fans with his play on the blue line. I was the youngest child by nine years in a family of seven children so I heard a lot of adult conversation. One evening, when I was four years old, during an exciting game, I jumped out of my chair (so they tell me) and endeavored to imitate Foster Hewitt as best I could while shouting, "King George comes down the ice; he jumps the fence; he shoots; he scores!" The facts were greatly distorted, but enthusiasm was not lacking.

That interest for hockey was nurtured as I grew up. The Birch Street Public School in Timmins, Ontario, was built just beyond a small field next to our house. The former school had been situated nine blocks from my home, and I would not have been able to participate in sports there as a "seven-year-old" child. With the new school next door, I never missed an opportunity to be involved in sports. Over 90% of our sports activities were arranged by those involved, and we would play for hours, not the few minutes that kids get today for a practice or a game. There were interschool

*Around 1945, Timmins. Birch Street Public School in background*

competitions that took place after classes, and I had the privilege of playing hockey, softball, and soccer on the Birch Street Public School teams.

As kids living in Timmins, we had the advantage of a long winter and each school had an outdoor rink that was ready for use before the Christmas break. Snow removal was the players' responsibility, but every day we would be there, and it was worth the effort in spite of the cold temperature just to spend the entire day playing pick-up hockey. Even in interschool hockey, it would have taken an extreme temperature before a game would be cancelled. Sometimes it became necessary to warm our feet in the school between periods.

At that time, the Porcupine district, including Timmins, always had many players in the OHA Junior A Major Hockey League, the professional teams, and even the NHL. I was privileged to grow up in Timmins and live next door to a school and have male teachers who on their own time would coach us. It was also my privilege to play at a time when hockey was a game of skill and sportsmanship. We would play for hours without ever thinking of fighting. One of our greatest joys was to stick handle through the opposition and score a goal. Even in the NHL, when spectators were on their feet it was because of the rink-long rushes, or a beautiful passing play, or skillful stick handling.

Today, often when the fans stand on their feet it is because there is a fight in progress on the ice. It is too bad that our own national sport and likely the event where parents take their children more than other in Canada has to be marred by things we do not allow on our streets or neighborhoods and bars owners do not allow in their bars. Fortunately, more and more fans today like to see good players demonstrate their skills in stick handling, skating, and scoring. When my dad took me to a game, it was hockey we enjoyed, not the spectacle that resembled a barroom brawl. I was indeed blessed to have played in the 1940's.

As for my mother, she was raised in Liverpool, England. Her mother allowed her to go to a youth group of a Methodist church where she heard the gospel and God opened her eyes to see that salvation came by repentance and faith in Jesus Christ. Years later, I too, believed, but much transpired in my life before that became a reality.

My mother grew up in an age when evangelical churches were legalistic, even restricting activities on Sundays, but she was tempered by compassion. For instance, Christians just did not swim on Sunday. But one very hot Sunday morning when I was about twelve years of age, while walking home from church my mother said, "You know, Ernie, we do not usually swim on Sunday, but today is so hot I think it would cool you down if you had a swim." As for hockey, in winter, I could not take my skates out on Sundays but she did allow me to play road hockey. Nevertheless, every Saturday I was on our school rink immediately following breakfast. When I came home at noon hour, my mother would put newspapers on the floor so I did not have to take my skates off. Immediately after dinner, I would return to the rink to play until darkness set in. After supper, I would settle down by the radio with a hot chocolate and a hot roll, fresh from the oven, waiting to hear the magical words from the unmistakable voice of Foster Hewitt, "It's hockey night in Canada." I remember the Imperial Oil commercials with the soft-spoken Esso station operator. In my young mind, I thought, when I grew up I would always buy Esso gas!

**Juvenile Hockey**

Hockey for children and teenagers was not arranged as it is today with many age levels and competitive divisions. When I was young, we played on a public school team up to grade eight and on a house league during the high school, if there was a teacher available to do the organization. Beyond that, there was Juvenile A Hockey, Junior B and Major Junior A. Sports writer Bill Boyd, in his book *Hockey Towns*, explains, "That was when juvenile hockey, with its age limit to eighteen, and not midget, was the stepping stone to Major Junior hockey."[1]

A player with aspirations of playing Major Junior hockey would try to break into Juvenile A Hockey when he was fifteen. I had turned fifteen that spring and was already playing Junior baseball (in the under-20 category) and wanted to break into Juvenile A hockey. My hockey equipment was laid out, my skates sharpened, and I was waiting for the try-out camps for Juvenile A. My heart sank when I learned that these were to be held Sunday mornings. At that time, Sunday hockey was non-existent, even in the Major Junior A league. With six teams in the Porcupine area, including four from Timmins alone (population over 40,000, with only two indoor arenas), there was just not enough ice available in the early fall to avoid Sunday morning try-outs. I entertained the thought that God would understand my predicament and would let me play but I was not at all sure about my mother's reaction. I was expected to be at Sunday School and church Sunday morning. In fact, I was not even supposed to take out my skates on Sundays.

As for try-outs for hockey, when I was fifteen she said:

I know there are hockey try-outs Sunday at church time. Your dad does not attend church, and I cannot follow you to see what a fifteen-year-old boy is doing, so I will leave the decision to you. There is one thing, however, that I want you to remember, and that is, if you put something ahead of the Lord, he can take it away from you.

The Holy Spirit etched those words of wisdom on my heart, even if they would only be recalled at a much later date. I went to the try-out, and earned a place on the Timmins Canadiens centering the third line between the Donovan brothers.

An unexpected event took place during the Christmas holidays. There were not enough players to have a regular practice; even the backup goalie was absent. In order to have a scrimmage, I volunteered to put on the goalie pads. At the end of the practice, Coach Arundel said to me, "I want you to play goal the next game."

I protested, stating that I had never played goal except with a tennis ball in street hockey. Coach Arundel retorted, "If you want to dress for the next game, you will have to put on the goalie equipment." Well, I thought, I am the youngest player on the team, and playing goal at this level is better than playing forward in a high school house league, so I put on the goalie pads!

It was with trepidation that I skated out on the ice for my first game ever as a goalie. To the surprise of everyone, and especially myself, I was named one of the three stars at the end of the game. On another occasion, the sports writer for the Timmins Press wrote, "Keefe in the nets, Aiken for his two goals, and Barilko for a steady game on defense, sparked the winners."[2] Yes, this was the same Bill Barilko who later starred on defense for Toronto Maple Leafs and whose sweater was later retired. He scored the winning goal for Toronto in the deciding game against the Montreal Canadiens in the 1951 Stanley Cup finals. When he played Juvenile, he kidded me, calling me Broda. Little did he know at that time that in two years he would be playing for Toronto in front of the real Maple Leafs' goalie, Turk Broda.

Tragically, Barilko was lost in the northern bush in an airplane crash and feared dead. Years later the plane was found. When I heard this news, events flashed across my mind – the year that he had played defense in front of me, and though I was two years his junior, we had also played on the same baseball team for two years. Those who had played with him were glad for his success and somewhat envious, but now it was all

*1946-47, Ernie was 17.*
***South Porcupine Red Wings***
***(Juvenile A)"***

over. The thought came to me, "The most important thing in this life is not the fame and success we have attained, but rather whether or not we have received pardon for our sins and the gift of eternal life through faith in Christ." Many years later, the plane in which Barilko was a passenger was found containing his remains and those of his dentist friend.

The following year I was back playing Juvenile hockey for the Timmins Canadiens, but not in goal. Many of our players had moved up to Junior hockey. It was a great honor for me to be named captain of the team, and this was a double honor because there were only three of us who were not French Canadian. The team was called the Timmins Canadians and represented the local French population. In my last year of Juvenile hockey, the Timmins Canadians disbanded, resulting in my move to South Porcupine to play under a renowned coach, Carlo Cattarello, whose team, the Red Wings, had won the All-Ontario Juvenile A championship the previous year. My position was to center the second line, play the

*1946-1947 South Porcupine Red Wings, Northern Ontario Juvenile A champions, Ontario Juvenile A finalists*

point in the power plays and on occasion, in crucial situations I was sent out to help on defense.

I had a good year and ended up fourth in scoring in a six-team league and led the Porcupine Red Wings in goals and total points in the play-offs. During the play-offs, we defeated Timmins, Schumacher, Iroquois Falls, Kirkland Lake, Copper Cliff (Sudbury area), and lost a heartbreaker to St. Catharines in the last minute of the third period of the final game in the All-Ontario finals.

Our line, with Gordie Hannigan (he later played with Toronto Maple Leafs) on left wing, Jimmy Campbell at centre, and myself on right wing, played well in the play-offs. In our first game against Kirkland Lake, we scored eight of our team's ten goals! The Timmins Press' report of the game noted that, "Jimmy Campbell copped top honors for the afternoon and piled up five goals and an assist, while Ernie Keefe scored two and assisted on five others."[3]

In our first game against Copper Cliff, our line did well again, but this time the scoring was turned around. The Timmins Press reported, "Shifty Ernie Keefe led the goal-getting parade with four counters, while his centreman, Jimmy Campbell, was the top point maker with two goals and five assists. Keefe had two assists to give him a six point night."[4]

John Sheddon, a big defenseman with whom I later played on the Barrie Major Junior team, told me that after our first play-off game against Kirkland Lake, he had been assigned to cover me for the next game. In the All-Ontario Juvenile A finals against St. Catharines, the St. Catharines players mentioned to me after the series that they had been told to watch Keefe around the goal. Although we lost the series, I was somewhat consoled when Rex Stimers, a leading sports broadcaster and journalist in the Niagara-St. Catharines area, looked me up and said, "You really know how to put the puck in the net." Gordie Hannigan, the hard checking winger and playmaker on our line, signed a *C form* with the Leafs through the Leafs' former player and scout, Bob Davidson. Hannigan played several seasons with Toronto. Nearly every member of our team graduated to Major

Junior A Teams and signed C contracts with professional teams. A *C Form* was a contract between a player and a professional hockey team. From that time it meant you were their property.

In those days, there were no drafts. Every professional team, and some Major Junior teams, had scouts. The All-Ontario Juvenile finals were one of their favorite scouting venues. Jimmy Campbell and I were the leading scorers on our team during the play-offs, yet neither of us was approached by a scout. Possibly it was because of our size. I measured 5'7½" and weighed 158. Jimmy was taller than I but weighed less. Players were much smaller in those days. We knew that we would move up to Major Junior hockey in the fall, but we had both hoped for more than that, and fans and sports writers were assuming that we would both have *C form* contracts before the end of the season.

### Moving up to Major Junior A and Signing with the Professionals

It finally worked out well for Jimmy and me. The following season we moved up to the Major Junior A with the Porcupine Combines in the Timmins area. At the same time and in the same place, seated together in the McIntyre arena in South Porcupine, Carlo Cattarello, New York Rangers Scout, signed us both to *C Forms*. At last, we signed a *C Form* with a professional team!

A few days later, we were playing against the Barrie Flyers for the Major Junior A Ontario championship. Following the second game, I attended the morning service at First Baptist Church in Timmins, a rare thing for me in those days. Coming out of the church at the end of the service, I heard someone call my name. It was a well-known businessman. He told me that Hap Emms, coach and part owner of the Barrie Flyers, wanted me to have dinner with him.

At dinner Hap asked me if I would sign to play with the Flyers the next year. Wow! Play for a team that had been in the Memorial Cup finals several times in the past few years and had a very good chance of a repeat in the next year. There was one hitch, however. Hap also wanted me to sign a *C contract* with the Buffalo Bisons of the American Hockey League. Since professional teams like their players to play in their system, I thought, "If I say I've just signed a *C form* with the New York Rangers, he might withdraw his offer to sign me with Barrie Flyers for the coming season." I was sure that most of those playing Major Junior hockey, or those hoping to move up into Major Junior in that era, would have jumped at an offer to play with the Barrie Flyers. What should I do? I decided to sign the *C Form* with Buffalo and let the New York Rangers and the Buffalo Bisons work it out. Meanwhile, I had a contract to play with the Barrie Flyers the following year.

In those days, every professional team in the NHL, or the AHL, had what they called a reserve list. This meant that besides the *C form*, each professional team could have up to twenty players on a list for their farm team. On signing with Buffalo, I was immediately put on their reserve list with their farm team in Houston, Texas. When the scout for the New York Rangers sent in the forms, the office in New York responded, stating that they could not touch Keefe as he was on Buffalo's reserve list in Houston. Hap Emms had lost no time in sending the contract signed to Buffalo and the AHL (American Hockey League) office.

As I was finishing the season with the Porcupine Combines we played for the Ontario Championship against the Barrie Flyers.

The team winning the Ontario championship would go on to play the winner of the Quebec and Maritime series. Then the winner of this series would go on to play in the Canadian championship for the Memorial Cup against the Western Champions.

## Maple Leaf Gardens

The Ontario Championship between my team, the Porcupine Combines, and the Barrie Flyers had started in Timmins but then moved to the Toronto Maple Leaf Gardens to complete the series. This was a great experience for an eighteen-year-old from Timmins, 700 kilometers (420 miles) north of Toronto. In the 1940's, the highway ended at Timmins. Just to visit the Gardens was a great pleasure, but to play in it was the thrill of a lifetime. As a child I never dreamed of such an experience.

When the Porcupine Combines entered the Gardens for a practice, the Toronto Maple Leafs were already practicing on the ice. We were proud that our coach Carlo was a friend of Turk Broda, the Toronto goalie, and Broda went to the boards to speak with him. The Combines players walked around the Gardens at ice level noting pictures of players they had idolized, and historic moments that had transpired there. I stopped in front of a photo of a player I could not identify, neither by his photo nor his name. I then read the gold plaque below the photo explaining that this player had been one of the Toronto Maple Leafs' best defense prospects, but he had been killed in a naval battle in the Atlantic towards the end of World War II. The plaque noted that he was only eighteen at the time of his death. I thought, "I'm eighteen. People can die at the age of eighteen, and hockey players are not exempt." I thought, "If I die at the age of eighteen, I'm not ready for eternity. I am not saved," as they would say at church. I quietly moved on to the next photo, oblivious of the other Combine players. The following night the Barrie Flyers beat us easily on the large ice surface and in front of their own fans. I had a good game, and of our three goals, I scored one and set up another. The Toronto Globe sports writer, who was seeing the Porcupine Combines play for the first time, made mention of the ability of four Combine players, and I was fortunate to be named as one of the four.

*Maple Leaf Garden*

**Move to Barrie**

Hap Emms, the Flyers' coach for whom I was to play the following year, was also pleased with my game and invited me to spend a week at Barrie and practice with the Barrie Flyers. Having played for the Combines that year, I was not eligible to play for Barrie that season, but I was signed to play for them in the following one, 1948-49. He also offered me summer employment in his electrical business if I wanted to move to Barrie immediately. Paul Meger, a Flyers player who later played with Buffalo and also for the Montreal Canadiens, worked for Hap Emms' company. I gladly accepted Hap's offer, and he arranged for me to live in one of the choice homes open to the Barrie Flyers players – the home of Wes Allsop, who was the arena manager. "Mom" Allsop, his wife, had been a mother to many teenage hockey players who laced their skates for the Barrie Flyers.

While Barrie was waiting for the Maritime Provinces and Quebec to finish their series, Barrie played an exhibition game against an all-star team from the Owen Sound area to keep in shape. Although I couldn't play a regular game for Barrie that season, I could replace the injured Rusty Aiken, another Timmins player, for this exhibition game. I fitted right in with the Barrie team and scored a picture-perfect goal in the second period. Between periods as the trainer was distributing oranges to the players, he told me that when I scored, Hap, obviously pleased, asked him, "Did you see that goal?" This was a long way from playing pick-up hockey on the school rink next door to our house. I had signed a *C form* with a professional team and was fitting in with the Flyers team, a team that was a contender for the Memorial Cup and would

*Barrie Arena*

likely be in the same position the following season. I was walking on a cloud, or should I say skating!

As the third period began, I wanted to score another goal. I received a pass from our defenseman and was speeding down the wing when I saw an opposing player coming across the ice to check me. I pushed the puck forward out of his reach. He lunged to get the puck and fell on my outstretched leg as I was pushing hard to pick up speed. I heard a cracking sound and felt a terrible pain shoot through my knee. I was carried off on a stretcher, afraid that I might have suffered a fracture, but I had the summer to recuperate, or so I thought.

In my first game with the Barrie Flyers, I scored a goal and assisted on another. My knee was hurting, and that was a problem because I was often described as a "smooth-skating centerman."[5] As the season progressed, my knee became more tender so I finally shared this with the trainer. (Former Toronto Maple Leaf Ron Ellis wrote in his book, Over the Boards, "The next day, I was in the hospital having an operation to remove cartilage! In 1965, it was a fairly major ordeal, which required two large incisions on either side of the knee. As a result, it took longer to recover."[6]) To have an operation would put me out for most of the season.

To avoid mid-season surgery and the loss of much of my season, the trainer gave me an elastic bandage. This definitely did not help; if it was tight it hampered my skating, which was key to my play; if it was loose, it gave no support.

I was reminded of my mother's words, "If you put something ahead of the Lord, He can take if from you."

Making my way slowly to the restaurant where the players gathered, the talk that evening was about rumors of a major trade between Barrie and Galt. I was so discouraged that I wanted to be traded. My future in hockey looked very doubtful. Réal (Chevy) Chevrefils, a fellow Barrie player, who also came from Timmins and later had an outstanding career with the Boston Bruins, said to me, "Ernie, what's the matter? When you were up North and started a rush, we couldn't get the puck away from you." I explained that it was my knee, that it was hurting all the time and that I couldn't put pressure on it. It was also hard to shift, to shoot, or to break away rapidly.

Coach Hap Emms had signed me to replace one of his centers, Reid, who had move back up to the professional ranks. But my knee injury had affected my play and I wasn't able to play up to my normal game; thus Hap Emms had no choice but to trade me, especially since he had his eye on winning the Memorial Cup. He needed three strong lines.

**ERNIE KEEFE**
*Dec. 9, 1948, p.14, Barrie Examiner*

> Ernie Keefe continues his flashy display at centre between George Ford and Ed Calhoun. In fact, Keefe and Sid McNabney have dominated the centre spotlight to late. McNabney has been working with Ken Green and Ed Down-

*Oct. 7, 1948, p.19, Barrie Examiner*

### New Hope Ends in Crisis

I was one of the players traded, but Galt knew nothing of my problem. When I started to put the bandage around my knee,

> the puck and outguessed Hendry. It was a beautiful effort. It placed the Flyers in front 5-1 as Ernie Keefe had banged home John Shedden's rebound earlier in the third period. Sullivan completed the scoring on a screened blueline shot. The absence of Jack Leckie from

*Nov. 25, 1948, p.15, Barrie Examiner*

the trainer asked me what I was doing. I explained that it was to help hold the injured knee in place. He said, "That's no good. I will give you a knee support that will help you." After the practice that day, George Ford, who had also been traded to Galt, said to me, "Ernie, you were flying in practice today." I replied, "Yes, I've been playing on a weak knee all season. The trainer gave me a knee support and I can skate as if I never had an injury." I could hardly wait for the Friday and Saturday home-and-home games with the

Stratford Kroehlers. I thought to myself, "I have two-thirds of the season left, and I'm going to make up for lost time."

Our line, with Green on left wing, Ford at right and myself at centre, started the game against Stratford's big line – O'Hearn, Lewicki and Flannigan. Lewicki went on to a good NHL career with Toronto and New York, and O'Hearn held the record for the fastest three goals scored in a Major Junior OHA game. We came very close to scoring against their top line. We started back to the bench satisfied with our first shift and confident that our line was going to score some goals that might help lead Galt to a victory. Our team received a penalty, so Coach Archie Moore, a former NHL goalie, sent George Ford and me out to kill the penalty. We had not played on the penalty-killing team at Barrie, but having seen it done in practice, we knew the play well. I said to Ford, "We'll try to pull off Barrie's play."

The play was that if the center-man won the face-off and got the puck back to his defenseman, he was to skate for a break-away, and the defense man would send him a pass rather than icing the puck. I faced off with Lewicki on the left side of the rink, a few feet outside our blue line, I won the face-off, and the puck went right to the stick of our big defenseman, Broughton, who was just inside our blue line behind me. The defenseman, not knowing the Barrie Flyers' play and not noticing me skating for a pass, did what a defenseman usually would do in this situation – he iced the puck. Without lifting his head, or hearing me call for a pass, this two-hundred-pound defenseman fired the puck towards the same opening toward which I was skating for a breakaway. I turned my head over my left shoulder, looking for a pass. Everybody in the area, except me, saw the puck soaring towards my head. The blow was unforgiving. I fell heavily to the ice. This happened before the players wore helmets. I was told after my recovery that the towel they wrapped around my head was soaked with blood. Four players carried me off the ice on a stretcher, but they did not leave me there for someone to complete the journey to the dressing room. Fearing the worst, they carried me right into the dressing room. A nurse who was at the game, later told my sister at the hospital that the way the puck hit me, and the way I fell to the ice, she had feared for my life. Since no one – referee, manager, players or doctor – came out of the players' room for some time, a rumor circulated in the arena that I had died.

While still in the dressing room, and for a very brief period, I regained consciousness. To my surprise, the four players were there, one at each corner of the stretcher. The referee was there, indicating that the game had been delayed. I heard the doctor say, "It is very serious. We must rush him to the hospital." I tried to ask what had happened after the face-off, but I couldn't utter a word. I wondered if the loss of speech was a first step toward death, followed by the loss of other faculties, and then death. I didn't have assurance of my salvation, even though I had often heard the gospel and had even made a decision when I was fourteen years of age. I did not walk with the Lord but continued to follow the path I had chosen. There was no communion with God, thus the Holy Spirit could not render testimony to my spirit that I was a child of God (as stated in Romans 8:16). I said to myself, "If I leave this world tonight, it is a step into darkness and uncertainty." One second after death, the fact that I had signed a *C form* with the New York Rangers and had played for one of the best Major Junior A teams in the country would mean nothing. Inwardly I cried out with a voice only God could hear, "Please let me live so that I may read the New Testament and come to the assurance of eternal life," something about which my mother had often spoken to me, as well as having heard it in Sunday School and church". I faintly remember the sound of an approaching ambulance before slipping back into unconsciousness, to awaken later in an operating room, still unable to talk.

A sister of Bill "the kid" Taylor, who played for the Toronto Maple Leafs, heard about my accident on the late news and notified my sister in St. Catharines. She and her husband left immediately for Stratford, about 160 kilometers (100 miles) away, while my parents prepared to make the long trip from Timmins. One of the examining doctors asked my sister how she thought I would take it if I recovered and found that I would never play hockey again. He then went on to say that brain surgery might be necessary, and there was no guarantee that I would regain normal speech. The team assured my family that all medical expenses would be covered, which was comforting in those pre-Medicare days.

My parents arrived from Timmins and of course, they were concerned. On the second day when my brother-in-law saw me at the hospital, he held little hope for my recovery. Thanks to God, on the third day, which, according to the doctor was crucial, there was a turn for the better and I was able to speak a few words. The crisis seemed to have passed.

On the fifth day, it was decided that I should be taken back to Galt (part of the city of Cambridge today). That weekend had been hard on the players. I had suffered a fractured skull in the Friday game in Stratford, and in the return game in Galt on Saturday, a Stratford defenseman broke his leg. An ambulance from Galt brought the injured player back to Stratford, and on the return trip transported me to Galt. Several players came in to see me, and I was able to converse haltingly with them. Whether it was the excitement of seeing my teammates or exertion, I do not know, but by the time the nurse passed to check on me, my speech had regressed considerably. I was alarmed that I was unable to ask for a glass of water. The doctor was called, who was angry that he had not been made aware of the seriousness of the case. Improvement came steadily, however, and a little after the second week I left the hospital and was permitted to go to my sister's home for convalescence because it was not too far from the team's home base.

While the danger was seemingly past, I knew that head injuries in sports were sometimes followed by a potentially fatal hemorrhaging. My sister and her husband had been warned that if they saw any change in my condition, I should be taken immediately to the Emergency Department. In view of this, upon retiring at night I was reticent to fall asleep in case of a hemorrhage during the night. I was still not ready to face eternity. What began as a hope to save my season after the knee injury became an ardent desire to save my life.

## Peace at Last

Soon after my arrival at my sister's home, Mr. and Mrs. Harper Beaver, friends of the family, dropped in for a visit. The husband, a zealous Christian, never missed an opportunity to witness and was often criticized for being too aggressive. Even the Apostle Paul, however, pled, "Pray also for me, that whenever I open my mouth, words may be given me so that I will fearlessly make known the mystery of the gospel, for which I am an ambassador ..." (Eph. 6:19,20).

The conversation around the table centered on Israel's becoming an autonomous nation for the first time in 2,500 years. This took place in May 1948, and my accident occurred in December 1948, so it was still a very recent event. I recalled my mother telling me that before Jesus' second coming, Israel would return to her land to be there when the Messiah would descend upon the Mount of Olives and come to her aid. The conclusion of those around the table was that one could not say that Jesus would come in the present generation, or even the present century, but, on the other hand, one of the key signs of Jesus' return would be the return of Israel to her country, since end-time prophecy was to take place around the country of Israel. Things were now in order for his return, but the Lord himself warned us that we could not know the precise date. What was important, and what impressed me, was that the scene was now ready for Jesus' return, and if he were to come at that time, I was not ready to meet him. My need of salvation seemed all the more urgent. I had escaped death for the moment, but having heard in my youth that the Lord's coming would take place in the twinkling of an eye, or like a thief in the night, I realized there were two ways I could meet Jesus – by death or by his coming.

Eventually everyone got up from the table and retired to the front room, and I found myself in the kitchen, face to face with Harper Beaver. He then said to me, "How are you with the Lord,

Ernie?" "Not very good," I replied. He said that even that very night I could have the assurance of pardon for all my sins, receive the gift of eternal life, and have a home reserved for me in heaven. I replied that there was nothing I would like more than that.

He showed me from the Bible that "All have sinned and come short of the glory of God" (Romans 3:23). I knew I was a sinner and that no one who was guilty of sin could enter heaven. He then showed me that, "God has demonstrated his love to us in that while we were yet sinners, Christ died for us" (Romans 5:8). I knew that, but what I didn't know was how I could receive God's forgiveness. At that moment, Mr. Beaver turned to one of the best known verses in the Bible, John 3:16, and read it to me: "For God so loved the world that he gave his only Son, that whoever believes in him shall not perish but have eternal life." It was like turning on a light switch in a dark room. I said to myself, "That's it! God would not deceive me, He has promised that whosoever trusts in his Son and believes that he died on the cross for his sins has everlasting life." In light of this, I said to God:

> Heavenly Father, you cannot lie and you wouldn't deceive me. You tell us through this verse that if I trust in your Son, you will give me eternal life. Therefore, the best way I know how, I am placing my faith in Jesus Christ and in Him alone. Give me this gift of eternal life.

I had a peace that I didn't know was possible.

When I went to bed that night, the thought that had haunted me since my accident, "What if I have a hemorrhage and die in my sleep?" crossed my mind, but I found that I no longer feared death. I sat up in my bed and said, "Lord, if I live five minutes or fifty years, it makes no difference now, because I know that if I die I will go to heaven."

## Back to Hockey

When my sister and brother-in-law arrived at the hospital and spoke with the doctor, they were advised that I would never play hockey again, and it was doubtful that I would recover normal speech. No one had told me, however, and as Bill Boyd wrote in his book, "Keefe made a surprisingly fast recovery and even played the last two (more correctly ten) games of Galt's schedule."[7] When I felt well enough to play, I simply showed up in the dressing room, put on my

*1948, in Saint Catharines in my sister's house. About a week after I had received Christ*

equipment and went out for the practice, and this without having an examination by a doctor. The only restriction was that I wear a helmet, something players didn't do in the 1940's. I returned to my pre-accident form and averaged close to two points a game.

I was very happy that God allowed me to return to hockey. It wasn't that I had to prove something, but I wanted to be able to make my own decision. This gave me the opportunity to leave hockey for Christ's sake and not because I could no longer play. I loved the game and I would have enjoyed staying in hockey and having a testimony as a professional player. My love for Christ was tested.

During my absence, Bronco Horvath took my place on the first line. He later starred with the Boston Bruins and was on his way to breaking Rocket Richard's record of fifty goals in fifty games when a broken toe sidelined him for several games. Horvath, Ford and Green were playing well together, and coach Alfie Moore didn't want to break up their line. Furthermore, he didn't know how my injury would affect my play, so I was put on a new line, often with rookies. I was just happy to be back in hockey, and with my newfound peace and assurance of eternal life, my whole outlook on life had changed. The aim of my life now was to glorify God and do his will, whether it was on the first line or elsewhere.

One game I won't forget, after my return to hockey, was against my former team, the Barrie Flyers. Though the Barrie team was a powerhouse, we tied them 4 to 4 on their own ice. On one play, I picked up the puck in our end and stick handled through the Barrie team to score. As I skated past the Flyers' bench, after the goal, I slapped my stick on the boards and said, "How did you like that one, Hap?" I guess I was a little too cocky, but he was a very competitive man himself and liked to see spunk in his players. A little later, the puck went into the Barrie end, and I went in to fore-check. I knew Barrie's play was to get the puck out of their end and where the one defenseman positioned himself for a pass. I coasted in and as soon as the first defenseman prepared to pass the puck, I put on a burst of speed and intercepted the pass. My wingman was skating toward the net, and I passed the puck to him. He let go a beautiful, hard shot into the top corner of the net. Our line played well and no goals were scored against us while we scored two.

After the game, as we were taking off our equipment, the door of our dressing room opened and in walked Hap Emms. It was a very unusual thing for a coach to enter the opposing team's dressing room after a game. All eyes were upon him. To my utter surprise, he walked across to me and shook my hand and congratulated me on my return to my pre-injury form of hockey.

### A Later Visit to Barrie

About seven years later, when I was beginning pastoral work, pastor Ernie Nullmeyer invited me to go to Barrie to preach in Emmanuel Baptist Church. He arranged for an interview on the Barrie television station, where I was questioned concerning my conversion and subsequent decision to leave hockey to go into missionary work. As well, Hap Emms had invited me to supper before a game that

Barrie was to play that Saturday night. His wife had received Jesus as her Savior about the same time as me. Hap asked many questions about the Bible as we waited for supper to be served. Later that night, I attended the game where Hap had reserved a seat for me behind the Barrie team's bench.

The Sunday evening service in Emmanuel Baptist Church that week was broadcast on the radio, and I was told that many sports fans had listened to the service to see why a young man would leave hockey to become a missionary for Jesus Christ. As I rose to speak, I was pleasantly surprised to see Hap and Mrs. Emms, the arena manager (Wes Allsop) and his wife (at whose home I boarded while in Barrie), team trainer (Harry Parsons) and one of Hap's employees (an electrician by the name of Gene with whom I had worked as an apprentice), all seated in the third row of the church. Hap and I remained good friends until his death.

This trip to Barrie revived many memories – my high hopes that the team I was playing on would win the Memorial Cup (this would have been a stepping stone to professional hockey, but my knee injury spoiled all that and caused me to become despondent, as I thought my career was going to end just when it had barely begun), and finally a fractured skull (after I had found a solution to my knee problem). On the other hand, these problems had brought back to me my mother's words, spoken when I was fifteen years of age, "If you put something in place of the Lord, He can take it away from you." This would not be to punish me, but rather that I might know him and follow him for his glory and my good. Hockey, and sports in general, were pushing Jesus to the periphery, if not altogether out of my life. At that time, those injuries were tragedies for me, but God used them to break my resistance and bring me the pardon of my sins and the gift of eternal life through faith in Jesus Christ.

## A Call to Missions

Shortly after my return to Galt, I discovered that a fan of the team, Fred Wilson, a businessman with a menswear store where the players bought their clothes, was a Christian. From the time I met Fred, his home became my home until the end of the season. A member of his family gave me a book entitled *Five Hundred Miles of Miracles in China,* which was the story of missionaries caught in the interior of China when the Communists came in, and how they made it to safety. That was the first Christian book I read – a missionary story.

Fred and his parents also took me to the large Central Baptist Church in London, Ontario for a Sunday evening service. I sat in the balcony and was overwhelmed by the number of people in attendance. At the end of the service, they sang the well-known hymn, "Just as I am." People who had never accepted Christ as Savior and/or wayward believers, were invited to go to the front, thus indicating their decision to accept Christ and receive counseling. But no one responded to the invitation. In my heart I said to God:

> I do not have to go forward for salvation, but I see how difficult it is to reach people with the gospel, and so in my heart tonight I come to you and promise that anything you want me to do to reach people with the gospel, even to leaving my career in hockey – I will do it.

Unknown to me, across the balcony, there was a small group of young men about my age. During my first year at London Bible Institute, one of this group came to me and asked me if I remembered being in the balcony at Central Baptist Church in the spring of 1949. I said I did, but wondered why he should ask. He went on to say that an usher had come to them and said that there was a young man on the other side of the balcony who was a hockey player, and that he had just been saved. He urged them to pray for him, and they did. The student was Bruce Woods, and I was able to tell him how God had spoken forcefully that night in answer to their prayers.

Later in the summer, Pastor P.B.Loney of Bethel Baptist Church in St. Catharines was teaching a Young People's class of which I was a member. He talked about Paul and the shipwreck in Acts chapter 27 and how they had to lighten the ship by throwing part of their cargo overboard. He made the application that sometimes we have to remove things from our lives in order to serve God. That irritated me somewhat, because it struck a chord too close to home for me.

By this time, I had developed the blooming of a friendship with Betty Merry, the pianist in the church and also part of the ladies' trio. Her father, a fine Christian, and Betty herself were a help to me as a young believer. The trio was invited to Maple Grove Church for special services. The husband of one of the trio members led the singing, and I was taken along to give my testimony. On the way back to St. Catharines, we visited in the James' home, a Christian family in Collingwood. The conversation turned to missions, as Mrs. James asked, "Did you hear about the tragedy of that missionary family in South America?" As we were unaware of this tragedy, she went on to explain. "Well, it is very sad. The husband was killed by those whom he tried to befriend. The natives were having a feast and became intoxicated and killed him with their machetes." There was a gasp on the part of those present, then one questioned as to what the missionary wife and mother would do. With four children, it would be impossible for her to remain in the jungle. When questioned if she regretted having gone as a missionary, we were told that her only regret was in having to leave a tribe without anyone to tell them about the Lord. This struck me like a load of bricks. It was as though God was saying to me, "Those people do not need to be born, to live and die without hearing the gospel. You could go, Ernie."

The next day I reported to training camp, and Rudy Pilous, Publicity director and the main scout of the Buffalo organization was there. When I checked in, he saw me and asked if I had been sick. I replied that I was just getting over the summer flu. The aftereffects of the flu did not help me at camp. Nevertheless, I was assigned to Washington, Buffalo's farm team in the Atlantic

Coast League. The New York Rangers and Boston Bruins also had farm teams in this league. I had two days to go home, gather my belongings, and report to Buffalo.

Before going to bed, it had become my practice since I had received Jesus as my Savior, to read in the Bible, meditate upon it, and to pray. This was the second time I was reading through the New Testament, and that night my reading was in Matthew, chapter four. Before I began to read, I pled with God to make his will clear to me so I could make the right decision about my future. As I read verses nineteen and twenty, God's will became clear. There was never a shadow of doubt. If Jesus had been there visibly, the answer to my prayer could not have been any clearer. Here are the words of Jesus found in these two verses, and the response of the disciples, "Follow me … and I will make you fishers of men. At once they left their nets and followed him." (Matt. 4:19, 20).

I not only knew what God's will for my life was but that it demanded an immediate response. I asked God for grace to obey Him, and I immediately got off my knees without even finishing the rest of the chapter, descended to the basement, found a nail, and literally hung up the skates that Buffalo had given me in my last year of Major Junior hockey.

---

### Written Testimonies

The testimony of this decision came to be written in a book, *Hockey Towns: Stories Of Small Town Hockey In Canada*,[8] by Bill Boyd. I was on a three-day visit to Timmins to celebrate the 75th anniversary of the First Baptist Church, where pioneer pastor Morley Hall had baptized my sisters and mother in the 1930's. Bill Boyd was on a cross-Canada trip gathering material for the book he was writing. He arrived in Timmins for a three-day stay the same weekend as me. As was my custom whenever I happened to be in Timmins, I phoned my former coach, Carlo Cattarello. Carlo answered that he couldn't see me that day because he was awaiting a call from a writer who had requested an interview with him, and he wasn't sure when he would arrive. At that moment the doorbell rang and Carlo asked me to hold the line. It was the writer in question at the door, and Carlo mentioned to him that if he was looking for hockey stories, he had a former player on the line who had an interesting story. He came to the telephone and asked if I would be free to meet with him. This led to a rendez-vous in a restaurant, where I answered his questions regarding hockey and also gave him an account of my conversion. Six weeks later I received a phone call from him in which he told me that he had chosen my experience for one of the hockey stories in the Timmins area.

The following is taken from what appears in his book:

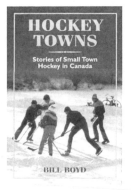

"It was against Stratford and I faced off outside our blue line with Danny Lewicki," he says. "I got the puck to one of our defensemen and broke for a pass but he tried to clear it; he really drove it hard, and it hit me in the head. When I came to in the dressing room I couldn't remember what had happened after the face-off. I tried to talk but I couldn't. Part of my brain was paralyzed. I heard the doctor say to the manager: 'We have to get him to hospital in a hurry.' Then I heard the ambulance siren. It was at that moment I realized that maybe this is what it's like when one is dying. And I was thinking that one second after death, the fact that I'd signed a 'C' form with the New York Rangers or that I'd played Junior A hockey, one second after I leave this life, those things don't count any more."[9]

Boyd also wrote about my recovery and return to hockey, as well as the decision I had to face. He wrote:

> That summer he began to think seriously of joining the ministry. On the one hand was the childhood dream of playing professional hockey, on the other the call from God … In the fall, he went to Buffalo's AHL training camp in Fort Erie … He was assigned to Washington in the Atlantic league but he said he wanted to go home to think about it. "I was only twenty, it was a big decision, but I decided to follow the Lord."[10]

It was not a religious book, but I am indebted to him for including my story in *Hockey Towns: Stories Of Small Town Hockey In Canada.* The Sovereign God, who arranged all this, can still use the few words to make people think of eternity and their need of Jesus Christ.

There was one article, among others, that clearly spelled out my testimony. Most hockey players who left Timmins did not return to make it their home, which is the centre of a mining and lumber district, 700 kilometers (420 miles) north of Toronto. When a player did return for a short visit, this was often noted in the *Timmins Press* by sportswriter Carlo Cattarello, who himself was an outstanding athlete, coach, scout for the New York Rangers, sports administrator and recent recipient of the Order of Canada. His article was entitled, "Ernie Keefe trades his skates to play on Christ's team." He wrote in part:

> A talented hockey player, Ernie Keefe, has traded his skates to play on Christ's team. The Baptist pastor, who now lives in Laval, Quebec, was in Timmins over the Thanksgiving weekend with his wife, Betty. … A head injury sidelined him for a time … "It was during convalescence, with the help of a friend of the family, that I learned from the gospel that Jesus died for me"

Keefe said. "I knew my first allegiance was to the one who died for my sins and gave me the gift of eternal life."[11]

A sister-in-law, Minnie Burgess, who sent me the clipping of Carlo's article, mentioned that it had caused a lot of positive discussion in the area. I was glad for this, because I often regretted having had very few opportunities to return to my home town to tell my friends, fellow hockey players and fans what Christ had done for me.

God's call to leave sports and enter the ministry is unusual, in that most professional Christian athletes stay in sports and render a good testimony. I thank God for every Christian athlete who maintains a vibrant testimony and lives a godly life. We did not have Christian hockey schools when I was a teenager, and I often wonder what influence that would have had on me, had that been the case. I made a decision for Christ when I was fourteen. Whether I was saved or not, God knows, but I do know that I did not have any positive male influence in my family, or in the church after my conversion, thus there was no growth and I lacked the assurance of salvation. Listening to testimonies of professional Christian hockey players, and being counseled by them, could have turned my life around in the early teen years. But in those days, many churches and Christians frowned on Christians being professional athletes, and I had often wondered about that question myself. Could I do both?

**Betty's Call to Missions**

As for Betty's background and call to missions, she related to me how, as a girl of eight, she had asked her Sunday School teacher what the word missionary meant. Her teacher explained that it was a person who left home and went far away, sometimes even

*April 1950, Ernest and Betty*

to the jungle, to take the gospel message to those who had never heard. Being a rather shy homebody, the idea of becoming a foreign missionary was almost repulsive to her young mind. Nevertheless, from that day onward, Betty was convinced that the Lord would call her into missionary service. This became a struggle throughout her adolescence, but with each yearly missionary conference, it became clearer that this was the Lord's will for her life. Finally, at about sixteen, she yielded completely to the Lord's leading, and from that time began to look forward to serving him wherever he should lead.

Our friendship flourished, and in a few months' time we announced our engagement. We were married in April of 1950 in Bethel Baptist Church. We began our studies at London Bible Institute and Theological Seminary in the fall of 1950. This institution later amalgamated with Toronto Bible College and it has since become Tyndale University College and Seminary. Four years later, we had the honor of becoming Bethel's first missionaries.

From the beginning, Bethel has been a missionary church and has had a strong missionary program. We were fortunate to have been in such a church that stood with us for fifty years in our missionary work. Bethel also gave us a place to exercise our gifts. For Betty it was mainly in music, but we were responsible for the Young People's group, which God blessed. It was at Bethel that I taught my first Sunday School class, which grew to include fourteen boys, one of whom was Bill Curry, who years later became the pastor of Bethel Baptist Church (1990-2000). He went to be with the Lord in March of 2000. Bethel was also where I preached my first sermon. I had followed the Lord in baptism on Mother's Day, 1949. We owe much to our home church, as well as all the churches and individuals who blessed us with their love, their prayers and financial support. Now, as a couple, we were ready to consider a Mission Board under which we could serve, and discern the will of God as to our field of service.

### Africa Bound? Where Should We Serve God?

The night Betty and I publicly dedicated ourselves to missionary work, the speaker was from Africa and spoke of the need, the hardships, and the culture of the people. From that moment onward, we took it for granted that Africa would be our field of service. We read missionary autobiographies and other biographies, as well as magazine articles covering missionary service in Africa.

Throughout our college years we attended the Africa prayer group, though there were many other fields represented. When nominations for the presidency of the missionary prayer groups were made, it was certain that we were headed for Africa. I was elected to the post of president by acclamation. When the college yearbook was being prepared, each section began with a picture of someone involved in that ministry. To represent foreign missions, I was asked to participate, and as a result I was photographed with a little black girl on one knee and a white boy standing on the other side. At a recent reunion of our alumni, after having labored fifty years in Quebec, a friend questioned us about the fact that we had been preparing to go to Africa. He remembered the picture on the first page of the missions section. That had been our plan at the time, but it is interesting how the change of field came about.

One day toward the end of my senior year, during a chapel service, a French Canadian, Ernest Tétreault, had been invited to speak. He talked about a Christian Youth Camp and Daily Vacation Bible Schools being conducted in Quebec and sponsored by the Canadian Sunday School Mission. During the message, the Holy Spirit spoke to me. At the close of the service, I felt compelled to speak to him about the summer program. I mentioned that I had been moved by his presentation, but went on to say that there were two obstacles to our working with him in Quebec. Firstly, we did not speak French, and secondly, at this time we had a nine-months -old baby. Ernest Tétreault responded that this would not hinder our working with them because the ministry was among the English minority, and that lodging, and even baby sitters, wouldn't be a problem.

At this news, Betty and I both rejoiced over how God had directed us for the summer. Arrangements had been made for the early part of the summer, when we were to replace George and Elaine White in the pastorate, in order to allow them to spend two months visiting their families in British Columbia, of whom many did not know the Lord.

After our stint in Michigan, we headed for Quebec in order to complete our commitment with the Sunday School Mission for the balance of the summer months.

### Summer Work in Quebec

The trip was more than 1,600 km. Our old wooden-bodied Plymouth station wagon held all our earthly possessions. We had intentionally not accumulated a lot of "stuff" because we were going to spend our life in Africa … or so we thought.

There was also a precious baby boy in the station-wagon, and he traveled very well. His name was Ernest James. Who named him? Our college president! There were five married couples in the class of 1953, with both husband and wife registered as full-time students. Each year, unknown to us, the faculty was anxious to see if all the wives were returning students. When the third year began and all five wives were there and looking forward to completing their third year of studies, the president came to us and said that we were making history for the school. The aspiration of the faculty members was that all the couples – husband and wife – would graduate together.

After the Christmas break, I went to see the president of the college, Dr. James Bedford. The reason for this rendez-vous was to tell him that we were expecting our first child in July, and to ask him if Betty could continue to attend classes and graduate. Before I could ask the question, he blurted out, "She isn't going to quit, is she?" I responded by saying that that was my reason for this meeting, to ask if she would be permitted to finish her year and graduate. (It was a very reserved culture in the 1950's, and so

we were asked not to discuss the pregnancy with other students!)
Dr. Bedford smiled and said that there was only one stipulation,
and that was that we name the baby Ernest James, James being his
first name. I rushed home to give the good news to Betty and tell
her about Dr. Bedford's witty remark. His suggestion pleased us,
and since we had not yet settled on a name, we thought it sounded
great and decided that our first-born would carry the name of Ernest
James Keefe. All five couples graduated together, thus making
history for the school.

The long trip from Michigan was nearly over and we were about
to enter the French- speaking Province of Quebec – a province
which neither one of us had ever visited. We looked at a map of
Quebec and discovered that a good part of the roads to the camp
would be on secondary highways. There was one red colored road
and we decided it would be a good choice for the first part of our
journey in Quebec. We were traveling through beautiful countryside
and thoroughly enjoying it, until a huge truck with a wide bulldozer
loaded on it appeared before us. The highway was too narrow to
pass safely, so we moseyed along behind it, nervously watching
the sun slip closer and closer to the horizon. This was unknown
country and we wanted to get to the camp before dark.

Finally reaching a village on the Richelieu River, we
experienced our first culture shock. All the major buildings belonged
to the Catholic Church. There was a cathedral-sized church with an
adjacent hotel-sized glebe house. Further on was a large convent,
followed by two Catholic schools – one for the girls and one for the
boys. To add to this, school had just finished for the summer and
black-robed teaching brothers, priests and nuns were everywhere;
all this in a small village. This was the pre-Quiet Revolution era. A
feeling of melancholy set in, especially knowing that most of the
people knew nothing about salvation by grace through faith or the
priesthood of Jesus Christ. The only encouraging thing was that
we lost the truck in the town.

I had grown up in Timmins, which was 40%, French Canadian.

Many of my childhood and teenage friends were French, and I was well known in the French quarters, having played two years with the Timmins Canadiens, the French Juvenile A team, coached by a well-known French athlete and managed by a priest. From our house, we could see a French Catholic school, and the English public school that I attended. My mother, who was an ardent Christian and knew the Bible well, explained to me why she had left the Catholic Church in her later teens, and showed me the differences between the Catholic Church and the Bible. I was not following the Lord at that time, so I did not try to witness to my Catholic friends. In Timmins, no church held a monopoly, and some of the French Catholics even left their church to attend Evangelical churches, although the Catholic Church vehemently opposed this. This village we had just visited was very different from Timmins and even more so to Betty, who had grown up in Southern Ontario.

We continued our journey with increased speed, deep in thought about what we had just seen. Finally, to change our sullen mood, I jokingly asked Betty what her reaction would be if God were to call us to serve him in Quebec. Her answer was swift and determined: "Not a chance! God has called us to Africa!"

We arrived at Camp Livingstone after dark. Our first responsibility was to hold a Daily Vacation Bible School at Cookshire while we were waiting for the camp season to begin. Little did we know that fifty years later we would still be in Quebec, and that at least three of the children in that Vacation Bible School – Sandra (Little) Fortin, her cousins Sharon (Hodge) Rothney and Margaret (Burns) MacKay – would be active in their local churches.

A family by the name of MacKay provided hospitality for us and kept our baby when we were teaching. The MacKay home became our home away from home, and the parents were like grandparents for our boys. The first French church that we planted was about 100 km. from Cookshire, and the MacKays and the Sawyerville Baptist Church became spiritual oases for us during the time of persecution in Quebec. This English church had been established by Baptist pastors from Fairfax, Vermont, in 1794, and was a blessing to our fledgling French churches.

At Camp Livingstone, I had an experience that further impressed upon me the need of Quebec. I became acquainted with the mechanic in the village of Fitch Bay. He was French Canadian. His mother had a French Bible, which was unusual in that era because the Catholic Church forbade its members to own a Bible. If the parish priest found that

*Wilson Ewin*

parishioners had one, he would confiscate it and scold them for having and reading the Bible. Nevertheless, we discussed the gospel together, and I would answer his and his mother's questions, using my English Bible. He would then show his mother the answers in her French Bible. She did not speak English and I did not speak French. I felt so incapable of helping this woman. She died suddenly. Betty and I asked one another, "What about the masses of French Canadians who never hear the New Testament truths in their churches, and are forbidden to have or read the Bible for themselves?" The late Kenneth Scott Latourette, Yale professor and renowned historian, wrote in his book *History of Christianity*, "In few countries did the Catholic Church have so firm a hold on all phases of the lives of its members as it did in French Canada."[12]

Wilson Ewin, who had been a pilot in World War II and a classmate at Bible College, had made application to go to Africa as a missionary pilot. He and his wife came to Quebec to study French in order to work in a French-speaking colony in Africa. God showed the Ewins, however, the need of Quebec and kept them there. We heard about this and wanted to see them and ask about their decision to stay in the province of Quebec. We had also learned that they were planning to start a church in the town of Coaticook, which was located about 25 kilometers (15 miles) from the camp but we did not have the address. We learned about a French-Canadian believer who had a shoe repair shop on the main street who was helping in the planting of this church. We were able to locate his shop by the sign, *Ovila Cotnoir – Cordonnier* (shoemaker). The proprietor, Ovila Cotnoir, was the first French-Canadian Christian that we met in the Province of Quebec, and the first convert in the town of Coaticook.

It was nearly closing time when we arrived, and we knew we were in the right place when we spotted a well-worn Bible near the cash register. I asked him if it was not risky to have a Bible on the counter where it could be seen by all entering the shop. Could this not cause persecution and also the loss of customers? Mr. Cotnoir had had his share of persecution being the first convert to the gospel in Coaticook, but his great fear was not of being persecuted, or losing customers because of the Bible. He was more concerned about people going out into eternity without hearing the gospel.

We introduced ourselves and told him we were missionaries and that we were trying to locate the Ewin home. At these words, he beamed. There were not many believers in the gospel in those days in French Canada, and missionaries or pastors were 'as scarce as hen's teeth.' There was a mere one-half of one per cent of the French population who were Evangelical Christians. In the town of Coaticook and the surrounding area, there were only thirty Evangelical Christians, including young people and children. As for his Bible, he wanted to show people the gospel of Jesus Christ and to show them, with the help of his Bible, that the religious practices and the sacrifices they were making were not in line with what Jesus and the Apostles taught.

One approach he used was to say that he had found purgatory in the Bible. Since Catholics knew that non-Catholics denied the existence of purgatory, stating that it could not be found in the Scriptures, this caught their interest. Of course, to show them where he had found it, he would have the persons in question look at the Scriptures with him. Ovila Cotnoir would then turn to 1 John 1:7 and read with them the words, "The blood of Jesus, his Son, purifies us from all sin." He would then say that purgatory is supposed to purge all sin from us, and God says that it is the blood of Christ, or his life, that he gave on Calvary's cross. This is God's purgatory, God's way of purging us from sin if we trust in his Son. If, as the Bible states, he purifies us from all sin, there would be no sins left to be cleansed in purgatory, even if it did exist. Depending on the interest, or desire, to discuss further, Mr. Cotnoir would continue the discussion. One way or another, he had planted a seed from the Bible – a seed that could make the person begin to question the teaching of his church on salvation, and as often happened, it sparked an interest in reading the Bible for himself to see what its teachings were.

How did Mr. Cotnoir come to knowledge of salvation? He first heard the gospel through a radio broadcast in which Arnold Reynolds, from a French Brethren Assembly in Sherbrooke, was the preacher. That memorable Sunday morning in 1949, the evangelist ended his message by inviting his listeners to a meeting, after which he quoted John 3:16, "For God so loved the world that he gave his only–begotten Son, that whoever believes in him should not perish but have everlasting life." He then repeated the verse and said that in case it had not been fully understood, he would repeat it one more time. Tears began to roll down the cheeks of Mr. Cotnoir. He turned to his wife, Agnes, and said, "We are going to that meeting tonight!" They got on a bus and rode the 40 kilometers (24 miles) to Sherbrooke. After the service, Mr. Cotnoir asked the speaker to come to his house and explain the gospel and answer his questions with the Bible. What a surprise was in store when Arnold Reynolds arrived at the Cotnoir home and found the house full. There were Mr. & Mrs. Cotnoir and many of their friends, as well as seven young people and children. After many meetings and discussions based on the Bible, thirty people came to know Jesus as Savior and, on a beautiful Sunday afternoon, thirty people were baptized in Lake

Wallace on the outskirts of the town of Coaticook. These were the first fruits of the gospel in that town.

The Cotnoirs suffered for their faith but God upheld them. At the time of his conversion, Mr. Cotnoir was working in a factory. The owner of this factory was a very pious Catholic, and he and members of his family were deeply involved in music at the Catholic Church. The conversion of Mr. & Mrs. Cotnoir and their family, and many of their friends, was the talk of the town, especially after the public baptism. The parish priest said to his employer that he would be obliged to fire Mr. Cotnoir, because he had left the Catholic Church. "Why should I release him?" asked the employer. "He has worked well for me for twenty years. He has never stolen a cent, and he is the key man in my operations."[13] Mr. Cotnoir retained his work and a short time later he was given an increase in salary. On the other hand, his two youngest boys, still in school, were expelled from the French Catholic school because they no longer practiced the Catholic religion.

We could have spent the night talking with Mr. Cotnoir, but he had offered to take us to the Ewin's home, and we were now approaching the house. Because of a threat the Ewins had recently experienced, they were hesitant to open the door. When he asked who was there, our guide responded that it was Ovila Cotnoir and the Keefes. The Ewins could hardly believe what they had just heard, but opened the door and ushered us into the house and wanted to know what we were doing in Quebec. After all, I was the leader of the prayer group for Africa at College. Wilson Ewin, who had aspired to go to French-speaking African colonies as a missionary pilot, had been a faithful member of the Africa prayer group. The Ewins related how they had come to Institut Biblique Béthel to study French, with a view of doing missionary work in Africa. During their studies at Béthel, they were overcome by the need for the New Testament message in Quebec, and became convinced that God had brought them to language school in Quebec to see first-hand one of the world's most needy and neglected mission fields. We then told of the Lord's leading in our lives and how our burden for French Canadians was growing.

The new school year was about to start at Institut Biblique Béthel, which offered a Bible course for French Canadians and a language course for missionaries aspiring to go to French-speaking countries. The fall session would be starting in about two weeks time. The Ewins lived only 20 kilometers (12 miles) from the school, and since the apartment was available on the second floor of their home, they offered to let us occupy it. This was timely, as our term with the Canadian Sunday School Mission was coming to an end, and we were in need of a base to call home. God was opening the door to Quebec for us.

## Getting Established in Quebec

Betty started the French course with me, but had to stop when our second son, Brian, arrived on the scene. We had no French Canada Mission Board at that time, and since we had gone to Quebec supposedly for a two-month period, which had by now stretched out to a full year, we had only fifty dollars monthly promised support. Today with our French Missions Board, arrangements are made for both husband and wife to study the French language, where necessary. Because by this time we had two small children, Betty had to learn French by living among the French people. I believe her ear for music helped her to learn the language easily. As a result, after moving into a French community a few months later, she was able to respond to telephone calls, although it must be said that it was with much apprehension. She always regretted not having had the opportunity of a good French course and would have desired to be as efficient in writing French as well as English. However, while working in the Montreal Fellowship House many years later, one of her responsibilities was to write articles for the section on French work for our denominational magazine, the *Evangelical Baptist.*

As for me, language studies were going well. The French course at Institut Biblique Béthel was excellent. One advantage was the presence of French-speaking students, enrolled in the Bible course, who were living on campus with us. There was a two-hour period weekday afternoons when students helped look after the grounds and the farm, and I usually worked with Ernest Houle, who did not speak English. We were exhorted to speak only French in our homes, on campus and in our contacts with other English- speaking students. Most students cooperated, even if it meant carrying a small English-French dictionary in their pocket.

I was faithful to my pledge to speak French everywhere I went, including a trip to the department store. In my effort to buy a pair of jeans, I asked the clerk for a pair of *pantoufles*. When she asked me what size, I said thirty-six. She looked at me quizzically and said that I would find the *pantoufles* in another department. I stated that I had seen some in this department and asked her if she would help me find my size. Finally I led her to the place where I had seen jeans, and pointed them out. She then helped me find the size I was wanting. I went home, proud of having made my first purchase in French. The next day, the word for pants came up in our vocabulary class and I learned that the word for pants was *pantalons,* not *pantoufles,* which was the word for *slippers.* No wonder the poor clerk was so confused. She could not imagine a pair of size 36 slippers in her department!

One of the students in the course was Bill Curry from our home church in St. Catharines, Ontario. Later in his ministry, and spanning several decades, he enjoyed many successful pastorates, including several years in his home church. He also served on missionary boards. He was a student in the first Sunday School class that I taught, a group of twelve and thirteen-year-old boys. Now we were studying French together. By the new year Bill and I felt comfortable enough in the French language to try our hand at door-to-door visitation. Ernest Houle, a converted Catholic, offered to help us. He had been a very active and devoted Catholic. When he was converted to the gospel, his zeal for spreading the gospel was well known. He was a tremendous help.

Then, Jack Cochrane, a newly arrived professor, along with his wife, Joyce, joined the team and offered the use of their house for weekly Bible studies. Out of this fledgling team, and despite the stumbling French of Bill Curry and myself, Église Baptiste Évangélique de Sherbrooke was born. This is one of our strong churches that has passed the fiftieth anniversary of its founding. After Bill and I left the Sherbrooke area at the end of our school year, Jack Cochrane and Ernest Houle carried on for some time. Later Houle went on to St. Georges in the Beauce region, to begin a church there. Cochrane then pastored the church until the arrival of Jacques Alexanian.

During the period of language study, Wilson Ewin asked me to accompany him on a trip to New Brunswick to pick up a trailer that he had lent to a missionary. We decided to count the towns and cities of 5,000 or more of a population, to find out how many French Evangelical churches there were. The distance was about 500 kilometers (300 miles). We counted more than fifteen towns and cities but there was not one Evangelical French church in any of them. There might have been the odd believer and some home Bible studies, but we were not aware of them. Furthermore, the Catholic Church had forbidden her members to have a copy of the Bible. How could a continent with thousands of Evangelical churches have left this French Province of Quebec in darkness for so many years? Did God not have an answer to this need? Yes, and the presence of the Ewins and ourselves as new missionaries, brought about by a providential, sovereign God, was a sign that God was at work. Near the end of the return trip, we stopped halfway up a hill at a picturesque lookout point to allow the car engines to cool. From there I saw, across the countryside, the mining town of Asbestos. God, in his strange but unmistakable manner, laid this city on my heart. It was about 95% French, and without one Evangelical believer among them. I still had months of language study left, and when I shared this burden with Betty, she wisely said, "We must pray about it." Then it was back to the books.

(Endnotes)
1    Bill Boyd, *Hockey Towns: Stories Of Small Town Hockey In Canada*
     (Toronto: Doubleday Canada Limited, 1998), p. 74.
2    Tom O'Loughlin, *The Timmins Press*, 1945.
3    Tom O'Loughlin, *The Timmins Press*, March 1947.
4    Tom O'Loughlin, *The Timmins Press*, March 1947.
5    Doug McLellan, *The Timmins Press*, April 19, 1961, p. 10.
6    Ron Ellis with Kevan Shea, Foreword by Paul Henderson, *Over the Boards:*
     *The Ron Ellis Story* (Bolton, Canada: HB Fenn and Company, 2002), 260 pages, p.59.
7    Bill Boyd, *Hockey Towns,* p. 78.
8    Bill Boyd, *Hockey Towns,* p. 78.
9    Bill Boyd, *Hockey Towns,* p. 78.
10   Bill Boyd, *Hockey Towns,* p. 78.
11   Carlo Cattarello, *The Timmins Press.*
12   Kenneth Scott Latourette, *A History of Christianity*
     (New York: Harper Brothers), 1953, p. 1281.
13   Interview with Marcel Cotnoir, December 22, 2003.

# Chapter 2

# *God Calls His Team For Quebec*

### The Need for God's Team

In the year 1940, very few evangelical churches served the French-speaking population of Quebec.

In the beginning of New France, later called Quebec, the situation was very different. Four of the first five expeditions to colonize New France were led by Huguenots, appointed by the king of France, and even men like Jacques Cartier and Samuel de Champlain had Huguenot supervisors. The Huguenots, sometimes called Calvinists, were the French evangelical Christians who came out of the Protestant Reformation of the 16th century. The Caën Trading Company had received its Charter from Henry IV, and two men – one Catholic and one Huguenot – administered it. Jean-Louis Lalonde called this period from 1524-1627 "Un bel espoir de cohabitation"[1] ("A beautiful hope of living together").

The situation changed, however, with the arrival of the Jesuits in 1625. Jesuits were described as being "aggressive and powerful, uncompromising opponents of Calvinism."[2]  With help from the King of France, the Jesuits barred the arrival of further Huguenots. If they did come, they were not allowed to practice their religion. Churches and schools for the Huguenots were banned and the

Catholic Church performed the only legal marriages. Therefore, Huguenots who wanted to marry were obliged to renounce their faith. Parents were forced to have their children baptized and educated by the Catholic Church.

As for commerce, the Caën Trading Company, comprised of both Catholics and Huguenots, had its rights revoked by Cardinal Richelieu, a powerful religious leader and the right-hand man of King Louis XIII of France. Under the leadership of Cardinal Richelieu, an exclusively Catholic company replaced the Caën Company. The new company was called *Les cents associés (The one hundred associates)* and each associate member was a Catholic. The cutting-off of Huguenot trade, and even their presence in New France, was the aim of the Jesuits. Mason Wade, a Catholic historian with good insight into Quebec's history, claimed "The Jesuits sought to establish in Canada the closed theocracy which they later achieved in Paraguay."[3] This effort to make Quebec "exclusively Catholic"[4] continued for three hundred years and ended with the Quiet Revolution in the 1960s, which will be treated later.

There was, however, one period during those three hundred years when the light of the gospel shone in Quebec. This was a spillover from the spiritual revival in Switzerland. Mme Henriette Feller and Louis Roussy were the first Swiss-French missionaries, but many others followed them. North American mainline churches also became involved. The French converts began to take leadership, and there were many outstanding conversions, including a doctor and a priest. Later years were marked by the conversion of a well-known French-Canadian priest, Charles Chiniquy, who was known as the Apostle of Temperance in the Catholic Church and an outstanding orator. After his conversion, he held large evangelical rallies where hundreds came to the Lord and new evangelical French churches were established. By 1894, "there were 63 French Protestant churches, or preaching points, with an estimated thirty to forty thousand adherents, 130 workers and four residents training schools—all this from scratch amidst stiff opposition, in just sixty years."[5]

Unfortunately, the revival of the 19th century did not continue into the 20th century. Wesley Peach calculated that "By 1940, evangelicals had been reduced to 23 churches, or preaching points, and only 24 workers."[6] As well, he lamented that the evangelical movement had almost disappeared at the dawn of the 1950s.

What caused this decline? Richard Strout (of the Brethren) and David Dobson (Fellowship of Evangelical Baptist Churches in Canada), who are still actively engaged in French work in Quebec, both wrote master's theses on the period of revival from 1834 to the beginning of the 20th century. Independently they came to the same conclusion that the cause of this was strong persecution, emigration (to English-speaking Canada and the United States due, at least in part, to persecution), liberal theology, and anglicization. Both men concluded, however, that the liberalism from Europe that penetrated mainline Protestant churches was the main cause. Richard Strout wrote, "Some churches that had not wavered under persecution succumbed to the changes brought in by modernistic Protestant theology."[7] Would God and evangelical Christians allow this situation to continue? The answer is a resounding "No!"

### The Master of the Harvest Calls His Workers

We have already written about the call of God to the Ewins and ourselves to evangelism among French Canadians. I trust it has been noticed how God used circumstances to bring both couples to Quebec, and although neither of us had any intention of staying in the province, once God brought us here he showed us "the fields white unto harvest", or should we say, he showed us the land that needed to be cleared, ploughed and seeded.

This work of God began in our denomination before the denomination itself existed as it does today. The Fellowship of Evangelical Baptist Churches in Canada came into being in 1953 when pastors from the Fellowship of the Independent Baptist Churches and the Union of Regular Baptist Churches believed that they could do more together than apart. They came from the same background. When liberalism was sweeping the mainline Protestant churches, some churches left their denominations to exist as independent churches rather than risk being assailed by liberalism, to which the leaders of many denominations had succumbed. The battle had been won for these churches; historic Christianity had been defended. The task now was to take this good news to the world, and combining our efforts could do this.

Among Baptists there were four associations of Evangelical Baptist Churches across Canada: The "Fellowship of Independent Baptist Churches," the "Union of Regular Baptist Churches of Ontario and Quebec," the "Regular Baptist Missionary Fellowship of the Prairies," and the "Convention of Regular Baptist Churches of British Columbia." Two groups, the "Fellowship of Independent Churches" and the "Union of Regular Baptist Churches of Ontario and Quebec" merged to form the "Evangelical Baptist Churches in Canada" in October 1953. Ten years later, each individual church of the "Regular Baptist Missionary Fellowship of the Prairies" joined the "Fellowship." Then in June 1965, the well-established Convention of Regular Baptist Churches of British Columbia was received into the Fellowship by their own request. We now had a "shore to shore" testimony for Jesus Christ with a small candle lit in French Canada, which would soon be a lighthouse. Let us look back in history to find how that candle was lit.

***W.S. Whitcombe at Toronto Baptist Seminary, 1945***

A conversation on a train traveling between Ottawa and Toronto left a profound mark upon a young pastor, influenced an entire denomination and brought joy and assurance of eternal salvation to thousands of French Canadians.

As W.S. Whitcombe sat on a train reading his Bible, two French-Canadian university students seated directly across from him asked him, in French, what he was reading. When they heard his reply, one of the students wondered if he was a priest, but Whitcombe stated that he was a believer in Jesus Christ. "Do you go to Mass?" one asked him. "No," he replied and proceeded to witness to them in his limited high school French. His heart had already been touched by a sermon he had heard preached by a missionary from Quebec who was working with the Grande Ligne Mission. [8] We don't know who the missionary was but we do know the work of evangelism was declining in Quebec at this time, as seen in the preceding chapter. It's easy to visualize this Spirit-filled preacher with a burden because of the decline in French work in Quebec. Little did that missionary know, that night he was sowing the seed for a revival in the heart of a young student, the fruit of which is still being seen.

*Toronto Baptist Seminary, 1934*

*Murray Heron, around 1949*

The personal encounter on the train convinced Dr. Whitcombe that something must be done to evangelize French Canada. This was God's doing!

W.S. Whitcombe was a professor at Toronto Baptist Seminary, founded by Dr. T.T. Shields, a leader in the fight against liberalism, in 1927. He persuaded the Board of Toronto Baptist Seminary to make the study of French mandatory because, he argued, the mandate of the seminary was to reach Canada with the gospel, and one-third of Canada's population at that time was French-speaking. Both the study of the French language and a burden for the French people were realized.

*Lorne Heron*

At the birth of the Fellowship in 1953, five pastors, all graduates of Toronto Baptist Seminary, were pastoring the infant French or bilingual churches in Quebec, namely Wilfred Wellington, Murray and Lorne Heron, Yvon Hurtubise, and Tom Carson.

The birth of these churches had not been easy. For a time the early missionaries were

*Lorne Heron in prison,*
*Life magazine, October 23, 1950*

harassed, physically attacked, falsely arrested, and unable to purchase property for a church building. In Val d'Or, "the Catholic Church had been given freely much land in the town, but objected to our receiving one small lot."[9]  Their radio broadcasts were censored by a priest before airing and finally rejected. These pioneer missionaries labored on with near starvation wages, often suffering extreme loneliness. They were denounced from the pulpit in Roman Catholic churches and purported to be heretics, even communists. The Catholic faithful were instructed not to accept any literature from the Baptists, not even a Catholic New Testament. In one case a priest ordered the workers at a local post office to destroy all mail coming from the Baptists. In other cases by-laws were changed in order to restrain missionaries from preaching in the open air, or even made *ultra vires* so they could be charged for deeds committed before the by-laws existed. The early missionaries, and those who dared to stand with them, spent a total of seven years in prison. Lorne Heron himself, over a period of six years (1949 to 1954) spent the equivalent of over one full year in prison for the gospel work. A full-page picture of him appeared in the popular *Life* magazine (October 23, 1950), showing him behind bars.

If the missionaries suffered, the lot of those who accepted the gospel message of salvation, and then showed others the differences between the Bible and the teachings of the Catholic Church, was even worse. Many were ostracized by their compatriots, disowned by their families, and suffered material loss through the burning or vandalizing of their homes. Others lost their employment due to pressure from local priests. In northwestern Quebec, free farmland was given to homesteaders, but the potential colonists had to be approved by the local priest and sign an agreement to help in the construction and maintenance of a Catholic church. Missionary Wilfred Wellington stated that some colonists who became interested were warned that "their land would be forfeited if they continued to receive us."[10]

*Wilfred Wellington around 1935*

*Tom Carson and family in Drummondville, 1952*

Tom Carson, another of the "famous five," began the first Fellowship French Church in the southern part of the province. The church building served both as chapel and parsonage; their front room became a chapel each weekend. The baptistry was concealed under a trap door, covered by a carpet when not in use. When the church in Asbestos began, 60 kilometers (36 miles) from Drummondville, we used the facilities of the Drummondville church for one of our first baptismal services. This church outgrew that building and, after a few years, a second much larger building was built. Recently they completed a third building, built in part by volunteer help, which seats over 350 people and is valued at $1,500,000.

---

### "Renounce Jesus, or I will pull the trigger"

Yvon Hurtubise was a Franco-Ontarian. John R. Boyd, pastor of an English church in Sudbury and W.S.Whitcombe's brother-in-law, undertook a mass mailing campaign offering tracts and a free New Testament to every French home in Northern and Eastern rural Ontario and Western Quebec. When the offer arrived at the Hurtubise home, Yvon requested a New Testament.

John Boyd and William-Henri Frey delivered the precious book in person and followed with numerous visits. One time, Boyd ploughed a field at the Hurtubise farm so that Yvon would be free to discuss the gospel with Frey. Yvon, and many members of his family, came to know Jesus personally, but his father strongly objected. One day he took his rifle and pointed it at Yvon's mother and said, "Renounce Jesus or I will pull the trigger." She explained that now she had come to know the Savior, nothing could make her abandon Him. He slowly lowered the gun to the floor. Another day Mme Hurtubise saw him take his gun and questioned his intentions. She discovered that he planned to kill Yvon and his brother, René, because of their stand for the gospel. Mme Hurtubise took another path, outran her husband to a field where her sons were working and warned them to hide in the bushes. God blessed her strong stand. Her son Yvon, who had been pastoring at Malartic at the time of the founding of the Fellowship, became the first Fellowship French pastor in Quebec. He and his wife Marion (née Ford) went on to minister at Valleyfield, then Drummondville, and three of Yvon's and Marion's daughters married pastors serving in French churches.[11]

*Yvon Hurtubise with his brother John, 1948*

## 1953 to 1963 –God Drafts His Players

In the decade following the formation of the Fellowship, God brought about important changes. The burden for reaching French Canadians with the gospel would no longer be borne by a handful of pioneers and served by one theological school. God stirred our entire Fellowship of churches by the stories of persecution and testimonies from Quebec. He began to call men and women from Europe (Switzerland, France, Czechoslovakia), the United States, Ontario, and French Canada.

The providential hand of God in evangelism and church planting in Quebec must be empasized. It has already been shown how the Ewins and ourselves were brought to Quebec in the 1950s, as for other workers, let's start with another young couple close to home.

William Phillips was among the seminary students who worked in Quebec in the pre-Fellowship era (late 1940s) and were jailed

*William and Blanche Phillips*

for preaching the gospel. During this period Blanche Ford had also gone to teach in a small French school in Northern Quebec. They were married in 1952. In 1951, Bill felt led to become a full-time worker in Quebec and had an interview with Rev. J.F. Holliday, at the time Home Missions Director of the Fellowship of Independent Baptist Churches. He learned that there were no funds available for French church planting. Although Pastor Holliday shared Bill Phillips' burden, all he could do was offer him the pastorate of the Ville-Émard English-language church in Montreal. Bill pastored this church, studied French, and was able to do some work among the French-speaking population with the help of the Ville-Émard church.

Finally the door opened. There was a need for a French pastor in Maniwaki and in 1954 the executives of the Fellowship voted to support the Phillips. When they moved to Maniwaki in 1954, the local priest announced from the pulpit that no one would be permitted to sell or rent property to the "communists that have come to town."[12] Bill Phillips wrote in his book, "A taxi driver who was in conflict with the priest, heard of the declaration and came to see me. He offered to sell us a lot for half price ... Soon after a building bearing the name of Maniwaki Baptist Church appeared."[13]

## From Dallas Theological Seminary
## to École Biblique Béthel

At the same time Jack Cochrane, a student at Dallas Theological Seminary, met a pastor from Moncton, New Brunswick. Cochrane was seeking the Lord's will for his life and later wrote to this pastor for information about *La Bonne Nouvelle Mission.* He responded, mentioning that the École Biblique Béthel near Sherbrooke was looking for a teacher. Cochrane applied for the position and was accepted.

In January 1956, three students at Béthel decided to begin visitation in view of beginning a French Baptist Church in Sherbrooke – a city of 60,000 whose only evangelical testimony was

*Jack Cochrane*

one small Brethren chapel. The Cochranes opened their home for weekly Bible studies and Jack participated in visitation and gave pastoral leadership to this church until Jacques Alexanian arrived in 1962. Jack Cochrane's and Germain Chouinard's production of French evangelical study literature is at the very forefront of anything produced in the last century in French. You will be made aware of this breakthrough later.

### From His Fields to God's Harvest Field

Ernest Houle was one of the students in the Bible course at École Biblique Béthel. He had been a farmer and a very committed Catholic. After becoming a Christian he showed this same zeal in serving Jesus Christ. Upon completion of Bible school, Ernest and Germaine Houle and their young family moved to St.Georges de Beauce in Eastern Quebec, where there were no evangelical believers. He purchased a house, added a third story, transformed the ground floor into a chapel, and opened for business. During the renovations he witnessed to people and told them he was going to start an Evangelical Baptist Church. The date for the opening was set for a Saturday evening in August. The Houles were certain that no one from the community would attend, so Houle invited Wilson Ewin and myself to the first service. It was decided to hold the meeting on the front verandah. As the service started we noted that as far as the eye could see there were lights from parked cars along the street. We took turns giving short messages and singing hymns, accompanied on the accordion. The crowd became agitated and started to throw stones. As the frenzy grew, so did the size of the stones. Rocks bounced off the house and around us, so we thought it wise to end the service *ex abrupto!*

Forty years later, I had the privilege of preaching at the anniversary service of the church in St. Georges. The mayor of the city and his wife were present and thanked the believers of the Baptist Church for their testimony and for the blessing they had been to the City of St. Georges. His daughter has attended services frequently.

## A Quebec Romance

Jean (John) Hamelin was a French-Canadian orphan boy. An elderly couple had adopted him but both died within a few months of one another. Misses Esther Bush and Beulah Courtney helped bring him to the Lord through Daily Vacation Bible School when he was a 12-year-old boy. Tom Carson, an unsung hero of French work, baptized Jean Hamelin.

Arrangements were made for him to study at the *École Biblique Béthel.* There he worked on a farm while completing his secondary education and later his Bible school studies. Walter Angst, the principal of the school, put his arm on Jean's shoulder and said

*John and Helen Hamelin*

"Jean, forget the girls you knew before coming here. Ask God to give you a wife of his choosing." Jean heard that a girl named Helen was coming to the school to improve her French. She had been helping in the Val d'Or/Rouyn-Noranda area and had seen the tremendous need of French schools for the children of the French Christians. During a time of prayer, Jean relates that God seemed to be saying to him, "Here is your future wife." Somewhat puzzled, Jean wondered how this could possibly be true when he hadn't even met her. To shorten the long story of this wonderful romance, Helen Hall, the daughter of Morley Hall, a well-known and beloved pioneer in the Fellowship, did become the bride of Jean Hamelin in 1958. He pastored in the Gaspé Peninsula and in the town of Malartic. Both Jean and Helen helped Murray Heron with music for his gospel television broadcasts. The Hamelins moved to Laval in 1968 and joined their efforts with those of missionary church planter Weldon Clark, establishing a church where they have been faithful workers ever since.

*Helping Murray Heron (center) with television broadcasts*
*(around 1959)*

## From Comfort to Conflict

The Lord was also at work calling missionaries in Europe. William-Henri and Betty Frey were a gifted and gracious couple. William-Henri was a linguist, a beloved pastor and an accomplished preacher; Betty came from a godly family. She was saved early in life and baptized by T.T. Shields[14]. She was a also skilled athlete and through her athletic ability she was able to pay her way through university as a playground supervisor. She not only coached teams but also led seven girls to the Lord, all of whom lived Christ-centered lives to the glory of God. She is the sister of Charles Tipp, who is well-known within and outside of the Fellowship.

William-Henri Frey had come from Switzerland to study at Toronto Baptist Seminary in 1938. His studies were interrupted by World War II, but resumed after the war, and he was chosen as valedictorian of his graduating class in 1945. Betty and William-Henri married the same year and left for Switzerland to take over the pastorate of the Baptist Church in Tramelan. There they enjoyed eleven fruitful years and were loved and appreciated, but at the

*William-Henri Frey publisher of "Le Phare"*

request of the Fellowship Home Missions Committee, they left a vibrant church of more than two hundred people for a church-planting assignment in the Province of Quebec. Just as God called Philip to leave the revival in Samaria to go into the desert where he met the Ethiopian eunuch, so he called the Freys to leave the thriving church in Tramelan to pioneer a work in the spiritual desert of Quebec. When the Fellowship began to negotiate with the Freys, there had been a small presence in Verdun, but by the time they arrived a crisis had reduced the church to only one man; but that man was pure gold. He was a solid Christian, and a great encouragement to the Freys.

Some time afterward, Dr Hall encouraged another experienced couple, the Langlois, to join Mr. Frey's fledgling congregation. They had experience in visitation and she was quite often the soloist in our early rallies.

### From Graduation in Switzerland, to Quebec, by Faith

The Holy Spirit used a professor, Dr. Homer Payne, at Emmaus Bible School in Switzerland, to touch the hearts of two couples. Both couples, Elisée and Marlene Beau and Jean and Charlene Flahaut, independently of each other, set out for Canada on cargo ships, which was the only mode of transportation they could afford.

*Élisée and Marlène Beau*

Neither couple had the financial support of a church or their family. Élisée relates, "We left by faith knowing nothing about Canada, except that God had called us to Quebec."[15] The voyage took nineteen days and it was one continual storm. After arriving in Canada on May 17, 1956, a pastor in Toronto received them, and Elisée immediately enrolled at Central Baptist Seminary in order to learn English and further his theological studies. The following year they moved to Montreal to help the Freys, who, after two years of hard work, had many contacts, but only M. Aubut and two other families were attending regularly.

Élisée Beau recently gave the writer a book covering the terrible suffering of the Huguenots, and how thousands of them had to flee France. The pastor who welcomed the Beaus in Toronto, coincidently enough, was also of Huguenot descent. God's sovereign, providential acts are so interesting to observe.

---

### Is This Canada?

The ship that the Flahauts sailed on had been scheduled to arrive at Montreal, but after eight days at sea the captain informed the passengers that they had been redirected to Fort Churchill on Hudson Bay. The danger of icebergs haunted the crew, and the captain hardly left the bridge during the last two weeks of the voyage. The sound of ice crashing against the sides of the boat was constant and they feared for their lives. When at last they reached Fort Churchill, Jean and Charlene expected to see a modern city (Montreal), but what they saw was a small Inuit village. "Is this Canada?" they asked. Charlene remarked to her husband that even the cars were strange in this land; it was the first time they had seen or heard of snowmobiles. Finally someone told them that large modern Canadian cities lay to the south. This was great news! Jean looked at his watch and questioned, "When will the next train be leaving?" "In three days," replied the Inuit man! Their train trip to Toronto, Ontario was as uncomfortable as it was memorable. They spent three sleepless nights on wooden benches on a train that stopped at every Indian village along the way. William-Henri Frey later introduced this young couple to Central Baptist Church in London, Ontario, and told of their step of faith in coming to Canada to bring the gospel to those whom most Canadians had neglected. The church took a spontaneous offering for them, which proved to be sufficient to meet their needs for their first year in Canada.[16]

*Jean Flahault*

## Late for Dinner by Divine Appointment

The team was not yet complete. Betty and I were invited to Moody Bible Institute in Chicago to speak to several classes about the work in Quebec. Due to tenuous circumstances along the way, the trip took four days and included two sleepless nights. After addressing four classes I was exhausted and was looking for a lounge where I could rest. A student encouraged me to go to the foyer, where a live radio broadcast was underway and the host would be interviewing visitors. I thanked him for this information but my tired body was aching for a place to relax. Betty, however, not knowing my intention, was already on her way to the broadcast, leaving me no choice but to follow. Within a short time I found myself in front of a microphone answering questions.

Meanwhile at Wheaton College, just west of Chicago, a student named Jacques Alexanian arrived home one hour later than usual for dinner. He was French-speaking and had already been moved in his spirit through a professor who spoke of a French-Canadian province where evangelical churches were almost nonexistent. Alexanian turned on the radio and heard an interview with a missionary from Quebec—my interview! He immediately telephoned Moody Bible Institute. I was contacted just before leaving the school and arrangements were made to meet over supper. I invited Alexanian to visit us in Quebec in order to see the spiritual needs firsthand.

While at our house, Jacques attended a small prayer meeting in a "basement chapel" with the half dozen believers who gathered

*Jacques Alexanian and his family, moving to Quebec in 1963*

for prayer. During the meeting, he heard one of the laymen of the church say a prayer that touched his heart. Lionel Gosselin called out to God, "O God, visit the province of Quebec after four centuries of darkness."

## Twice Liberated

The final missionary God called to Quebec in this period was Jan Gazdik. He was caught in the Second World War when his country, Central Slovakia, was invaded by Germany. During the final days of WWII, the Germans were retreating and evacuating men with them. Jan describes what happened:

Five young men and myself deserted, to hide in the depths of the forest as we waited for the Russian Army to bring liberation. One day, when I was out for a short walk, I heard a loud voice behind me that shouted the words, "Halte. Hande hoch" (Stop. Hands up). I dove to the ground and cried, "I want to live, not die! God, deliver me and I will be converted."[17]

The bullets meant for Jan were embedded in a tree. After the soldiers left, presuming that he was dead or dying, Jan made his way across an icy stream to safety.

God had another liberation planned for Jan Gazdik. He came to Christ through the ministry of missionaries in Czechoslovakia, and later enrolled in a Bible school in Switzerland. Meanwhile, back home, the Russians had imposed communism and all missionaries were expelled. He was advised not to return. He obtained refugee status in France, but the communists were searching for Czechoslovakian students outside the country in order to repatriate them. He then fled to the United States. While studying in Cleveland he met Alice and they were married in 1950. The following year they left for France to plant a church in the city of Dijon.

After eleven years overseas, God brought them back to North America. They settled in Trois-Rivières, a city situated midway

*The Gazdik Family, 1961*

between Quebec City and Montreal, which was established in 1634 under the orders of Samuel de Champlain. When the Gazdiks arrived in 1961, this city still did not have an evangelical church within its borders. By God's grace, an Evangelical Baptist Church was established and today more than 300 people attend the recently enlarged church. The congregation is still growing and the church is considering planting a daughter church on the south shore of the St. Lawrence River.

### God's Life Line for the Missionaries – The French Board

With the increase of workers and the establishment of French-language churches, we were invited to send a French worker to sit as a member on the Home Missions Board of the Fellowship. I was elected to that position but from our very first Board meeting in Toronto it was clear that this wouldn't be the answer to our situation in French Canada. Although we did appreciate the English churches' recognition of our existence and our needs. The needs, plans, and problems of the English-language churches, however, were totally different from ours. We needed a Board to deal with a cross-cultural situation, the challenges, plans, persecution, language, and ecclesiastical environment of which were fundamentally different to those of English Canada. At a meeting of French workers in Montreal we asked Pastor E.S. Kerr of Snowdon Baptist Church, who was a member of the Executive Council of our Fellowship, to explain our plight to the Executive Council and request a separate Board for French Canada. The English members of the Council recognized the cross-cultural situation and graciously conceded to the request and, "on November 28, 1958, Dr. Morley Hall, General Secretary of the Fellowship, was authorized to write, "This is to announce the formation of a French Missions Committee by the Executive Council."[18] The French workers were ecstatic.

> This not only joined the French workers in a unified effort, but it brought English and French language churches together under the guidance of the Holy Spirit to accomplish the seemingly impossible task of evangelizing French Canada. The list of the first members of the French Board demonstrates that both English and French churches were represented from the outset, a practice that continues to the present. The initial members were E.S. Kerr (chair person), W. Gordon Brown, and pastors Lorne Heron, Ernest Keefe, W.H. Frey, Harold Hindry, D.A. Loveday and Jack Scott.[19]

### The French Board's First New Missionary

After the founding of the French Board, the majority of missionaries already working in Quebec in cooperation with the Fellowship were accepted under the newly formed French Board. The salvation of the Cotnoir family has already been mentioned, and one of the sons, Gabriel, was a student at Institut Biblique Béthel when the Ewins were studying French there. Wilson encouraged him to apply to the French Board to become a missionary with the Fellowship. Was this a sign of good things to come, that this first new missionary was a French Canadian?

*Gabriel and Nita Cotnoir, 1958*

The church in Asbestos invited Gabriel to help start a work in Victoriaville, a neighbouring city, where there were some contacts and one Christian family, the Elphège Paillés, who lived about 10 kilometers (6 miles) from town. Gabriel and his wife Nita went on to pioneer and serve in a number of other churches, and also helped to found two Bible camps (Camp des Bouleaux and Camp Patmos). He also led in building the beautiful, spacious church in St. Hyacinthe when he pastored in that city.

### The Need of God's Team in Quebec

Two conversions that took place in the late forties and fifties depict the need of workers to preach the gospel in Quebec. They also demonstrate why the missionaries were so motivated to reach people with the good news despite misconceptions within the communities, rejection, persecution, and the danger of arrest by the civil authorities, which were greatly influenced by the ecclesiastical powers.

One conversion took place on a lonely farm in the backwoods of Northwestern Quebec, while the second took place in Southeastern Quebec in the mining town of Asbestos. More than 700 kilometers (420 miles) separate the two residences of the two families concerned, but their testimonies are similar and equally touching.

The account of the first conversion will be quoted verbatim from Murray Heron's book, *Footprints Across Quebec*:

Pastor J.R. Boyd, a fellow pastor from Sudbury, Ontario, sponsored a French radio program to reach northwestern Quebec from the town of Kirkland Lake, just across the Quebec-Ontario border. Occasionally some of us ministering in Quebec were asked to conduct follow-up visits to people who had requested Christian literature or a New Testament. Thus, Pastor Wellington and Les Barnhart, a deacon from the Noranda church, went to visit M. Dallaire who lived about 90 kilometers (54 miles) south of Noranda. Although this man was illiterate, he had been listening to the radio program and was intensely interested in the gospel. He had become so preoccupied with his salvation that he asked his wife to write and request a copy of the Bible and a hymnbook.

When Pastor Wellington and Les Barnhart arrived at M. Dallaire's isolated home in the country, he greeted these servants of the Lord with great joy. He told them how he had hired a taxi and traveled 90 kilometers (54 miles) to Rouyn-Noranda in search of someone to explain the message of the Bible to him in French. But his journey had proved unsuccessful. Anyone he talked to was either unfriendly or unable to help him, and he had returned home without the knowledge he sought.

Still, there was a burning desire in this poor farmer's heart, so once again he hired a taxi, and this time went 60 kilometers (24 miles) across the Quebec-Ontario border into the town of New Liskeard. He thought that in Ontario someone would certainly point him to the way of salvation, since this was "the province of Protestants." However, because he was unable to communicate in English, no one could help him and he again returned home disappointed.

The arrival of Pastor Wellington and Les Barnhart was an answer from God. After several hours of conversation, they asked M. Dallaire if he wanted to give his life to Christ. He answered that he had been waiting for this moment for years. Following a prayer for salvation, M. Dallaire asked if they could sing a hymn together. To the delight and amazement of the two visitors, this man who had never been to *an evangelical* (*evangelical* added by author) church service in his life sang verse after verse in French of the beautiful hymn, "I found a Friend, oh, such a Friend, He loved me ere I knew Him." His wife had read the words to him from the hymn book they had received in the mail, and he had memorized them while listening to the melody on the radio!

When M. Dallaire was able to make the long trip to the Rouyn-Noranda church, Murray Heron had the joy of baptizing him. Murray Heron concluded, "The conversion of Georges Dallaire touched us all deeply. It convinced us that there was a host of people like this country farmer who were desperately seeking peace and hope through salvation in Jesus Christ."[20]

The second testimony begins with a door-to-door visitation. A retired farmer and his wife, living in a small three-room house, welcomed my visit and accepted a New Testament. One of the things this man said during the first visit impressed me. He said that today there are many who are called Monseigneurs, but Mon Seigneur is Jesus. Monseigneur is a French word that literally translates to *My Lord,* in English. It is also the term used for bishops, archbishops, princes, and other persons of eminence. This was a revelation to me that he had lost his confidence in his religious leaders but knew nothing about salvation. I went over passages like 1 John 5:13 where we read, "And this is the testimony: I write these things to you who believe in the name of the Son of God so that you may know that you have eternal life." We studied other passages in the Epistle to the Hebrews showing that Jesus Christ was the great high priest who saves perfectly all those who approach God through him (Heb. 7:25). We read together verses that emphasized the fact that Christ died once for all, as a sacrifice for our sins (Heb. 7:27; 190:11-14). Still M. Tellier didn't seem to grasp that he could only be saved by grace through faith, and not his merits, but that it is the gift of God, nor could it be through good works so that no one could boast (Eph. 2:8, 9). He believed that he was too great a sinner for God to save him by grace through faith.

I had given the Telliers a New Testament on my first visit but later I found that they faced two difficulties. In the first place, M. Tellier was illiterate, and secondly, Mme Tellier had lost muscle tone in her eyelids and was unable to keep her eyes open. She managed to function with the help of scotch tape, which held her eyelids open and permitted her to do limited reading. The characters in the New Testament I had left were too small for her to see. It took some time for our relationship to come to the point where they felt comfortable telling me this.

On the very next deputation trip to Ontario, I was staying in the home of Pastor McLeary in Toronto. During my stay he said to me, "I received some books and among them is one that might interest you. It is in French." I couldn't believe my eyes when he showed me a French pulpit Bible more than 100 years old with the name of the owner, and showing that it had come from the Hebrides islands off the west coast of Scotland. "Could you use it?" he asked me. I assured him that I knew just where I could use it, and related my contact with M. and Mme Tellier. He then gave me the Bible. I could hardly wait to finish the week of deputation!

You should have seen the faces of the Telliers when I presented them this Bible with extra-large print. From that time on, each evening they would position the kitchen table directly under the single light that hung from the ceiling. There Mme Tellier would read the Bible to her husband, as he sat rocking in his chair listening to the Scriptures, as long as her eyes permitted. Like Mary of old, they were seated at Jesus' feet listening to his Word.

This was early in my ministry. I had much to learn in witnessing to Catholics because most of my prior witnessing had been to people who had already heard the gospel and, in general, had a Bible. I had to learn to be patient and let them compare, with the help of the Holy Spirit, what they had been taught with what the Bible teaches (Acts 27:10-11). Even then there was always the fear of persecution, because as one grasped the teaching of salvation by grace through faith and not by works or sacraments, there was often a great price to pay for becoming a believer and following the Bible. What I didn't realize, in the case of the Telliers, was that a close relative had already warned them that if they left the Catholic Church she would never again set foot in their home. Because of my ignorance of these facts in my early ministry, I interpreted their slowness to make a decision for Christ as a lack of interest and didn't visit them for about three or four months.

I had also left a New Testament with a couple who lived on the family farm. Unknown to me, it was one of their daughters and son-in-law. When the couple came into town for their weekly shopping, they would stop at the parents' home. The father would always ask if the man with the Bibles had been by. The answer was, " No" and the 72-year-old M. Tellier went on to explain his interest, "Our church does not teach us the way to heaven, but this young man seemed to have the answer. I fear that he has gone to another city to give his Bibles and we will die without knowing the way to heaven."

Then one day I decided to revisit the Telliers to see if they were reading their Bible and showing any spiritual hunger. I was received like the prodigal son. Soon he, and later his wife, as well as their daughter and son-in-law, all came to know Jesus as Savior. I asked myself, "How many other Octave Telliers are there in Quebec who are waiting for someone to show them the way to heaven?"

M. Tellier related another incident in his life, which had a profound impact upon him. He was fifty years old and had become seriously ill. Family members sent their son into town with the horse and wagon to ask the priest to return with him to give his grandfather the last rites of the church. When the priest saw that he would have to go by horse and buggy, he said he could not do that because the wet snow that was falling might cause him to be sick. He instructed the grandson to get a taxi. The young man did not have the money and so returned without the priest. This took place in 1940 when most farmers did not own cars.

Though totally unexpected, he did recover, and when the family told him what had happened, he came to the conclusion that the priests were not the real servants of God. He further concluded that either the sacrament did not have any power to prepare him for dying or that priest didn't take his office seriously. In either case, he could no longer believe that the priests were God's representatives. But if they weren't, who were his true representatives? Where were they? Why do they not come to us? He went on to explain that when I arrived with the Bible and answered his questions from the Bible, and told him that he could have assurance of eternal life, his interest grew. Also, he was impressed by the way I prayed—not something out of a book, but in my own words. To him, God seemed to be someone that I knew personally. How pleased I was that God had sent me to answer his questions and show him that God did have servants, and like Cornelius and the Apostle Peter (Acts 10), he sends his servants to those who seek him.

The night M. Tellier passed into Jesus' presence I visited him in the hospital. Just before leaving I said to him, "Jesus is important." He took my hand in his big farmer's hand and replied, "Jesus is the only one who is really important." By the time I arrived home, Betty had received a message for me – M. Tellier had passed away. Because of his limited French, the doctor had requested that I go and break the news to his wife. As I made my way through town to their humble home to give Mme Tellier this difficult message, and assure her once again that her husband was with Jesus, I said to myself, "No trophy or honor in sports could compare with the joy of leading a soul to Christ, especially when one sees him pass into eternity." I was glad that God had saved me, and despite all my limitations and shortcomings had made me, by grace, a player on his team along with the other missionaries who had been called to Quebec.

---

### The Sacrament of the Last Rite

Many Protestants do not know what the Catholic Church teaches about the sacrament of the last rite. The following paragraph is self-explanatory.

In a catechism based on Vatican II and published "For the 20th anniversary of the close of the Council"[21] under the order of John Paul II and entrusted to "a commission of twelve Cardinals and Bishops, chaired by Cardinal Joseph Ratzinger,"[22] the sacrament called Extreme Unction for centuries is now called "the sacrament of anointing the sick"[23] and it no longer puts the emphasis on people at the point of death, but it is more a prayer for help and mercy from God, as well as healing of the sick person in any state of illness. In the time of M. Tellier "it was conferred … more exclusively on those at the point of death." [24]

(Endnotes)

1  Jean-Louis Lalonde, *Les loups dans la bergerie, Les Protestants de la langue française au Québec, 1534-2000* (Montréal: Fides, 2002), p. 27.

2  Thomas Guthrie Marquis, *The Jesuit Mission* (Toronto : University of Toronto Press, 1916), p. 11.

3  Mason Wade, *The French Canadians 1760 – 1945* (Toronto: MacMillan, 1955), p. 15.

4  Michel Gaudette, *Guerres de religion d'ici : catholicisme et protestantisme face à l'histoire* (Trois-Rivières, Québec: Éditions Souffle de vent, 2001), p. 45.

5  Wesley Peach, *Evangelism – Distinctly Quebec*, in A. Motz, ed., *Reclaiming a Nation* (Richmond, VA, Church Leadership Library, 1990, p. 156.

6  Wesley Peach, *Histoire du Protestantisme au Québec Depuis 1960* (Québec: La Clairière, 1999).

7  David R Dobson, *A Legacy of Suffering, The Persecution of French Protestants,* to Dr. Bruce Guenther A.C.T.S. Seminary, p. 21.

8  Ernie & Betty Keefe, interview with Leila Whitcombe, November 2002.

9  Rev. and Mrs. Wilfred Wellington, *Rome's Challenge Accepted,* (Published by the author, 1949), p. 35.

10  Wilfred Wellington, *Rome's Challenge Accepted*, p. 36.

11  Ernie & Betty Keefe, interview with Lois Hurtubise Tessier, May 2003.

12  Ernie & Betty Keefe, Interview with William and Blanche Phillips, May 2005.

13  William Phillips, *Modern Day Missionary Miracles*, Published by Fellowship French Missions, 7415, boul. Gouin, Montréal, H4K 1B8, 1998, p.25.

14  Betty Frey, *Mon Mari-William-Henri Frey*, Published by l'Église Baptiste Évangélique de Rosemont, p.10.

15  Ernie Keefe, Interview with Élisée and Marlène Beau, March 2003.

16  Ernie Keefe, Interview with Jean and Charlene Flahaut, March 2003.

17  Jan Gazdik, adapted from *The Evangelical Baptist*, September 1988.

18  Ernest Keefe with Ginette Cotnoir, *A Glorious Fellowship of Churches, Fellowship Baptist Churches in French Canada*, published by The Fellowship of Evangelical Baptist Churches in Canada, Guelph, Ontario, 2004, p. 73.

19  Ernest Keefe with Ginette Cotnoir, *A Glorious Fellowship of Churches*, p.73.

20  Murray Heron, *Footprints across Quebec* (Dundas, Ontario: Joshua Press, 1999), p. 28-29.

21  *Catechism of the Catholic Church*, Libreria Editrice Vaticana, Paulist Press, p.2.

22  *Catechism of the Catholic Church*, p.3.

23  *Catechism of the Catholic Church*, p. 378.

24  *Catechism of the Catholic Church*, p. 378.

# Chapter 3

# *Asbestos on Fire*

*Whenever you are arrested and brought to trial,*
*do not worry beforehand about what to say.*
*Just say whatever is given you at the time,*
*for it is not you speaking, but the Holy Spirit.*
*(Mark 13:11)*

Ever since viewing the city of Asbestos from a scenic lookout on highway 116, our hearts burned to share the gospel with the people of that city and the surrounding villages and rural areas. As previously mentioned, Wilson Ewin and I were returning from New Brunswick. It was 1955, and in the 500 kilometers (350 miles) from Richmond, Quebec to the border of New Brunswick there was not one French evangelical church. Asbestos was one of the first cities we passed through, situated 70 kilometers (42 miles) north of Sherbrooke.

Wilson, a former RCAF pilot, was a highly disciplined man and was always anxious to be doing something. He has related that, while driving in to the city for his courses at London Bible Institute one morning, he was impatiently waiting for the traffic light to change. After what seemed like too long a period of waiting to him, he said to his wife, "Here, take the wheel. That light is not working." He jumped out of his car and stopped the cars passing through the green light. When he had succeeded in directing the traffic and was about to flag the waiting cars through on the red light, the light changed. He was embarrassed by the incident, but it describes his desire to keep things moving! The Lord did use his disciplined nature and zeal for his service, but sometimes the Lord had to apply the brakes and redirect him, too!

Wilson suggested that we take advantage of the Christmas holidays to go to Asbestos for three days to do some door-to-door evangelism. This sounded like a great idea and we thought it might give us some contacts to follow up when we moved to Asbestos in the spring. We contacted a young couple, Marcel and Verna Cotnoir, who had recently moved to Asbestos because of his work with the Shawinigan Light and Power Company. They offered to provide us with hospitality during our visit.

The day following our arrival, we put a few New Testaments (provided by Scripture Gift Mission) and a few Catholic New Testaments in our briefcases. It was not simply a matter of giving out New Testaments, but an effort was made to show people how to use them and to explain how they could be saved. A Catholic New Testament was used for this purpose because it gave us easier access to the homes. When people began to see the differences between the New Testament and what the Catholic Church taught, they would not be able to say that we were using a Protestant Bible.

I would usually begin with 1 John 5:13 to show that one could be saved *now*, and have the assurance of eternal life. We would then refer to verses like Ephesians 2:8,9 to show that we are saved by grace through faith, and not by sacraments or works, lest any man should boast. We also used the book of Hebrews to show Christ's once-for-all sacrifice, and that he is the priest we can go to, in order to be saved perfectly by

> 1 John 5:13
> I write these things to you who believe in the name of the Son of God so that you may know that you have eternal life
>
> Ephesians 2:8-9
> For it is by grace you have been saved, through faith – and this not from yourselves, it is the gift of God – not by works, so that no one can boast.
>
> Hebrew 7:25
> Therefore, he is able to save completely those who come to God through him, because he always lives to intercede for them.

him (Hebrews 7:21-28). This approach usually opened the door for further discussion, because Catholic theology doesn't teach that one can have eternal life and know it. Their teaching is based on a mixture of grace and works, but Romans 11:6 states "if by grace, then it is no longer by works; if it were, grace would no longer be grace."

With this approach, we weren't coming in to upset anyone but wanted to start the fire of the gospel in the hearts of people. However, the people misunderstood our purpose. Usually, Asbestos is a material that does not burn, but our presence there upset many, and another type of fire was lit against us: a fire of opposition.

### The Arrest

It was our first day of visitation. I was just leaving the third house when I noticed the police were waiting for me in their patrol car.

*Ernie Keefe and Wilson Ewin, in door-to-door visitations*

Wilson came out of a house on the opposite side of the street and saw me talking with the police. "That's great," he thought. "Ernie is witnessing to a policeman." There were no more arrests in the North, so we were not expecting opposition from the authorities. In reality, the opposite was taking place. The police officer asked what we were doing. I explained that we were encouraging the people to read the gospel for themselves and that we offered them a Scripture Gift New Testament or sold them a Catholic New Testament at cost, which at that time was fifty cents. The police officer responded, "Get your friend, hop in your car and follow us to the Police Station."

We were left in the Police Station under the watchful eye of another officer. He was very friendly and we began to converse with him. When we asked what the charge was against us, he replied that he was not sure, and he didn't think that the other officers knew either. He went on to say that the Chief of Police was in his office with the parish priest, and they were going through our material to see if they could find a reason to charge us. Eventually the Chief of Police came through the door and declared that we were being arrested for selling New Testaments without a license. We were surprised by this announcement and told him that we did not know that it was necessary to have a license to give or sell New Testaments. We asked if we might see a copy of the by-law, to which they complied. When we had read it, Wilson and I saw that it permitted the distribution of literature *"concerning religion."* The New Testaments we were distributing would certainly fall into this category. When we pointed this out to them, the Chief of Police retorted that this by-law only applied to the diocese of the Catholic Church. We were locked up in jail without having an opportunity to buy a license or explain that we were pastors.

The young man who delivered our supper must have thought we were dangerous criminals, as he looked frightened and kept a safe distance while serving us. At that moment, we realized that we should have been eating at the Cotnoir home, and to further complicate the situation, we had Marcel's car, which he had graciously lent us in place of my old wooden-bodied station wagon.

We asked for the use of a telephone and called the Cotnoirs to tell them we were in jail. They weren't overly surprised at the outcome of our visits.

There were two other important calls that had to be made. We wanted to get the news to our wives, and since this would be long distance, to which we did not have access, Marcel phoned Trudy and Betty. At that time, Betty and I lived in an upstairs apartment in the Ewins' home. When the Ewin girls learned that we were in prison, the oldest one, who was about ten years of age, was troubled. When her mother asked her if there was something bothering her, she said, "Yes. Are they in chains?" Her only knowledge of the inside of a prison was what she had seen in Sunday school lessons, where the apostles were put in chains. Trudy explained that this was not the case. They all had a good laugh, which was, under the circumstances, a good remedy for them.

The second call that was made was to Pastor E.S. Kerr in Montreal, the closest member of the Fellowship executive. He enquired as to our whereabouts. "In prison in Asbestos," we answered, to which he asked, "What are you doing in Asbestos? Who told you to go there? What did you do to get arrested?" After the initial shock he realized that we didn't have a Mission Board at that time to give direction, but we had gone seeking the Lord's will as to where we should go to reach French Canadians with the gospel. All we had was a call from God and the words of Jesus at the end of every gospel, as well as the first chapter of Acts, telling us to go in the power of the Holy Spirit and preach the gospel to all the nations. French Canada was one of those nations, and one of the most neglected.

After Pastor Kerr ended his conversation with us, he arranged an appointment with a Montreal lawyer who was an Orangeman and had defended several religious groups in similar situations, including the Salvation Army and our own Fellowship of Baptist Churches. Pastor Kerr also changed his advice to us. The first suggestion was to let the City of Asbestos keep us in jail until our

*Procès à Asbestos*
*Samedi, 7 janvier*
*10.00 A.M.*

ARTICLE 16  COLPORTEURS - SOLLICITEURS

　　Colporteurs, sollociteurs, marchands,
ambulants dans toutes les autres lignes de marchandises
y compris les revues, journaux annonces, livres, à
l'exception cependant des livres, revues, journaux ou
annonces concernant la religion ou des oeuvres de charité
diocéssaines.　　　$ 25.00

Province de Quebecé

　　Ville d'Asbestos.

December 28th,  -

Illégalment sollioiter la vente de livres, savoir la bible
dans la ville d'Asbestos, sans avoir obtenu au préalable
obtenu une licence ou un permis du Secrétaire-trésorier
de la ville à cet effet.

Le tout contrairement aux dispositions de l'article 16,
de règlement municipal 285, et de ses amendements.

### The By-law used against us

trial, as was done up North, in order to underline the injustice of
our situation. This would have meant separation from our families
for the Christmas holidays. However, the lawyer wanted us to get
to Montreal as soon as possible in order to meet with him, before
the city could make any changes to the by-law.

When Marcel Cotnoir arrived to get his car, he had a Christian
friend with him. Mr. Webb was a member of a small English church
in Danville. It was the only Protestant church among the English
minority that understood why we would evangelize Catholics. There
were three main English Protestant churches in the adjoining town
of Danville, where most of the English-speaking minority lived,
but they were liberal.

Mr. Webb was a longtime resident of Asbestos and knew the police officer on duty very well. Speaking in French in a friendly tone to his friend, the police officer, he said, "Why in the world were two pastors arrested in our town for giving away New Testaments?" The police officer replied that he could not understand either, but that he was just carrying out orders. He went on to say that evidently the Chief of Police thought otherwise. When we moved to Asbestos the Webbs became close friends.

Pastor E.S. Kerr had warned the Chief of Police that our Association was holding him responsible for the arrest, and if the charge was not withdrawn, he would release the story to the Canadian Press. Bail was paid and we were allowed to leave the prison late that evening. We were expected to be in the lawyer's office in Montreal at 9 o'clock the next morning. Tom and Margaret Carson, who had planted our first French church in the southern part of the province, lived an hour's drive from Asbestos in the direction of Montreal. After phoning to see is they could accommodate a couple of jailbirds for the night, they received us royally and listened with patience to our account of the predicament in which we found ourselves. After a short period of discussion over a lunch and a cup of tea, we went off to bed. Wilson's last words that night, as we bedded down, were, "Well Ernie, we can say that we have been in jail for the cause of Christ."

Because it was extremely cold at that time, Tom Carson had suggested that we put our car in his garage so that it would be easier to start in the morning, and somewhat more comfortable. What had seemed a gracious idea turned out to be a bad decision! At about three o'clock in the morning, our sleep was interrupted by the voice of Tom Carson. When we opened our eyes we did not need to ask why he had awakened us; we could see the glow of flames dancing on the walls and ceiling of the bedroom. The garage next door was on fire. We had to get out of the house and get my car out of the garage, which was situated between the house and the flaming garage.

*The bail receipts*

We dressed quickly and ran outside to move the cars. After
starting my car, I noted in the light of the flames that Tom Carson's
car had not been moved and that he and Wilson were trying to get
it started. I did not know what to do. The lawn next to the garage
would have provided an escape route in summer, but it was now
covered with at least three feet of snow. By this time, the adrenalin
level was so high that I believe we could have almost carried it out
of harm's way ourselves. We finally got both cars out to the street
and it was safe to go back into the house. Nobody, however, seemed
calm enough to return to bed. Most of the night was gone and we
were as wound up as a child's toy on Christmas day.

Mrs. Carson prepared a sumptuous breakfast and we ate and we
talked; Tom Carson read a passage of Scripture and led us in prayer.
We were leaving about the time we would have normally been eating
breakfast, but we were glad, in view of the frigid weather and the
age of my car, to be on our way with little time to spare. I tried to
get a newscast but anything resembling one was accompanied by
so much static that it was incomprehensible. Then, like lightning

out of a stormy sky, the *Back to the Bible* broadcast came over the airwaves with unbelievable clarity. The words of an old hymn brought tears to our eyes as we meditated upon them against the background of the past twenty hours. The words were:

> For this one thing I know
> That when the crimson flow
> Fell to this world below,
> It fell on me …

### Wilson and Ernie before the Judge

We were seated in the lawyer's office with Article 16 of the By-laws of the City of Asbestos, as well as the charge against us, held safely in our hands. The lawyer ushered us into his office, asked a few questions and requested to see the documents relative to our arrest. After reading the by-law and the charge against us, he looked at us and said, "They have no case against you, unless they make a new retroactive law." The lawyer's young assistant was alarmed and said, "They cannot do that. It's against a certain article of the law," which he then cited. The old lawyer pulled his glasses down on his nose and, peering over the top, abruptly stated, "I have seen them do it!" He had already defended people such as workers from the Salvation Army.

To have kept us in jail over Christmas time for giving or selling New Testaments would have been bad publicity for the town and its main industry, the American Johns-Manville mine and factory, as well as for the Catholic Church. It was more important however to win the case and the right to give out God's Word in Quebec, as was done by our missionaries and other evangelical workers in North Western Quebec. A Brethren missionary, Roy Buttery was also arrested in Drummondville for going door-to-door and selling New Testaments that were approved by Cardinal Léger. He wrote, "The matter went into the hands of the lawyers. Our cause had a precedent in a case dismissed against a Baptist worker who was doing the same thing."[1] He was probably referring to our case because we were the only ones who had been arrested in that part of the province for giving out literature.

Thanks to lawyer Wherry's intervention and the prayers of God's people, we received a letter stating that the City of Asbestos had withdrawn the charge and that we should appear before the judge to have it withdrawn.

---

**COUR MUNICIPALE**
Casier Postal 20

**HUGUETTE HINSE**
Greffier.

Tél. 170
469

ASBESTOS, Qué.

*Le 4 Janvier 1956.*

*Monsieur Ernest Wilfrid Keefe
69, rue Victoria
COATICOOK, P.Q.*

*Monsieur,*

*Je désire vous aviser que vous devrez vous présenter Devant LA Cour Municipale d'Asbestos, samedi le 7 Janvier 1956, à 10:00 heures a.m. et la plainte va être retirée par le plaignant.*

*Bien à vous,*

*HUGUETTE HINSE, G.C.M.*

*HH:lb*

---

*Letter from the court advising of the withdrawal of charges*

At our court appearance, we were obliged to sign an agreement that we would not take legal action against the City of Asbestos. We did sign the document and assured the judge:

One of our practices as Evangelical Baptists is to be good citizens and, according to the Bible, be submissive to every authority instituted among men. If, however, these authorities transgressed the will of God, who is the supreme authority, in that case we are to obey God.

At the completion of the court session and after having signed that there would be no legal action taken against the city, we were released, but not before the judge delivered a stern warning that we should not return to Asbestos. He further warned, "You will not have any converts and, in all possibilities you could be mistreated, in which case you would be held responsible for provoking the situation." Jesus assured his disciples that when they would appear to trial, the Holy Spirit would give them the words to say. Our response to the judge, given in a quiet, friendly manner, was, "It is not a case of whether or not we will have converts, or that we will possibly be mistreated or arrested. Rather, if Jesus Christ wants us to preach the gospel in Asbestos, we will have no choice but to do just that." Little did he know that God was already leading us to return to the Asbestos-Danville area in the spring. The arrest came to the attention of our churches and other Christians across Canada, and people began to pray for an unknown missionary and a small mining town in Quebec, the town of Asbestos.

It's strange, but the verse that God brought to our minds was Acts 18:9-11, "Do not be afraid; keep on speaking, do not be silent. For I am with you, and no one is going to attack and harm you, because I have many people in this city. So Paul stayed for a year and a half, teaching them the word of God. " This was an encouragement for us, especially the words, "I have many people in this city." We recognized that this promise was given to the apostle Paul, but we were doing the same task for the same Lord. Surely he had called and sent us forth to bear fruit for him, fruit which would remain (John 15:16). We went forth trusting his promises and reassured that Jesus had many people in the city of Asbestos whom the Holy Spirit was preparing to receive the message of the gospel. Despite opposition and threats, God kept us safe, and as in Corinth, there were many who "heard him (us) and believed and were baptized" (Acts 18:8). In this same vein of thought, Jesus himself said, "I have other sheep that are not of this sheep pen. I must bring them also" (John 10:16).

## Arrival at Asbestos

In June of 1955, Betty and I along with our children, Ernest, who was nearly three years old, and his three-month-old brother, Brian, moved to the Asbestos-Danville area. Six months had passed since the arrest and the ensuing warning and intimidating threats of the judge. When we arrived, Marcel and Verna Cotnoir were the only French-speaking evangelical believers in Asbestos. God in his sovereignty had Marcel transferred to Asbestos, just before our arrival, to stand with us in the work.

One month before our arrival we sent out a mailing to Asbestos homes, offering a New Testament. Many people were exhorted for the first time to read the Bible in order to know the Christ of the Bible. From the beginning of Catholic rule, they were usually forbidden to own a Bible. However, this changed with the Quiet Revolution, when Catholic Church scholars made a translation of the New Testament. It was published in Quebec and had the imprimatur of the well-known Cardinal Léger (The word *imprimatur* means it was examined and authorized by the ecclesiastical authorities). It was that Catholic version that we offered to the people of Asbestos. They would be more likely to read it, knowing it was approved by their church. If they found something in it that was not in agreement with their religion – which they usually did – they could not blame us for the differences.

Out of several thousands letters that were sent, we received only eight requests for New Testaments, and when we endeavored to deliver them, only six would accept one. Despite the fact that it was a Catholic Bible, people were still afraid to accept it. It's worth mentioning that no one converted following that effort. We were warned by this experience that much plowing lay ahead and the ground was hard. James wrote, "Brothers, as an example of patience in the face of suffering, take the prophets who spoke in the name of the Lord. As you know, we consider blessed those who have persevered" (James 5:10,11).

***Door-to-door visitations, around 1960***

The next step was door-to-door visitation. Generally, I visited Monday to Friday afternoons and Monday, Tuesday and Thursday evenings. It was not an easy task. The disciples were fearful as they followed Jesus back to Judea (John 11:7, 8); Paul went to Corinth with "fear, and with much trembling" (1 Corinthians 2:3); and Ernie Keefe was scared to death as he knocked on the first door every time he went out to do door-to-door visitation. I often spent about 10 minutes in the car in prayer and repeating such verses as Joshua 1:9; 2 Chronicles 32:7, 8; Isaiah 41:9-13; Matthew 28:18-20; Luke 24:46-49; Acts 1:8; 18:9-11 before knocking on that first door. After contact with the occupant of the house had been made, whether I was welcomed or refused, I was ready for the day's work and had no hesitation or fear of knocking on other doors that day. The French have a saying, "la glace a été cassée" (the ice has been broken), but the first visit the next day I found that "la glace était gelée de nouveau" (the ice was frozen over again)! Sometimes I would say to Betty, "One thing I am going to like about heaven is that there will be no door-to-door visitation there." Nevertheless, in our eleven years at Asbestos, I visited the entire town of 11,000 people and all the homes within a radius of about nine miles surrounding the city, including other towns and villages and the rural area. About 80% of those approached allowed me to present the gospel, and once in conversation with them, I was perfectly at ease. On return visits, I had no difficulty, and my prayer was that the contact had begun to read the New Testament, and that members of the family, or acquaintances, or even the parish priest had not succeeded in discouraging them. Often I was filled with joy after visitations, as I had explained the gospel and left a New Testament, or I had made a return visit to find the contacts reading God's Word. The Psalmist wrote, "The unfolding of your words gives light; it gives understanding to the simple" (Psalm 119:130).

The greatest number of New Testaments that I was able to leave in one afternoon, including an explanation of the gospel, was eight. The most profitable afternoons or evenings were when I was able to make longer, but fewer visits. After a day when I gave a record number of New Testaments, I had a follow-up visit about two weeks later only to find that the priest had confiscated them or ordered them to be burned. Many times I paraphrased the words of Jesus on the cross and prayed, "Father, open their eyes, for they do not realize what they are doing."

Soon I was joined by the first fruits of evangelism, and all the new converts seemed to be zealous to share the errors of the Church of Rome with everyone they knew. Below is the testimony of one couple who was among our first fruits.

---

**Lionel Gosselin**

Though I (Lionel) must go back forty-seven years to share with you the beginnings of my personal walk with God, the details remain so very clear as I remember understanding and believing in salvation by faith in Jesus Christ alone.

Following nearly 300 years of religious darkness in Quebec, God visited our people. In our region (the mining town of Asbestos), Pastor Ernest Keefe and his wife Betty arrived among us to proclaim the good news of the gospel. They first learned our language, then started to visit the homes of the area. Far from our minds was the thought that we would be among the first converts!

Following several meetings and profound discussions with Pastor Keefe, I came to the conclusion that his interpretation of the Scriptures must be false. It was so different from what we had been taught all our lives. In response, my wife and I decided to purchase a "good" Bible – one approved by our Church. We actually bought two approved versions and started reading them.

But what surprises were in store for us! In our Catholic religion, the worship of the Virgin Mary was very prominent. This is what I was looking to confirm in my study of the New Testament. I had a blue pencil and underlined every verse talking about Mary. I was troubled to observe how very little she was mentioned.

We pursued our study of God's Word. We realized we needed more proof, so we asked to visit with our priest. He knew us and we knew him, and we were sure he would give us the answers we were looking for. However, to our great surprise we were told that, for the Catholic Church, the Bible is not the final authority. The final authority rests with the Pope and with church tradition. The Bible, our priest told us, is only a reference book, and not the final authority.

We were a busy young couple. We had our first child by now, and we had built a new home in Asbestos. However, my wife, Jeanne, was a seeker. She continued studying God's Word, but I was afraid to take a public stand for the gospel. The Church of Rome had almost total control over all our lives, our schools, and our hospitals.

To become a believer meant to embark on a direction totally opposite to the ruling system. I was very aware that the consequences of renouncing the Church of Rome would label me as "unfrocked," and invite mockery from my family, my friends, and my colleagues. I felt I was before a stone wall – an insurmountable stone wall. So, I kept going to Mass, in spite of all the Biblical evidences I now knew. I felt like a weakling and a hypocrite. God's Spirit was working in me.

Then on Easter morning, as was my habit, I decided to go to Mass. My young wife was in tears. She understood from reading the book of Hebrews that the Mass was a sacrilege and that Jesus could not be offered again on the altar because he is now beside his Father in heaven. She knew that I understood it too but was still willing to go to Mass because of my fear of persecution. I went to the garage to take out my car. However, something unexplainable happened; it felt as though a strong hand was holding the garage door shut and I was unable to open it. Then the Spirit of God convicted me. The words of the Lord came to me, "My friend, I am not

*Lionel Gosselin with Ernest Keefe*

on the altar of the place where you are going. They cannot sacrifice me again. I am living. I am risen." These words struck me, and I knew it was the Spirit of God speaking to me. I went back upstairs, and on that Easter morning, I was saved. The brick wall came down.

We did suffer the consequences – we were mocked, rejected. Our children could not go to the French Catholic School anymore. We were constantly threatened. Often we would get anonymous calls in the night. But God's power and grace kept us.

This is not the end of the testimony of the Gosselin family. It's only the beginning. As fifty years of evangelical history of Quebec are recounted, this name will appear frequently. There is much more background to Lionel and Jeanne's testimony that is very interesting. First, while most of our contacts were the fruit of door-to-door visitation, it was different in the case of this family. Roland Lacombe was a friend of Lionel Gosselin's father. Like several converts of the era here in Quebec, both had been very active members of the French arm of the Social Credit party. Roland Lacombe had been converted and had become an evangelist but had yet to witness to his friend Rosaire. The working of the Holy Spirit is seen here again because just as we were beginning the church at Asbestos, Roland Lacombe, a zealous Brethren evangelist, suddenly had a burden to visit this man who was living 40 miles away. After a good visit and sharing the gospel, he referred this contact to us because we were starting an evangelical church in Asbestos. He could have organized a Bible study and kept the contact for himself, but he chose not to, but graciously turned the follow-up of his friend over to me.

**Discovering the Teachings of the Bible**

*Rosaire Gosselin*

It was not long before I contacted Rosaire Gosselin. I was very impressed by his gracious character, his intelligence, wisdom, and sincerity. It was his perception that the Catholic Church, with all its riches, did not have the needs of the people at heart and would not even consider a political philosophy that he felt could solve the problem of poverty in Quebec. His confidence in the Catholic Church waned, but being a moral man who was seeking God, he had no choice as a French Canadian but to attend the Catholic Church. There was no other French church in his city. Thus, within the context of the Catholic Church he sought a pious person in whom he could trust, which brought him to the point of putting his confidence in the Virgin Mary.

An event that could have influenced this man was the declaration of the dogma of the Assumption of Mary. This dogma was declared officially in 1950, just six years before I met Rosaire Gosselin. The renowned Catholic theologian, Karl Rahner, in his book on Mary describes this doctrine. He writes:

> So it is that since the Feast of All Saints, 1950, we finally know ... through the infallible definition of the Roman pontiff, that the immaculate virgin mother of God, after completing her earthly course, the Pope in his teaching capacity, has given every Christian supreme certainty that this truth belongs to the content of the divine and apostolic revelation[2]

In conversation, the subject of Mary came up, and I said to Mr. Gosselin that we should look at what the New Testament says about Mary. Hebrews 1:1,2 underlines the fact that in the past God spoke "to our forefathers through the prophets at many times and in various ways, but in these last days he has spoken to us by his Son." I explained that this teaching of Jesus is in the New Testament and we must not add to it! Jesus told the disciples to make disciples of all nations, "teaching them to obey everything I have commanded you" (Matthew 28:20). Furthermore, the apostolic church devoted itself to the teaching of the apostles (Acts 2:42). I suggested that we see what Jesus and the apostles said and wrote about Mary, and if they acted on the same principles as some churches do today.

> This is how the birth of Jesus Christ came about: His mother Mary was pledged to be married to Joseph, but before they came together, she was found to be with child through the Holy Spirit. Because Joseph her husband was a righteous man and did not want to expose her to public disgrace, he had in mind to divorce her quietly. But after he had considered this, an angel of the Lord appeared to him in a dream and said, 'Joseph son of David, do not be afraid to take Mary home as your wife, because what is conceived in her is from the Holy Spirit. She will give birth to a son, and you are to give him the name Jesus, because he will save his people from their sins.' All this took place to fulfill what the Lord had said through the prophet: 'The virgin will be with child and will give birth to a son, and they will call

him Immanuel' – which means, 'God with us.' When Joseph woke up, he did what the angel of the Lord had commanded him and took Mary home as his wife. But he had no union with her until she gave birth to a son. And he gave him the name Jesus (Matthew 1:18-25).

I pointed out that one could not read this passage and doubt that Jesus Christ was born of a virgin. Mention was also made of those who confirmed this fact, the prophets, Isaiah, the angel Gabriel, Matthew who wrote the Gospel, and Joseph who did not send Mary away because he believed the message of the angel. However, there was another point in the passage that is mentioned in very matter-of-fact language, that after the birth of Jesus the marriage was consummated. "Does this seem a sacrilege?" I queried. He seemed to take this in very thoughtfully, so I added, "If so, our marriage is sinful as well and every married person is an adulterer. This cannot be, because God planned marriage in creation." Being an upright moral man, he agreed with this reasoning.

I mentioned that there was another passage that sheds light on this subject and he was eager to see it, and so we read Matthew 13:53-58 together:

When Jesus had finished these parables, he moved on from there. Coming to his hometown, he began teaching the people in their synagogue, and they were amazed. 'Where did this man get this wisdom and these miraculous powers?' they asked. 'Isn't this the carpenter's son? Isn't his mother's name Mary, and aren't his brothers James, Joseph, Simon and Judas? Aren't all his sisters with us? Where then did this man get all these things?' And they took offense at him. But Jesus said to them, 'Only in his hometown and in his own house is a prophet without honor.' And he did not do many miracles there because of their lack of faith.

Does this not appear to be a normal family setting? First, the parents are identified; secondly, the brothers of Jesus are named, and the fact that he also had sisters is underlined. And who said this?

His fellow citizens in a small town. This cannot refer to cousins; it refers to Jesus' half-brothers.

Mr. Gosselin did not speak much, but he read every verse carefully. This was the same New Testament that he had requested from an evangelical broadcast. He had started to read it, but when he talked to his friends about what he was reading he found that they had no interest, so he put it aside. Now he was seeing something that he had overlooked.

We read the account of two other incidents that took place in Jesus' ministry which reveal Mary had no special place in the spiritual realm. The first is found in Matthew 12:46-50:

While Jesus was still talking to the crowd, his mother and brothers stood outside, wanting to speak to him. Someone told him, 'Your mother and brothers are standing outside, wanting to speak to you.' He replied to him, 'Who is my mother, and who are my brothers?' Pointing to his disciples, he said, 'Here are my mother and my brothers. For whoever does the will of my Father in heaven is my brother and sister and mother.'

We discussed what the man expected when he spoke to Jesus and the significance of Jesus' reply. It was evident that Mary had had a special privilege in the human earthly realm, but that in the spiritual realm, all true believers in God who do his will are on the same level and are his family.

The second event is found in the Gospel of Luke. In this case, Jesus teaches the same lesson and the response of Jesus is so forceful that it resembles a rebuttal. "As Jesus was saying these things, a woman in the crowd called out, 'Blessed is the mother who gave you birth and nursed you.' He replied, 'Blessed rather are those who hear the word of God and obey it' " (Luke 11:27,28).

I questioned him:

What do you think of the fact that Jesus reproached the woman who wanted to worship Mary in saying, "Blessed rather are those who hear the word of God and obey it"? Would you say that Mary was blessed because she obeyed the Word of God? The same holds true for us as well. Would God have used Mary if she had disobeyed his Word which was spoken to her by the angel (Luke 1:26-38)?

Mary's answer to the angel Gabriel was, "I am the Lord's servant … May it be to me as you have said." Mr. Gosselin thought this was very logical, and he was amazed that Jesus did not do what Mary requested in Matthew 12:46-50.

I pointed out that Satan is very subtle and that one must read God's Word and accept it exactly as it is written. Satan seduced Eve by twisting God's Word, and he would want to turn attention and adoration away from Jesus to Mary. We then read the account of what Peter said about Jesus in Acts 4:8-13:

> Then Peter, filled with the Holy Spirit, said to them. "Rulers and elders of the people! If we are being called to account today for an act of kindness shown to a cripple and are asked how he was healed, then know this, you and all the people of Israel: It is by the name of Jesus Christ of Nazareth, whom you crucified but whom God raised from the dead, that this man stands before you healed. He is 'the stone you builders rejected, which has become the capstone.' Salvation is found in no one else, for there is no other name under heaven given to men by which we must be saved." When they saw the courage of Peter and John and realized that they were unschooled, ordinary men, they were astonished and they took note that these men had been with Jesus.

Mr. Gosselin was astounded by this passage. I learned that after I had left he turned to his son, Henri-Georges, who had also been present at the time, and said, "If that young man is right, we are wrong. We must study the Bible." The determination on the part of this man resembled that of the Berean people of whom the Apostle Paul spoke as having a noble character because they received the message with great eagerness and examined the Scriptures every day to see if what Paul said was true (Acts 17:11). I continued to visit Mr. Gosselin regularly and discussed subjects such as salvation, the priesthood of Jesus Christ, the inspiration and trustworthiness of the Bible, and the current teaching of religion in the light of the New Testament.

## "We Are Going to Baptize the Baptists"

It was at this time, 1957, that the Eglise Baptiste Evangélique de Coaticook (The Coaticook French Baptist Church) received permission to hold open-air meetings in the town's main park. This small church with few believers asked for help, and Christians came from Sherbrooke, St. Georges de Beauce, St. Jean, and Montreal (including English speaking people from Bethel Baptist Church in Ville St. Laurent). Two or three carloads drove down from Asbestos. It was a trip of 100 kilometers (60 miles) and others had come from even further, but with the beautiful Quebec countryside and the cool evening air, it was a pleasant drive, except for the apprehension caused by some hecklers present at the previous Friday evening service.

Élisée Beau and his family, who had just arrived from France, had quite a shock, this being his first experience of evangelization in Quebec. Following is Élisée's account of this experience:

In the beginning, everything proceeded normally. We sang (hymns) and several had given their testimonies. Several pastors and Christians had come for this occasion from all across the province. It was evening, at sunset, when a group of men accompanied by a Catholic priest suddenly appeared. They were half drunk and seemed intent to stir up trouble. They began by calling out insults and threats. Then, all of a sudden, they began to yell, "*We are going to baptize the Baptists.*" In the middle of the park, there was a fountain in a large pool of water. The men began to pursue the evangelicals to throw them into the pool.[3]

I was one of the men thrown into the small pool surrounding the fountain. The pastors who were giving testimonies and short messages were separated one from another. Some men in the crowd pushed an unlit cigarette in my mouth as I tried to speak. By the time I was dragged to the pool, the others had already been thrown in, having been carried there on the rioters' shoulders. In my case, a young police officer was doing his best to help me but he too was being pushed by the crowd. Arriving at the pool, I saw Ernest Houle, Wilson Ewin, and Jean Flahaut all standing in the water. Jean Flahaut was in the pool with the water from the fountain falling on his head, a New Testament in his hand, and still preaching. The police officer and I had our feet braced against the wall of the pool, resisting the crowd. I reasoned that there was no way I could continue to hold back against the crowd and that it would be safer to go in standing up rather than head first. At this point, I stopped resisting and landed on my feet in the pool. I should have tried to tell the police officer my intentions because when I stopped resisting the pushing, he was overpowered and went in head first, thankfully without injury. It was total chaos!

Élisée Beau further remarked:

> We left, safe and sound, but several of us had had a bath. After this tumultuous meeting, we gathered at the home of the pastor who received several threatening phone calls. It was only with God's protection that we were able to spend some time at that place without harm. This visit gave us a general idea of the climate that was reigning in Quebec, our future mission field. We were able to see the power that the Catholic Church had over the people. Quebec really needed the Gospel of peace, the peace of Jesus Christ.[4]

A very popular tabloid in those years, Allo Police, reported, "On the 2nd and 9th of August the Baptists were interrupted in their evangelistic work by a crowd of several hundred people."[5]

From an interview with the police chief of Coaticook, Allo Police reported as follows:

*Newspaper article reporting the incident*

On August 2nd a group of men came to turn the meeting into a tumultuous mob: one single policeman did everything he could to establish order. The police chief Groleau was observing all this from the Police Station but no effort was made to call for back up from the provincial or local police forces." He said that, "these men, while under the influence of alcohol, would have been able to cause greater problems and that it was only by a miracle that nothing worse took place."[6]

Our God protected us, permitting us to return and preach the following week.

I was reminded of what the apostle Paul wrote in Ephesians 6:12, " ... our struggle is not against flesh and blood, but against the rulers, against the authorities, against the powers of this dark world and against the spiritual forces of evil in the heavenly realms." Paul then terminated this section with a request, "Pray also for me, that whenever I open my mouth, words may be given me so that I will fearlessly make known the mystery of the gospel ... " (Ephesians 6:19). I realized that we were in a spiritual warfare and the opposition had great resources both in the heavens and on earth. On the other hand, did God not promise victory to Israel over "nations greater and stronger than you, with large cities that have walls up to the sky" (Deuteronomy 9:1)?

### Home Sweet Home

Leaving home for an afternoon or evening of visitation, I knew that I had a wife who was a prayer warrior. As well, upon arriving at home after the visits, there were two little boys there, whom God had given us; Ernie was four years old and Brian just a few months. They helped relieve the stress of visitation. Our favorite game was similar to soccer and involved a small air-filled ball. I would hold Brian with both hands and put his feet under the ball and he would give it a little kick. He usually chuckled when the ball became airborne. Ernie, for his part, got under the kitchen table and used the open area between the two legs as a goal. Things went well for weeks until one day I must have lifted Brian's feet too high, because the ball soared over the table and went crashing through the window. Ernie ran to his mother who was in another room. He was afraid Betty would be upset with me and also that our soccer season would come to an abrupt end, so he explained, "Brian broke the window!"

*Ernest Keefe with children*

### Getting to know the "Once for All" Sacrifice of Christ

We continued to visit, explain the gospel, and place New Testaments in homes that would accept one. God was at work and he began to save people. One night I dropped into Henri-Georges Gosselin's home to have a visit and hopefully to have an occasion to discuss the gospel. The phone rang and I understood by what was said that his brother, Lionel, had lost his wallet. Someone had found it and wanted to give it to Henri-Georges so he could pass it on to Lionel. Henri-Georges said that he had no vehicle because his car was being repaired. I offered immediately to drive him to Lionel's house so he could deliver the wallet. You have already read Lionel's testimony, but it is interesting how God opened the door, which led to numerous discussions before he accepted the Lord of whom the Bible speaks. I had no idea how I would be received, even though I was returning the lost wallet. I reasoned that they might not want me to go and knock on their door with a Bible, but returning a lost wallet would be acceptable. Henri-Georges accepted my offer and Lionel and his wife, Jeanne, knew that we were on our way. Timidly I followed Henri-Georges into the house. Jeanne appeared and said, "Do you have something good from the Bible for us tonight?" Somewhat surprised, I questioned, "Are you reading the Bible?" She answered affirmatively and went on to explain that she had read the book of Hebrews and could not, and would not go back to Mass. All her life she had thought Jesus was being offered bodily in the Mass, and that it was a literal sacrifice of Jesus Christ. The book of Hebrews had enlightened her. It taught her that Jesus died once for all for her sins and now he is at God's right hand as her great high priest.

***Lionel and Jeanne Gosselin***

Jeanne was right, for this epistle does teach that Jesus died for our sins *once for all* (Hebrews 7:27). Hebrews 10:1-14 also states this truth very plainly. First of all, chapter ten shows why sacrifices are repeated:

The law is only a shadow of the good things that are coming – not the realities themselves. For this reason it can never, by the same sacrifices repeated endlessly year after year, make perfect those who draw near to worship. If it could, would they not have stopped being offered? For the worshipers would have been cleansed once for all, and would no longer have felt guilty for their sins. But those sacrifices are an annual reminder of sins, because it is impossible for the blood of bulls and goats to take away sins. (Hebrews 10:1-4).

Jesus knew the Old Testament. He also knew that animal sacrifices that were offered repeatedly could not cleanse a sinner or please his heavenly Father, otherwise once cleansed from sin, sacrifices would cease. As verses 5 to 10 state:

Therefore, when Christ came into the world, he said: ... 'Sacrifices and offerings, burnt offerings and sin offerings you did not desire, nor were you pleased with them' (although the law required them to be made). Then he said, 'Here I am, I have come to do your will.' He sets aside the first to establish the second. And by that will, we have been made holy through the sacrifice of the body of Jesus Christ once for all (Hebrews 10:5-10).

To Jeanne Gosselin, these verses jumped out of the text as she read them. But in spite of Jesus' and the apostles' explicit teaching of Christ's *once for all sacrifice*, the Jewish priests continued to offer daily sacrifices, but they did not take away sins, as confirmed by verse 11, "Day after day every priest stands and performs his religious duties; again and again he offers the same sacrifices, which can never take away sins."

After the destruction of the Jewish temple by the Romans in 70 A.D., the Jewish priests did not offer animal sacrifices. Furthermore, Jesus replaced the Levitical or Jewish priesthood by himself. However, there are churches that try to imitate the Jewish priesthood and they pretend to offer Jesus anew in their services.

This is a sacrilege because Jesus himself said he offered himself *once for all*. On the cross Jesus cried out, "*It is finished.*" That is, his sacrifice for sin. Here is what Hebrews 10:12-14 says about Jesus' priesthood and his sacrifice, "But when this priest had offered for all time *one* sacrifice for sins, he sat down at the right hand of God. Since that time he waits for his enemies to be made his footstool, because by *one* sacrifice he has made *perfect forever* those who are being made holy."

Jeanne Gosselin reasoned that the priests who claim to offer Jesus Christ anew, even if they say it is the continual sacrifice of Jesus, make the same mistake as the Jewish priests, and she likened the verse Hebrews 10:11 to Catholic priests who offer the sacrifice of the Mass every day. The Holy Spirit had enlightened this woman to this great truth that Jesus had paid for her sins *once for all* on the cross. To continue to offer him anew in the Mass was, in her understanding, blasphemy. As the Bible states, God the Father "did not spare his own Son, but gave him up for us all" (Romans 8:32). Note that this is in the past tense, thus a completed work. The same passage of the Bible continues in regard to Jesus' part in salvation, and declares, "Christ Jesus, who died – more than that, who was raised to life – is at the right hand of God and is also interceding for us" (Romans 8:34). Jeanne grasped the fact that he is not in the sacrifice of the Mass but at the right hand of God.

That same week we had invited two young women from l'École Biblique Béthel (Bethel Bible School) to spend the weekend with us, as they lived 700 miles from the school and could not get home during the school term. While Réjeanne Trudel and Huguette Vézina were with us, Betty and the two young women visited Jeanne. During the visit, she asked if she had to read the entire Bible before she could be saved. They explained to her that since she knew that Jesus had died for her sins, she could be saved through faith in Him, as Hebrews 7:25 explains, "Therefore he (Jesus) is able to save completely those who come to God through him, because he always lives to intercede for them." That day Jeanne went to God through faith in Christ and was saved. She became a vibrant witness to this truth, and along with her husband, has led many to the Lord through the great high priest, Jesus Christ. Lionel also studied the Bible, especially regarding Mary and found that the Mary of the Bible, as shown primarily in Jesus' teaching, was not the same Mary as he had been taught in his church, as has been cited previously in his testimony.

There was another family by the name of Fortier. The first day I contacted this family in door-to-door visitation, Mme Fortier showed a hunger for the Word of God, and she convinced her husband to read the Bible as well. In a relatively short time she, and later her husband, confessed faith in Christ for salvation. I recall her as a young believer telling us, "It's amazing. My choices of television programs have completely changed since becoming a Christian."

God was also working in other hearts. Mme Annette Gosselin, Lionel's mother, had also begun to read the New Testament. She became convinced of the truth of the gospel but was fearful that if she became a believer the Catholic Church would no longer permit her to visit her daughter, who was a nun. She kept reading her New Testament, however, and came across the verse, " … anyone who loves his son or daughter more than me, is not worthy of me" (Matthew 10:37). Finally, she reasoned with the Lord that if she followed him in obedience to his word, he could surely take care of her daughter; no convent walls would be too high for him. This was the woman who told me that her husband would not be able to accept the gospel and take an open stand for the Lord because of the burnout he had suffered due to his political connections, and this because she was sure it would be much more stressful than what he experienced in politics. She had already decided to follow Jesus whatever the cost, and what a witness she became! She then began to pray for her husband's salvation.

**I Want to Buy a Fifty Dollars New Testament**

Another touching story is a family that moved to our area when the company for which the husband worked was awarded a contract in Asbestos. It was to last a year or two. Once again, it was in door-to-door visitation that the acquaintance of this couple was made. On the first visit the husband was not at home, so I showed the New Testament to his wife, spoke of salvation, and explained that we had a Scripture Gift New Testament that we could give her, or a Catholic New Testament that she could buy for fifty cents. I suggested that I come back when her husband would be at the home, at which time she could decide which one she would like. She told her husband about the visit and said that she would like to buy the Catholic New Testament. Upon my return, she mentioned that she would like to see the Catholic New Testament that she could buy for fifty dollars. Somewhat surprised, I told her that it cost fifty cents and not fifty dollars. I saw relief in the husband's face, but his wife went on to explain that she thought I had said fifty cents but couldn't possibly believe that such an important book could be so inexpensive. She then bought a New Testament and began to read it avidly. Since her husband would be in Asbestos only for the duration of the contract, the Christians were anxious for her to be saved before returning to Montreal. Despite all the efforts of the women in the church, she could not grasp salvation as a gift of God that was received by faith in Christ. Then one Sunday morning she arrived for the morning service and she was beaming. She went from one Christian to another telling them, "I really saw it. It was so clear. Jesus said, 'He who believes in me has eternal life.' I said, 'Heavenly Father, I believe in Jesus with all my heart; now I know I have eternal life.'"

> What a joy to know that one plants the seed and another waters it, but it is only God who can give the increase. In writing to the Corinthians Paul said, "I planted the seed, Apollos watered it, but God made it grow" (1 Corinthians 3:6). God also gives the assurance of salvation for "The Spirit himself testifies with our spirit that we are God's children" (Romans 8:16).

One day a fellow pastor dropped in for a visit. As we talked about the Lord's work and evangelism, I mentioned this very special contact that I had. He was a man in his early sixties, and it was evident that he was not well. On the other hand, he was one of the most gracious, intellectual, and wisest men that I had ever known. I invited this pastor to make a visit with me and we went to visit Mr. Gosselin.

This man had talked to me previously about his activities in politics. The Great Depression of the thirties – seeing so many people live in poverty, seeing able-bodied men wanting to work but being unemployed in a country such as Canada with all her natural resources – left a mark on his life. I could sympathize with him. I was a child born during that period. Men often came to our door asking for a meal and my mother, moved by Christian compassion, never turned anyone away. She reasoned that if we fed them, God would give us the food to help others and feed ourselves. One day a young man came by our home begging for a meal. My mother asked my older brother if he would get something ready for him. When questioned if bacon and eggs would be all right, the young man replied that when one had not eaten for three days, anything would taste good.

In the face of this injustice, Mr. Gosselin related how he had studied different philosophies and political movements, even some more radical ones, seeking an answer. He came to the conclusion that the Social Credit Movement that came out of the Canadian West had put their finger upon the problem in our society and offered a logical solution. In view of this, he, along with his wife, gave all they could to this movement by means of participation, money, and energy. This caused him much fatigue, opposition, and ostracism – some resulting from his confrontations with the Catholic Church, which did not welcome a political movement from Western Canada that had many evangelicals among its leaders. Furthermore, the Catholic Church had a good relationship with both federal and provincial parties, which proved advantageous to it. Whether Mr. Gosselin was right or not is not the question that concerns us here. Rather, it was the fact that he was so sure it was the solution that he stopped at nothing to try to popularize this movement. This caused the burnout of which his wife had spoken and from which he had not yet recovered. He was obliged to withdraw from politics, and as Mme Gosselin had said, to follow the gospel in Quebec in the Duplessis era would be more stressful and he would meet with more opposition than he had been subjected to in his political involvement. Furthermore, he was now in his sixties.

During the visit, we discussed the gospel. Mr. Gosselin also mentioned different religious movements, including the one into which he was born as a French Canadian. In his judgment, they all fell short. Then he added, "There is a great love between me and men like Roland Lacombe and Ernest Keefe, who led me to my Savior." I could not believe what I was hearing from his lips. I asked him if he had received Jesus as his personal Savior. "Yes," he replied. "On your last visit you said that all my life I had sought peace in general for our world and also peace for myself, but I never found it because I had never gone to the Prince of Peace to receive it. After you left, I went into my bedroom, knelt by my bed and prayed to God. I told him, 'I want to receive your Son, the Prince of Peace, as my Lord and Savior.'" I could not recall having told him those words, but sometimes God uses our simple statements rather than some great argument so that the glory will be his and not ours.

There are difficult times in missionary work. Good contacts are lost because of the threat of persecution, sometimes Christians are not faithful, and missionaries often have to survive on a small salary. Then there was the pressure of being marked people, living in a small city where we were considered odd or even religious fanatics. We didn't have the favor of local liberal Protestants either, who wondered why we would evangelize people who already considered themselves Christians. However, when someone like Mr. Gosselin came through for the Lord, it was a time of rejoicing in heaven and on earth. I could not wait to get home to give Betty the good news. If someone had been following me, I think they would have seen my Volkswagen beetle hopping up and down all the way home!

As we entered the house, I announced to Betty that I had a pleasant surprise for her. Immediately she asked if Mr. Gosselin had accepted the Lord. I explained that it was after my last visit that, all alone, he had made his decision. She replied, "What is impossible to man is possible with God," and tears ran down our cheeks as we embraced one another. "This a great answer to prayer," she said, "and his testimony is going to have an effect upon Asbestos and on our church." Jesus was surely building his church at Asbestos.

## The City of Asbestos Turned Upside Down

New converts were being baptized and were sending their abjurations to the Catholic Church. Abjuration was a document advising that you no longer believed in the Catholic Church, that you were no longer in agreement with their theology, and that you wanted them to take your name off their registers. You were then protected against any claims to yourself or your property or your school taxes. Though you sent in your abjuration, the Catholic Church did not take your name off their registers, because according to their teachings, once you were baptized in a Catholic church, you were a Catholic for life. In a family when only one member left the Catholic Church, there has been some instances when the believer died, the family took them quickly, and did a catholic funeral and burial for them despite their desire.

A Knights of Columbus member invited one of our new believers to his house, where he tried to dissuade him from being baptized in the Baptist Church. The Christian replied that the Second Vatican Council had declared that the Catholic Church now recognized baptisms performed in non-Catholic churches. This Knight of Columbus warned that it applied only to people who were baptized outside of the Catholic Church, but if one had been baptized in a Catholic Church – the true church of Jesus Christ – to be baptized again in another church would be blasphemous. That held the risk of excommunication.

The following is an excerpt directly from Vatican II (The Second Ecumenical Council of the Vatican, from 1962 to 1965) which shows the position of the Catholic Church on the question of baptism, "The Church's practice in this matter is governed by two principles: that baptism is necessary for salvation, and that it can be conferred only once."[7] Evangelicals do not agree with this statement because salvation is by faith, not by baptism. Note in the following excerpt one of the principal concerns of Vatican II, "The restoration of unity among all Christians is one of the principal concerns of the Second Vatican Council. Christ the Lord founded one Church and one Church only."[8] Therefore, the unity of all Christians in one church is the aim of the Roman Catholic Church, according to their teaching. The eminent Catholic theologian, Gregory Baum, states, "The last end of ecumenism is the return of separated Christians to the Church of Christ, that is, to the Roman Catholic Church."[9] To simplify this, the Vatican II Council accepts the baptism and the baptized of other Christian denominations into the Catholic Church. Regarding people who have been baptized in churches outside of the Catholic Church Vatican II declares:

> For men who believe in Christ and have been properly baptized are brought into a certain, though imperfect, communion with the Catholic Church ... all who have been justified by faith in baptism are incorporated into Christ; they therefore have a right to be called Christians, and with good reason are accepted

as brothers by the children of the Catholic church. (Decree on Ecumenism, n.3).[10]

Lionel Gosselin asked, "Does this document mean that a former Catholic who is then rebaptized outside of the Church would not be accepted back into the Catholic Church?" The Knight of Columbus responded what Vatican II declares:

The Decree on Ecumenism makes clear that the brethren born and baptized outside the visible communion of the Catholic Church should be carefully distinguished from those who, though baptized in the Catholic Church, have knowingly and publicly abjured her faith … What Canon 2314 prescribes is only applicable to those who, after culpably giving up the Catholic faith or communion, repent and ask to be reconciled with mother Church.[11]

For other Christians who have been baptized in a non-Catholic Church and then rebaptized in another church, once again Vatican II Council teaches:

one cannot charge with the sin of separation those who at present are born into these communities and in them are brought up in the faith of Christ. Hence, in the absence of such blame, if they freely wish to embrace the Catholic faith, they have no need to be absolved from excommunication, but after making profession of their faith according to the regulations set down by the ordinary of the place they should be admitted to the full communion of the Catholic Church.[12]

This means that anyone who is baptized in any church bearing the name of Christian is welcome into the Catholic Church. Those, on the other hand, that have been baptized in the Catholic Church, and then have been rebaptized according to believers' baptism because they have become convinced that infant baptism and the teaching that baptism is necessary to salvation are not biblical, are not welcome in the Catholic Church. If one wishes to return to the Catholic Church, he must repent of his terrible sin and ask to be reconciled with the Catholic Church.

### Infant Baptism Falsely Understood as Regeneration

I once attended a funeral of a relative of one of our members in a Catholic Church. During the service, the priest said that we did not need to worry about our sister's death because, he said, she was born again. However, the priest was referring to her infant baptism, which, according to Catholic teaching, has several sacramental effects.

The new Catholic Catechism edited by the Vatican Library in 1994, and bearing the imprimatur of Joseph Cardinal Ratzinger, declares that, "the two principal effects (of baptism) are purification from sins and new birth in the Holy Spirit"[13]

However, the Bible says that we are saved by grace through faith (Ephesians 2:8-9), and not by baptism. Evangelical Christians hearing the priest's statement could conclude that she was born again. They could have easily left the church stating that they had attended a Catholic funeral in which the priest and the deceased were born-again Christians. This bears witness to the danger of not understanding Catholic teaching and interpreting biblical terms in the evangelical sense, which is not at all what Catholic doctrine teaches.

There was another man who fought against the gospel and lost! I knocked on the door of his home one afternoon as he was just getting home from work. I told him that I was visiting the homes in town to encourage folk to read the New Testament.

He began to ask questions that made me think he had heard Christians talking at work or had read some gospel tracts. He had questions about the forgiveness of sin. Where does one go after death, and can one know in this life that he has eternal life. Can your pastors marry? Do you pray to Mary and the saints? What do you think of confession to a priest? Can ordinary people understand the Bible? Can we be sure the Bible is reliable? Do you have a pope?

As I answered every question from the Bible, he became so interested that he went beyond his supper hour, while the family went ahead and ate their supper. His wife was a fervent Catholic and was not happy about her husband discussing with me and finding answers in the book that ordinary people were forbidden to read – the Bible. Finally, he said to me, "That's enough." Many biblical answers had surprised and even bothered him. Then he said again, "That is enough. I have missed my supper. Do not come back. I do not want to talk any more about the Bible." Despite his request, I wrote on the card in my visitation file, "Go back to this home. The man asked good questions and is troubled by the answers. Revisit in two months."

In about two months, I returned to his home and again I was permitted to enter. The visit was much like the first one with different questions, or others related to what we had studied previously. The main difference this time was that he went and served his own dinner, put the plate on the corner of the table between us, and ate during our discussion. After a good visit and evidence of progress by the questions he asked, he suddenly interrupted the conversation and said, "Hey, I thought I told you not to come back!" "That's right, you did. But when I see a man with a hunger for answers to very important spiritual questions, I can't help but return." He then assured me that this would be the last visit. "This is final," he affirmed.

He was a truck driver in the open pit, and the mammoth truck he drove from the pit to the mill had a two-hundred-ton capacity. The cab on the shovel was large enough to accommodate the entire team when the weather was bad. This man chose to stay outside in the frigid weather because if he went inside he would find himself with the shovel operator, who was a Christian, whom he feared would talk to him about the gospel. Generally the men on the team, after they had moved the huge wires or helped the operator with some other operation, would be glad of the opportunity to go inside and warm up, and eventually this man did find the courage to meet the Christian face to face, who did indeed talk to him about the Lord and eventually helped lead him to Christ. As for his wife, she began to read the Bible in order to defend her Catholic faith, but as has been the experience of so many others, she saw vast differences between the Bible and her church. Before long, she became a strong believer and was devoted and faithful to the end.

In our travels, and in reading articles concerning the French work, we find there's a notion that it was mainly nominal Catholics who were responding to the gospel message. What we and other fellow workers have found is that the more devout Catholics became stronger Christians. Many are the pious and committed Catholics who have come to the Lord. Their struggle was fiercer and longer, but once the decision was made, nothing could deter them in their witness and service for the one who had saved them and given them assurance of eternal life.

This was my baptism into Quebec evangelization. I learned so much and studied deeply about Catholicism. I learned much more through visitations and chatting with the converts from Catholicism to Christ. In my later studies, the subject of one of my master's degrees was *Historical Theology With A Special Emphasis On The Catholic Church*. The subject of my thesis was *From Trent to Vatican II, a Study in Change*.

(Endnotes)
1   Roy Buttery, *Arrest*, in *News of Québec* (Sherbrooke, Québec: Editor Arthur C. Hill,
    1959), p. 33.
2   Karl Rahner, *Mary Mother of the Lord, Theological Meditations* (Montreal: Palm
    Publishers, Imprimatur E. Morrogh Bernard Vic. Gen. Westmonasterii, die 30.
    Novembris, 1962), p.84-85.
3   Élisée Beau, *Une vie sous l'appel du Berger, autobiographie d'Élisée Beau,
    Missionnaire pionnier au Québec* (Montreal : Édition SEMBEQ, Collection « Notre
    histoire », 7415 boul Gouin Ouest, Montreal (Québec) H4K 1B8 Canada, 2005),
    p. 77,78.
4   Élisée Beau, *Une vie sous l'appel du Berger*, p.78.
5   *Allo Police*, August 25, 1957, p. 11.
6   *Allo Police*, August 25, 1957, p. 11.
7   Austin P. Flannery, *Documents of Vatican II, Decree 35 II, The Validity of Baptism
    Conferred by Ministers of Churches and Ecclesial Communities separated from Us*
    (Grand Rapids, Michigan: William B. Eerdmans Publishing Company, 1975), p. 487.
8   *Decree on Ecumenism 32 Vatican II, Unitatis Redintegratio* (November 1964),
    p. 452,1.
9   Gregory Baum, O.S.A., *That They May be One* (Westminster, Maryland:
    The Newman Press, 1958), p.98.
10  Austin P. Flannery, *Documents of Vatican II, Decree 35 II, The Validity of Baptism
    Conferred by Ministers of Churches and Ecclesial Communities separated from Us*
    (Grand Rapids, Michigan: William B. Eerdmans Publishing Company, 1975),
    p. 487, No. 10.
11  Austin P. Flannery, *Documents of Vatican II*, p. 490, No. 19.
12  Austin P. Flannery, *Documents of Vatican II*, p. 490, No. 19.
13  *Catechism of the Catholic Church*, Imprimatur Joseph Cardinal Ratzinger
    (Libreria Editrice Vaticana , Paulist Press, Mahwah, New Jersey, 1994) p. 321. e

# Chapter 4

## *The Catholic Church Goes on the Defensive at Asbestos*

Just before moving from Asbestos in 1967, I had two months to fill before my resignation became effective, and I wondered what I should do to be fruitful during this time. A new street had recently been completed and was home to a housing development I had never visited. This was a good project for door-to-door visitation. At the second house I visited, I found the man very friendly. Finally, he said, "Do you realize that when you came to town about ten years ago and started to visit and talk about the Bible, *the whole town was turned upside down?"* His wife interrupted him and said, "And no one was more upset than you!" I was able to continue to share the gospel with him and encourage him to read his own Catholic New Testament, or if he preferred I could supply one. I assured him that our aim was not to upset people but help them find peace for this life and full assurance of spending eternity with God through faith in Christ.

Going back to the beginning of our work, Asbestos was a town of 11,000 people, almost exclusively French Canadian. Danville, a town with a population of about 4,000, was situated five kilometers (three miles) away. There was also a rich farming area around these two towns, with several small villages. Asbestos was a one-industry town. It was here that the Canadian Johns-Manville Company had an underground and open pit mine, a modern mill, and a factory to produce asbestos by-products. The great majority of the men worked at the mine; everyone knew each other and news traveled quickly. This both helped and hindered evangelism. It helped in the sense that the Christians "preached the Word wherever they went" (as in Acts 8:4). Their enthusiasm, joy and knowledge of the Bible were impressive. The trouble came when someone saw one of the Christians or myself visiting a family or individual; they would often soon be harassed. Those who dared to attend our church, or let it be known that they were reading the Bible, would be badgered and even ostracized by family, friends, relatives, or neighbors. Many a good contact couldn't stand the pressure and refused to receive further visits, and many destroyed their New Testaments. Nevertheless, many were reflecting on the teachings of their church and their salvation. Priests were being asked questions about the Bible and their Catholic religion that oftentimes they found difficult and embarrassing to answer.

### The Means for the Reaction

The Catholic Church found this situation intolerable and it came to a head in the summer of 1959, three years after our move to Asbestos. They sent a team called "*Les Messagers de la Bible Catholique*" (The Messengers of the Catholic Bible),[1] which was founded by R.P. Henri Roy and sanctioned by the Catholic Church.

> On March 25, 1952, this organization received the official church approval for all the rules and regulations of its charter … An appeal was made to laymen to spread the message of Christ to the homes. After receiving serious preparation, these laymen went out two by two to accomplish their mission: to bring the message of Christ to the homes, door to door. In order to awaken sleeping consciences, in order to restore solid religious convictions to negligent Catholics, in order to shake up the apathy of the world, it was necessary to find a means of entering homes to transmit the Word of Christ.[2]

Unfortunately, the message of salvation by grace through faith in Christ alone was not presented by the Messengers. Furthermore, the message of the Bible was mixed with Church tradition. Tradition was having the same effects for which Jesus condemned the Jews when he said to them, "You have let go of the commands of God and are holding on to the traditions of men" (Mark 7:8).

This team arrived in Asbestos with two huge trailers; one was to house the team while the other was used for literature and a place for interested people to discuss with the members of the team and/or the priest who happened to be present. "Usually when the mobile vehicle arrived in an average sized parish, it remained there for a week. In less populated parishes, the Messengers would remain for two or three days."[3] In Asbestos, however, the team spent a whole month!

LE CITOYEN, ASBESTOS.  VENDREDI, LE 14 AOUT 1959

# Les Messagers, porteurs
# de la Parole du Christ

*The large trailers of the "Messengers" parked
in the centre of Asbestos*

### The Purpose of their Visit

The purpose of their visit was no secret, as explained in the local paper, *Le Citoyen*:

> During a period of four week the 'Messengers' visited every home in Asbestos, endeavoring to set many things right ... Indeed, no one is ignorant of the fact that for a couple of years numerous false prophets have come to sow the tares of error and doubt in the hearts of our citizens.[4]

The expression "false prophets" targeted the pastor and members of the newly founded French Baptist Church. What was called "the tares sown among the wheat" meant the message of the Bible that is preached by evangelical churches the world over. However, this can be verified by the contents of the New Testament and the testimonies of the French Canadians who chose to follow the Word of Christ rather than the tradition of men.

As for saying there were *numerous* so-called "false prophets" coming to Asbestos, this was totally untrue. I began to visit door-to-door in Asbestos in June 1956. During those first three years no one from the outside ever came to help us in the evangelization of Asbestos. Not one! It was new converts who turned the city of Asbestos and the surrounding area upside down. As for me, what could a young, inexperienced English pastor from Ontario do to upset this city? It was the new converts, strengthened by the Holy Spirit, who upset the city. It was also many others, reading their Bible and not yet converted but who were visiting their priests with questions even the clergy found hard to answer. In my experience with numerous priests I've known, they don't have a deep knowledge of the Bible. But the new converts knew their Bibles and succeeded in confounding the priests by what they had found therein.

### The Bearers of the Light

Raymond Edman, past president of Wheaton College, in his book *The Light in Dark Ages*, covering a period of "Eighteen centuries of

Missions, from the giving of the Great Commission to the beginning of modern missions under William Carey"[5] states:

> In the long and deepening twilight of empire and gods, the gospel message shone brightly in ever-enlarging areas, beginning at Jerusalem until it reached the utmost borders of the Roman rule, and even beyond them into regions as widely separated as Ethiopia and India ... Who were the bearers of the light, the witnesses of the transforming power of the message of life? In the earliest centuries of expansion of Christianity the messengers and the methods of evangelization began with the spontaneous and unplanned enthusiasm of those who had themselves come out of spiritual darkness into light, and only gradually did ecclesiasticism and priestly professionalism replace the powerful preaching and witnessing of the primitive church.[6]

The new believers in Quebec followed this long line of *light bearers*. Like the apostles they said, "We cannot help speaking about what we have seen and heard" (Acts 4:20). One of the first things they saw in the Scriptures was Ephesians 2:8,9, "For it is by grace you have been saved, through faith – and this not from yourselves, it is the gift of God – not by works, so that no one can boast."

Prior to this knowledge of the gospel, their hope was not to die in a state of mortal sin so that they wouldn't go to hell but rather to purgatory. There, by their suffering and the prayers and Masses said on their behalf, they would eventually be released and fit for heaven. The state of anxiety resulting from this doctrine became clear to me when I was visiting the Ringuette family. A question that came up that day was, "Does purgatory exist?" I said, "No," unequivocally, "purgatory does not exist." The young teenage daughter, Gisèle, who was sitting in the corner of the kitchen and listening very carefully, said to me, "If purgatory doesn't exist, that scares me." I questioned as to why she should be afraid and she replied, "I do not believe I am bad enough to go to hell, but I am not good enough to go to heaven. If purgatory doesn't exist, I have a problem."

In view of Gisèle's question, I explained that those who claim it exists have twisted a few Scriptural passages to try to prove their point. If such an important place existed it would be clearly spelled out on the pages of the Bible. To the contrary, the Scriptures claim that "The blood of Jesus Christ cleanses us from all sin" (1 John 1:7) so there is no need of purgatory. The term *blood of Christ* means he gave his life for us, for the Bible teaches that "the life of the body is in the blood"(Leviticus 17:11). Jesus died for our sins and if we trust wholly in him and his death for our sins, God pardons us from all sin. The apostle Paul, in view of Jesus Christ's revelation to him, declares, "I want you to know that through Jesus the forgiveness of sins is proclaimed to you" (Acts 13:38). Despite that visit and many subsequent visits, not one of the Ringuette family accepted the Lord before I left Asbestos.

About fifteen years later I was invited to the Asbestos church to preach. We got caught in heavy traffic and arrived about ten minutes late. As we entered the church there was a woman singing a solo. I asked Betty if she recognized the soloist. She did not, so I very excitedly said, "That's Gisèle Ringuette! She was the young teenager who told me she was fearful if purgatory did not exist. She has been saved!" Gisèle could now sing because to her "to live is Christ and to die is gain" (Philippians 1:21). She no longer had reason to fear!

It was not only Gisèle who had accepted the Lord, but also all the Ringuette family except one member who was converted later, to whom I had repeatedly presented the gospel. They had discovered the Biblical message of salvation that "all have sinned and fall short of the glory of God, and are justified freely by his grace through the redemption that came by Christ Jesus" (Romans 3:23, 24). You can imagine how many people in Asbestos heard from this one family that one need not worry about purgatory because it doesn't exist! The Bible says it's Jesus who cleanses us from all sin. The Ringuette family could not keep this to themselves. Upon hearing this and other Catholic doctrines, Catholic friends and acquaintances would begin to have doubts about some of the teachings of their church. That is why the local newspaper journalist wrote that "false prophets" had been sowing tares among the wheat in the citizens of Asbestos. The "false prophets," however, were not people who came from the outside. They were citizens of the city of Asbestos who themselves had passed from darkness into light by faith in Jesus Christ "and preached the word wherever they went" (Acts 8:4).

### Anecdotes Relating to the Work of the Messengers

Three things are noteworthy, which took place after the departure of the *Messengers*. First, there was a visit with the editor of the local newspaper, *Le Citoyen*. Secondly, the real reason for the coming of the Messengers to Asbestos was revealed, and thirdly, what happened to the New Testaments that were given or sold by the believers and me in Asbestos and surrounding area.

### The First Anecdote – A Visit to the Newspaper Editor

I went to the office of *Le Citoyen* and asked to see the editor. He greeted me, and I could see that he knew who I was. He was also aware of my hockey background and asked what it was like to play for the coach, Hap Emms, a former NHL player who was, in his day, one of the most successful Junior A Major coaches in Canada. We had some discussion before getting to the purpose of my visit.

I started by saying:

> I have come to discuss an article that appeared in *Le Citoyen*. I do not believe that you wrote it, because it is not your style. Nevertheless, a full page was given to this article along with corresponding pictures. This article does not name our church, but the description and some of the facts clearly do point to us. I would like to ask your permission to write a rebuttal, or at least to be allowed to defend ourselves.

I knew ahead of time that in the Quebec of the 1950s this editor, even if he wanted to, could not give us the right to defend ourselves against the Catholic Church and this incriminating article. The occasion, however, allowed time for a testimony and a defense of ourselves, as well as an illustration that showed that in the light of the Bible, it was the Catholic Church, which was sowing tares, not us.

After some discussion, the subject changed and I was able to give my testimony – starting with the fractured skull in hockey that resulted in a brush with death, which ultimately brought me to the Savior and the assurance of eternal life. I explained that since that time I have had a burden to share this good news with others and tell how they can be saved and have the assurance of eternal life, and that's why I left hockey to become a pastor.

"Do you have a Bible?" I asked him, to which he answered, "No." I then asked him if he had ever read the Bible and his reply was again negative. "You don't know what you are missing," I continued. "It's God's personal letter to mankind. As a Catholic and an educated man you have heard of Eusebius Jerome, or more commonly known as Saint Jerome?" He agreed that he was well aware of that name. I continued:

> He was a great linguist in the fourth century and it was he who translated the Bible into Latin. This version, called The Vulgate, became the official Bible of the Catholic Church. He also wrote commentaries on most of the books of the Bible. He asserted that ' ... the ignorance of the Bible is ignorance of Christ.'[7] Would you let me show you an example of that statement, that ignorance of the Scriptures is ignorance of Christ?

He agreed.

I began:

> We all know that in the beginning of this decade, 1950, Pope Pius XII declared that the Virgin Mary was 'assumed body and soul into heavenly glory ... '[8] The Bible teaches, however, that as long as we are in the body, we are away from the Lord (2

Corinthians 5:6), not with the Lord. The apostle Paul wrote, that he "would prefer to be away from the body and at home with the Lord" (2 Corinthians 5:8). How could people, therefore, in the centuries that followed, claim that Mary went to heaven in her body? The Bible also teaches about the resurrection of the body at Christ's return, but there is a definite order in the resurrection. The Bible teaches that Christ is the first fruit of the resurrection, then when he comes those who belong to him will be resurrected (1 Corinthians 15:23). The text does not say Christ was the first resurrected, then Mary the second, and finally all believers at his resurrection. In fact, it says the opposite. Let's take the Bible and see if it throws any light on this subject.

I opened my Catholic New Testament at John's Gospel, chapter three, verse thirteen where I read, "No one has ever gone into heaven except the one who came from heaven – the Son of Man" (a name Jesus applies to Himself about eighty times in the gospels). The editor got the point without any further commentary from me. He said, "That is why I don't read the Bible. My conscience is at peace now, but if I read the Bible I will be troubled."

Even in Jesus' day people asked him, "Why don't your disciples live according to the tradition of the elders?" (Mark 7:5). Jesus replied, "You have let go of the commands of God and are holding on to the traditions of men ... Thus you nullify the Word of God by your tradition" (Mark 7:8, 13).

However, not all people had this attitude. In door-to-door visitation, I tried to knock on every door, rich or poor. In fact, as a rule my last visit in a parish was to the presbytery of the priest. This resulted in different reactions, from interesting, profitable discussions to outright refusals to communicate with me. One young priest, however, who was helping the senior priest for the summer, did want me to visit him at the presbytery. He suggested that I arrive at 3:30 p.m., which would give him half an hour before he was scheduled to hear confessions at 4 p.m. He became so interested in the gospel, and especially the assurance of eternal life, that he asked me to wait while he found someone to replace him in the confessional. That being accomplished, I spent another two hours with him, and he confessed that he would have liked to invite me to stay for supper but was unable to because the senior priest was not at all favorable to this visit. I mentioned that supper would be ready for me at home, but he still had questions. We finally parted, but I regret to this day that I did not try to keep contact with that young priest after he left the Asbestos area to return to further studies. Maybe he is one of the great number of priests who left the priesthood and found salvation through reading the New Testament.

It was nearly seven o'clock when I got home. In my mind, I thought Betty would be rejoicing because I was able to spend so much time with this good contact. She had other thoughts. She was well aware of how in the past workers had agreed to meet someone at a designated place, only to find that they had been trapped. Some were kidnapped and sent out of town on a train or in a car, and told not to return. Some were even warned that if they did, the next time they would be leaving in a wooden box! She was trying desperately to keep calm so the children would not be upset. Having fed them supper, they were already bathed and ready for bed. She reasoned that as soon as they were settled in their beds, she would get in touch with Pastor Sid Kerr in Montreal to make him aware of the situation and seek his advice in the matter. One can only imagine the relief when I arrived. She then rejoiced that I was safe and sound, and that the time spent with the young priest had been extremely profitable.

One evening in my visitation, I came to the home of a very special person. It was the home of the local Member of Parliament in the Quebec government. After pacing back and forth in front of the house, the Holy Spirit gave me the courage to proceed. He invited me in, and after I had identified myself I told him that the reason for my visit was to encourage people to read the Bible for themselves. I asked him if he had a Bible and he went to his bookshelf and took down a Catholic Bible, which was identical to the one that I carried in my briefcase. It was the version known as *La Sainte Bible du Chanoine Crampon* and bore the imprimatur of the Archbishop of Paris. It was as much a surprise to him as it was to me that we both had the same version. I asked him if he had ever read this Bible and he replied that he did not recall ever having done so. I explained that it was an interesting and a vital book, and that it reveals Jesus' present ministry in heaven, just as the Gospels reveal his earthly ministry. I opened my *Chanoine Crampon* Catholic version and read passages from the book of Hebrews, such as chapter 4:14-16, 7:21-28 and chapter 10:11-18. He remarked that the book of Hebrews was very interesting and that he should study it for himself. I did not feel it was right to take too much of his time as he was a busy man, so we bid each other a friendly goodbye. This was the case of a man who, when being introduced to something new and even contradictory to his religion, did not turn away from the Bible. Contrary to the editor's reaction, this man, the Honorable Émilien Lafrance, wanted to study it further.

### The Second Anecdote –
### The Secret Behind the Coming of the Messengers

Why did the Messengers come to Asbestos? We knew in a general way from the articles in the newspaper why they had come, but there was another reason of which we were totally unaware. This was revealed to us by a business couple who was sympathetic to our work, after they had had a confrontation with the Catholic Church. Unfortunately, they were never converted. Nevertheless, when the representative of the Messengers knocked on their door, the wife feigned being a very pious but confused Catholic. She explained that all her life she had been told by the priests that she should not have a Bible, much less read it. According to them, it was a book that only specially trained people could read. For an ordinary person like her, it was dangerous and could cause bewilderment and even mental disorders. She went on to say that now they were at her door in the name of the Catholic Church to sell her a Bible, and she was completely perplexed and did not know what to believe. She even added that she was thinking of abandoning religion altogether. The two representatives of the Messengers team said:

> Madame, we will tell you something very confidential. Mr. Rosaire Gosselin is about to leave the Catholic Church, and we are afraid there are about two hundred families that might follow him. We are visiting all the homes in this area to see where the Baptist pastor has left a New Testament.

This is the extent to which Mr. Gosselin was esteemed in Asbestos. With his involvement in politics, perhaps Les Messagers feared that those who had been influenced by him politically might accept his religious views as well.

Two hundred families did not follow Mr. Gosselin when he left the Catholic Church, but over the years, many of those who came to the Lord told how this man and his family had influenced their thinking. It also made them consider the Baptist Church as a legitimate church rather than a sect, for Mr. Gosselin was too wise a man to make such a critical decision, with the numerous consequences and risks, without having solid reasons for his decision.

### The Third Anecdote: Two Very Special New Testaments

The third anecdote relating to the Messengers' visit to Asbestos was what happened to all the New Testaments that had been given, or the Catholic ones that we had sold at cost. I knew from experience that in the 1950s the priests ordered people to either give them their New Testaments or destroy them. On one occasion, in the same afternoon, I had left eight New Testaments in eight different homes, with an explanation of the gospel and advice on how to go about reading them. Two weeks later I revisited these homes and found that the parish priest had gone by and confiscated every copy from each one of the families. Would this be the fate of all the other New Testaments that had been given? Two incredible anecdotes reveal how God protects and accomplishes his Word according to his plan, despite man's efforts to thwart it.

## "I Heard Every Word"

The first involves an elderly woman and a Christian social worker who had been assigned to her case. She asked the woman if there was anything she could do for her beyond her regular duties. The elderly woman asked her what she could do. The social worker offered to play cassettes and read Psalms. This woman responded excitedly, "You are an angel. God has sent you!" Week after week they sang hymns, read Psalms, and studied from the New Testament that the woman had in her possession, and before long she made a decision to receive Christ.

One day when the social worker arrived, she found her client very weak but she requested that her caregiver make a promise, "Would you explain the gospel to my husband after the Lord takes me to heaven? I want him also to know about salvation by faith in Christ alone before he dies. I want him to go to heaven as well." This seemed to be a difficult promise to keep. How could she witness to this well-known businessman? This man had been singing daily in the Catholic Church for forty years, as well as for marriages and funerals, and had been the right-hand man of the priests. She wondered if he would be vexed because of her teaching his wife the Bible. Nevertheless, she could not fail in her promise to this woman who had become a close friend and fellow believer. She thought of verses such as Acts 1:8 where Jesus stated, "you will receive power when the Holy Spirit comes on you; and you will be my witnesses." This verse gave her courage, and so she prayed and obeyed.

After the death of this person, the Christian social worker approached her husband and started to explain what his late wife had made her promise. The man said, "You don't need to explain anything to me. We have an intercom system in our house and because my wife was very ill I left it on at all times. I heard all that you and my wife discussed and I, too, agree with what the Bible teaches. I know now that I cannot gain heaven by sacraments, or works, or through earthly priests, or saints. I believe and I know

now that I am saved by grace through faith in Jesus Christ." This man lived about four years after his conversion. He obeyed the New Testament and was baptized by immersion after giving his testimony. He became an active member of the *Église Baptiste Évangélique d'Asbestos.*

He was so anxious to tell people why he had made his decision and how they had to believe in Jesus Christ alone for salvation, otherwise they would not enter heaven. He also recorded a cassette to be played at his funeral. His rich voice, that had touched many people in religious services and attracted their attention when he made announcements over his mobile loud speaker for many years in Asbestos, was to be heard once more. This time he was announcing the message of Christ, who had died, was resurrected and is now seated at God's right hand to intercede for us (Romans 8:34). I had been told about this outstanding testimony, but when we visited the Asbestos church in September 2005 we were in for a surprise.

The social worker of whom we have been speaking was six years old when I presented the gospel to her parents, and according to her testimony she was interested in the Bible from that time on. I asked her about her parents and she said they had both come to the Lord. Her father accepted the Lord two years before his death and was soundly persecuted, but he remained faithful to the end. She even reminded me about the time a rat came into the kitchen in their farm home during one of our visits and her father and I killed it with a baseball bat!

Then she asked me if I recognized the New Testament that she had brought with her. It was a Scripture Gift Mission New Testament and I replied that I knew it well, as I had given out literally hundreds of them, always taking time to explain the gospel and answer questions. "Look at the inside cover," she said. To my great surprise there were written the words in my handwriting, "Presented by Ernest W. Keefe" with the address of the church. I have no idea to whom I had presented this New Testament or why

I had written my name in it, as it wasn't my practice to do so. It had to have been given between the years 1956 and 1967, the period when we lived and worked in Asbestos. One thing I was sure of was that I had not given it to this family. I distinctly remember visiting their home in the 1950s and being told by the man of the house that he didn't want to discuss the Bible, because he was satisfied with his religion. I asked him if he was certain that God was satisfied with his religion, and the conversation ended there. Because he had been a good friend of Mr. Gosselin, we thought this would have helped to open the door, but in the twilight of his life, God, through a social worker, once again brought the gospel to his home. After his conversion he said, "If only I had understood that this was what Rosaire Gosselin had discovered in the Bible, I would have embraced it then. I would have been able to raise my children in the gospel and tell my friends about the plan of salvation." Though he did not accept a New Testament when I visited him, somebody had received one at least thirty years prior to his conversion. As God hid Moses, so he wouldn't be killed and then placed him in Pharaoh's daughter's hands, so he took this New Testament and hid it from those who would have destroyed it and placed it in the hands of someone who profited from it. This experience reminded me of the exhortation of 1 Corinthians 15:58, "Always give yourselves fully to the work of the Lord, because you know that your labor in the Lord is not in vain. " What's remarkable about this New Testament is that, in the years when they were destroyed and when the Catholic Church had a well-organized effort to find all the copies that I had given out, it was protected by God and had somehow found its way into the house of Mr. and Mrs. Pelletier. This is living proof of Isaiah 55:10,11:

> As the rain and the snow come down from heaven, and do not return to it without watering the earth and making it bud and flourish, so that it yields seed for the sower and bread for the eater, so is my word that goes out from my mouth: It will not return to me empty, but will accomplish what I desire and achieve the purpose for which I sent it.

### "I Want to See the Man of God Again"

The second illustration that I would like to relate is about a Catholic New Testament and how God used it. The woman who received it, along with her husband, had just suffered a setback and were strapped financially, so I gave them a copy of a Catholic New Testament. After their financial situation improved, they moved and I lost contact with them.

Some years later, they moved next door to members of the French Baptist Church in Asbestos. One day when the women were visiting together, the Catholic woman said to her neighbor that she was glad to have someone who attended the Baptist Church for a neighbor. The Christian had noticed that their new neighbors had taken the statue of Mary off the front lawn and put it under the porch when they moved in, but she did not know why. This woman told that she had received a New Testament from a man of God forty years ago, and that she had read it daily from then on. She went on to say that she had cancer in both lungs and didn't have long to live. "I would love to see that man of God before I die," she said to Gisèle, her Christian neighbor. Gisèle testified to her to make sure she really understood salvation. Then she went on to say that she knew that man of God and that she was sure he would come from Montreal to see her, and offered to get in touch with me.

After receiving the request from Gisèle, I made arrangements to go to Asbestos. Upon arrival at the contact's home I realized that one of her married daughters was present, and that her husband had left work early to make sure he would be home in time for this visit. For the benefit of the daughter and the husband, I explained the gospel message, using the Epistle to the Hebrews. We explained that Jesus was the great sinless priest seated at God's right hand in order to intercede for us. Furthermore, I pointed out that Jesus could save perfectly those who come to God by him, because he offered himself once for all as an offering for our sins (Hebrews 7:25). When I finished explaining the gospel the woman exclaimed, "That is exactly what you told me forty years ago!"

The husband then told me his part of the story. Somehow, his wife had lost her New Testament. She couldn't figure where it had gone and was very upset. But at that time, he happened to be demolishing a house and in the walls he found, of all things, a New Testament exactly like the one I had given his wife. How it got there was as much of a mystery as what had happened to the first one, but God wanted her to have his Word.

This woman had never read Psalm 119, as she only had a New Testament, but if she had, she would have seen how many verses reflected her feelings as they did those of the Psalmists'. With the writer of this Psalm, I believe she would have said, "I delight in your commandments because I love them. I reach out my hands for your commandments which I love, and I meditate on your decrees" (Psalm 119:47, 48). How I thank God that he led me to visit the farms along the concession line where she and her husband lived.

(Endnotes)
1   *La Tribune de Sherbrooke*, August 1959.
2   *Le Citoyen d'Asbestos*, August 14, 1959.
3   *Le Citoyen d'Asbestos*, August 14, 1959.
4   *Le Citoyen d'Asbestos*, August 14, 1959.
5   Raymond Edman, *Light in Dark Ages* (Wheaton, Illinois: Van Kampen Press, 1949), Preface.
6   Raymond Edman, *Light in Dark Ages*, p. 32.
7   *The New Testament* (Fides and Imprimatur Cardinal Léger, Jerome), Preface.
8   Karl Rahner, *Mary Mother of the Lord, Theological Meditations* (Montreal: Palm Publishers, Imprimatur E. Morrogh Bernard Vic. Gen. Westmonasterii, die 30. Novembris, 1962), p.85.

# Chapter 5

# *The Church under Attack from Within*

The apostle Paul exhorted the elders of the church in Ephesus to keep watch over themselves and all the flock of which the Holy Spirit had made them overseers. He warned them, "I know that after I leave, savage wolves will come in among you and will not spare the flock. Even from your own number men will arise and distort the truth in order to draw away disciples after them" (Acts 20:29-31).

What Paul foresaw in Ephesus also happened in Asbestos. It did not come from men but from a woman. She and her husband had been stalwarts from the early days of the work and they became very good friends. She obtained books of liberal theology, however, and added many of her own interpretations. She was destroying the cardinal doctrines of the Word of God (Liberal theology is a religious movement that infiltrated Catholic and Protestant churches. It rejects that the Bible is the inspired Word of God and undermines some central doctrines of Christianity such as the divinity of Christ). We did our best to help that woman and her husband over many weeks. Jack Cochrane, a professor at École Biblique Béthel and pastor of Église Baptiste Évangélique de Sherbrooke, helped as well and gave written refutations to her errors. Rather than concede to these corrections, she began to reproduce her writings and distribute them among the members of the church.

We had been patient with this couple because of their work and sacrifice for the church in its early days. Furthermore, when they identified themselves as evangelical Christians, they were ostracized by family and friends. On one occasion, the husband represented his workers' union at a meeting of union and Catholic Church leaders. He did not kiss the bishop's ring, as was customary, but simply shook hands with the bishop. This caused an uproar.

French Canadians are very family-oriented and as such, family gatherings, weddings, and holidays are very special occasions for them. Once someone became an evangelical Christian, the family usually treated them coldly, and very often, they were no longer welcome at family functions such as the famous French Canadian *réveillon*. To remove a member of our church would cut them off from other Christians and put them in no-man's-land, as they were already cut-off from family and friends.

It was a hard decision, but because this person continued to hand out copies of her studies despite our exhortations not to do so, we had to act. The words found in Revelation 2:18-20 spoke to me. It is written:

These are the words of the Son of God, whose eyes are like blazing fire and whose feet are like burnished bronze. I know your deeds, your love and faith, your service and perseverance, and that you are now doing more than you did at first. Nevertheless, I have this against you: You tolerate that woman … who calls herself a prophetess.

Though the circumstances were not exactly the same, the principles were and we couldn't tolerate a situation that was damaging the church any longer. A church meeting to remove this couple from the list of members was held, and the Christians were advised to break fellowship with them (2 John 7-10). It was one of the hardest things I've ever had to do in my ministry. I often think, however, of Old Testament prophets who had to deliver messages from God, such as Nathan, who had to take a message to his king and friend, David.

**The Aftermath**

The following Sunday, instead of having members from fifteen families, we only had seven families represented. I remember Rosaire Gosselin saying to me, "Mr. Keefe, it's better to have three families with the Bible than one hundred without it." This showed great wisdom and faith on the part of a new convert.

One of the leaders in our Fellowship, who was a good friend and had been a successful pastor in several of our churches, came to visit us and suggested we move to a larger centre like Quebec City. He advised us that it would be better because a split like the one we had would take years to heal. That night in our devotions we were beginning to read the book of Joshua and when we read chapter one, verses six and seven, we just looked at one another. The verses read as follows, "Be strong and courageous, because you will lead these people to inherit the land I swore to their forefathers ... Be strong and very courageous." We both believed the Lord was using that Scripture to show us that we must stay in Asbestos. One day, as I was on my way to visit one of the church families, the thought came to me, "If we were to leave Asbestos now, who would we be leaving behind?" Perhaps the better word would be *abandoning*, rather than *leaving*. It would be those who left Roman Catholicism at a great price under our evangelism. They stood with us in making the truth of the gospel known to others. They suffered persecution, ostracism, and sometimes financial loss for their faith, but they "regarded disgrace for the sake of Christ as of greater value" (Hebrews 11:26). How could we abandon them?

God gave us a precious promise which is found in James 5:10-11. After reading these verses, I turned to the last chapter of Job to recall how God had blessed Job after he had permitted his great trial. God allowed Job's trial in order to prove his love for God and to prove that Satan was wrong. Job's trial hurt the heart of God, who is "full of compassion and mercy" (James 5:11), and, "The Lord ... blessed the latter part of Job's life more than the first" (Job 42:12).

I had a blackboard in my office, which also served as a Sunday school classroom. At the height of the problem, I wrote this part of the passage on the board, "You have heard of Job's perseverance and have seen what the Lord finally brought about. The Lord is full of compassion and mercy" (James 5:11). I resolved in my heart and said to the Lord, "I am not going to erase that verse until I see what you do for your church in Asbestos. You are full of compassion and mercy toward us and it's your honor and your gospel that are at stake here."

## Blessings According to James 5:11
### First Blessing – Believers Return to the Church

Mme Fortier was one who returned. She missed fellowship with the believers and the church very much. She had followed those who went to a Protestant church in a neighboring town, but this situation had soon petered out. In her hunger for fellowship and Bible study, she began to attend studies with the Jehovah's Witnesses, thinking that she could detect their errors and resist them. Satan, however, seduced her (2 Corinthians 11:3) and she began to question the divinity of Christ. One morning, in her personal devotions, she came upon Isaiah 9:6. Chapter 9 prophesied the coming of the Messiah (Christ) and in verse six it stated, "He will be called ... Mighty God." The Holy Spirit opened her eyes and her doubts vanished; Jesus is Mighty God! She began to call the ladies in our church and tell them of her doubt and how God had removed it. Then she called us, relating her experience in detail asking if she could return to the church. We received her with open arms. Except for the detour mentioned above, she has been an outstanding believer from her conversion.

She told us something interesting about the Jehovah's Witnesses. Apparently, they were angry with me because, due to my efforts in evangelism, I had caused them to lose many contacts. Sometimes people would ask me if I were a Jehovah's Witness. I would answer, "Oh no. I could never be a Jehovah's Witness because this sect does not believe that Jesus is God manifest in the flesh" (John 1:1,2,14). In those days all Catholics in Quebec believed in the Trinity, so, I would show the error of the Witnesses by not accepting the doctrine of the Trinity and they were readily seen as heretics. From there, I could show that they didn't believe one could be assured of having eternal life. They believed in works as a means of salvation rather than grace, and if they worked hard enough they would merit a place on the new earth. This allowed me to explain salvation by grace through faith as revealed in the Bible. And while I was revealing the errors of the Witnesses, I was also showing them something that was new to them, salvation by grace through faith, "For it is by grace you have been saved, through faith – and this not from yourselves, it is the gift of God – not by works, so that no one can boast" (Eph 2:8-9). I was really surprised that our evangelism could have a twofold effect. Mme Fortier was not the only one to return. Nearly all returned except the couple who had erred in doctrine and one or two others.

## Second Blessing – New Converts

God also blessed us with new converts. Every conversion is a miracle, be it a child or a hardened atheist; in every conversion the person passes "from death to life" (John 5:24), "from the dominion of darkness ... into the kingdom of the Son he loves" (Colossians 1:13). Some conversions, however, are out of the ordinary as we see them. M. Lamontagne and his family fall into that category. He was a simple man and one whom, I believe, would have found it hard, maybe even impossible, to gain entrance to a college.

While we met the Lamontagne family through door-to-door visitation, at some point he became curious as to the time of our services and decided to turn the tables and make a visit to our place in search of the desired information. It was early evening and I wasn't home when Betty looked out the kitchen window and saw three big men coming toward the house. Responding to their knock on the door, she let them in, answered their questions and told them the time of the Sunday morning worship service. They were in the house long enough for the next-door neighbor, who was a Christian and had seen the three men pass in front of her home and enter our house, to become concerned. She telephoned to see if everything was in order, or if she had reason to be anxious. Betty assured her that nothing was amiss, and after the phone call, the men left. They were M. Lamontagne, his son and his nephew.

M. Lamontagne had begun to devour the New Testament, thinking that this book, written by the apostles, would teach him more about his religion. To his surprise, he began to find differences between what his church taught and what he was reading in the New Testament. Jesus said that God hides things from the wise and the learned, but reveals them to little children (Matthew 11:25). It surprised me one day that he had lost twenty pounds since he began studying the New Testament and comparing it with what was being taught at his church. He realized that he would be obliged to make a decision and that it wouldn't be easy.

Finally, he made a plan. It was Easter weekend and he decided that he would do all that his church expected of him: attend the Mass on Good Friday, confess his sins on Saturday, and attend early Mass on Sunday morning. Then he would go to the Evangelical Baptist Church for their morning service, as he had already done on a few occasions. He decided to ask God to show him the truth beyond any shadow of doubt, and then he would be able to make the right decision, no matter what it might cost him.

I was on deputation in Ontario that Sunday, but we had a good pastoral team. I was the elder set aside to serve the Lord full-time (1 Timothy 5:17). (The Asbestos church was the first church in our Association to have a plurality of elders/pastors.) Elder Marcel Cotnoir was giving the message that morning.

True to his plan, M. Lamontagne did go to Mass on Good Friday, followed by confession on Saturday. He began his confession by saying, "I confess to God and to … " He paused. The words, "and to you my *Father*" (the priest), which should have followed, just would not come out. Finally, looking up, he blurted out, "And to Jesus, my great high priest!" This time it was the priest who was speechless. He didn't know what to say so he immediately dismissed his penitent one. On a lighter note, M. Lamontagne later mused that he'd never in his life received absolution so quickly!

Nevertheless, he went to Mass early Sunday morning as planned, after which he drove across town and attended the morning service at the Baptist Church. The Holy Spirit led Marcel Cotnoir to speak that morning on the great high priest, based on the Epistle to the Hebrews. Marcel is a compassionate preacher who, years earlier had had to make the same painful decision that M. Lamontagne was facing that morning. He poured his heart out and passages from the book of Hebrews convinced this hungry soul concerning Jesus, the great high priest:

Therefore, since we have a great high priest who has gone through the heavens, Jesus the Son of God, let us hold firmly to the faith we profess. For we do not have a high priest who is unable to sympathize with our weaknesses, but we have one who has been tempted in every way, just as we are – yet was without sin. Let us then approach the throne of grace with confidence, so that we may receive mercy and find grace to help us in our time of need. (Hebrews 4: 14-16)

Did this passage not point us to the great high priest and a promise that we would receive mercy and grace if we were to approach the throne of grace through him? Is Jesus not seated at the right hand of God and is he not interceding for us? (Romans 8:34). Then there was the beautiful chapter seven of Hebrews where Jesus, the eternal priest, replaced the mortal priesthood of the Old Testament.

**The Priesthood of Jesus**

Here are the inspired words of Hebrews 7: And it was not without an oath! Others became priests without any oath, but he became a priest with an oath when God said to him: 'The Lord has sworn and will not change his mind: 'You are a priest forever." Because of this oath, Jesus has become the guarantee of a better covenant. Now there were many of those priests, since death prevented them from continuing in office; but because Jesus lives forever, he has a permanent priesthood. Therefore, he is able to save completely those who come to God through him, because he always lives to intercede for them. Such a high priest meets our need – one who is holy, blameless, pure, set apart from sinners, exalted above the heavens. Unlike the other high priests, he does not need to offer sacrifices day after day, first for his own sins, and then for the sins of the people. He sacrificed for their sins once for all when he offered himself. For the law appoints as high priests men who are weak; but the oath, which came after the law, appointed the Son, who has been made perfect forever (Hebrews 7:20-28).

First, in verses 20-21 Jesus alone was established as a priest forever, as prophesied in Psalm 110:4. Secondly, the oath made by his Father God, is a guarantee that the New Testament covenant is true and Jesus is its priest (verse 22). Thirdly, the other priests in the Old Testament were mortals. They died and needed replacements. Jesus rose from the dead and is alive forevermore and does not need to be replaced (verse 24). Fourthly, because Jesus is living today and is seated at God's right hand, he can SAVE COMPLETELY those who come to God THROUGH HIM. To go to God by anyone else (saint, pastor, priest, etc.) is disobedience to the Word of God and an insult to Jesus (verse 25). Fifthly, he has a sterling, sinless character and is exalted above the heavens (verse 26). Sixthly, other priests

repeatedly offer sacrifices that cannot cleanse the sinner, but
Jesus, by one sacrifice, offered once for all, cleanses from
all sin the person who trusts in him (verse 27). Finally, other
priests are weak. Jesus is forever perfect (verse 28).

As M. Lamontagne left the church that morning he shook hands
warmly with Marcel Cotnoir and said, "This morning I decided to
receive Jesus as my personal and eternal priest in order to be saved."
After his conversion, he handed out so many gospel tracts that he
earned the nickname "the postman" at the mine where he worked.
He was also faithful in his duties to the Lord. Sunday services and
weeknight prayer meetings, he was always seated in the same place
with his family. Furthermore, the harassment and mistreatment he
received for his stand for Jesus could never turn him from his great
and wonderful Saviour and priest, Jesus Christ.

The family who lived next door to the Lamontagnes, and to
whom I was also witnessing, said to me, "We don't understand
the Lamontagnes. The more they are persecuted, the happier they
are." I showed them 1 Thessalonians 1:6 where Paul wrote to the
Thessalonians, "You became imitators of us and of the Lord; in
spite of severe suffering, you welcomed the message with the joy
given by the Holy Spirit." By the grace of God these neighbors
some time later found the joy of the Holy Spirit themselves, when
they too put their faith in Jesus Christ. M. and Mme Lamontagne
and their family were part of the new believers who were God's
blessing to us in view of James 5:10,11.

### The Priesthood and the Mass

Perhaps after reading the testimony of M. Lamontagne and hearing
about the preaching of Marcel Cotnoir you ask, "Where does the
church's practice of the priesthood come from?" The traditional
Catholic teaching is that:

Within the Church are men who are specially ordained as
priests to consecrate and offer the body and blood of Christ in

the Mass. The Apostles were the first ordained priests, when on Holy Thursday night Christ told them to do in his memory what he had done at the Last Supper.[1]

According to the Catholic theologian Dr. Richard McBrien, nowhere in the New Testament, are either the apostles, or the leaders of the church called priests. They are rather designated as pastors/ elders or overseers (bishops). Dr. Richard P. McBrien, a post-Vatican II Catholic theologian, in his two-volume theology states that the accepted Catholic statement of Jesus Christ ordaining the apostles as priests, is wrong. "This historical record requires some modification of the traditional Catholic notion that Jesus directly and explicitly instituted the Catholic priesthood at the Last Supper."[2] Further to this statement about Jesus not ordaining the apostles as priests, one might ask when the church began to transition from the memorial breaking of bread to start viewing it as an actual sacrifice.

This idea did not appear until the end of the 1st century or the beginning of the second. It is therefore not in Christ's teaching nor in the apostolic teachings, because the apostles' time had passed. Furthermore, for this to be a sacrifice the elements would have to be changed into the actual blood and body, but that wasn't even considered before the 9th century. The great theologian Augustine (354-430) held the position " ... that Christ's presence in the supper is spiritual."[3] It was in 1059 that the Catholic Church propagated the doctrine that the elements (bread and wine) " ... are changed into the actual body and blood of Jesus Christ."[4] The concept of the Lord's Supper being the actual body and blood was not accepted until nine centuries after the passing of the apostles and confirmed by the Council of Trent (1545-63). It is, therefore, a doctrine of man, not of Jesus Christ as taught by the apostles. Jesus commanded the apostles to "go and make disciples of all nations, baptizing them in the name of the Father and of the Son and of the Holy Spirit, and teaching them to obey everything I have commanded you" (Matthew 28:19,20). The Mass is definitely something Jesus did not teach the apostles.

## A Third Blessing – A Church Building

The need for a church building was urgent. The meetings were being held in our basement and our numbers were growing. Our attendance had increased beyond what the membership had been before the crisis, and the basement chapel had been crowded at that time. It wasn't safe with only one exit from the basement, and Betty was finding it difficult having fifty or more people in our small bungalow. We once even had a funeral service in our basement chapel. An elderly single man who attended our church, who was boarding with one of our families, died suddenly and his family would have nothing to do with a Protestant service, so our church took over. To keep expenses to a minimum, the wake was held in the basement chapel and we conducted the service there also. It was indeed a rarity to have a corpse in one's basement for three days. To say we needed a church building was an understatement.

We didn't want to push the project ourselves, but rather wanted it to come from the members. Teaching new French converts to give was an difficult task. The Catholic Church had a legal right to levy a mortgage on the property of each member of the parish to help pay for the church building. The churches they built were massive. Mason Wade, in his history of Quebec, has a picture of the church in Ste-Anne de la Pérade. He states that this church, with its twin steeples, was built in 1855, obviously under the influence of the Notre Dame Cathedral in Montreal. "This was a disastrous venture in a style foreign to Quebec's tradition and an example of the *folie de grandeur* ["delusion of grandeur"] which was to burden many a small community with a cathedral rather than a church."[5]

The parsonage was another building that caused much dissension. It was a very large, two-storey house built adjacent to the church. Most of the time, it was used by the priest, an assistant priest, and the housekeeper. It also housed the church office and was used to accommodate visiting clergy and/or important visitors. All of this was paid for by the parishioners. In the 1950s and 60s Catholics would often say to me, "It's not fair. The priest is single and we are married with large families. We paid for that house and it should belong to us."

Besides this, every service rendered by the Catholic Church had a price tag – marriages, funerals, Masses held for the departed, etc. In view of this, French Catholics were not motivated to give to the Sunday offering. When they became Christians they increased their giving, but not to the extent that evangelical Christians were giving. If they had given one dollar to the offering when they were Catholic and then began to attend an evangelical church and gave five dollars, that represented an increase of 500% and they thought they were being generous. Others, of course, surprised us with their kindness.

In view of these facts, I wanted the members themselves to come up with the suggestion to build. Another reason for this was that they knew that sister English churches gave gifts to the French work, and we didn't want them to expect that English churches would come and build their church for them. We were working toward self-reliance for the Asbestos church, and the building was a good project to start with. We prayed that God would put it upon their hearts to come to us. God answered our prayers and a few men came to us with a plan not only to build but a plan to finance the building as well.

Two and a half acres of land had already been purchased with a fairly new house on it. Our research for a plan led us to a building that could be used for many different purposes. It was made out of British Columbian fir and required an arch every thirty inches. These arches were built by the men of the church in the field behind the church property. When the basement and floor were in place, we had a building blitz that began early in the morning and ended around suppertime. Workers arriving in the morning saw a basement and a floor, but on the way home all the arches were in place. It seemed like a miracle, and for us it was a miracle. Even the judge who had told us we would not have any converts was obliged to pass the church on his way to and from his office, built by the converts that we weren't supposed to have! Samuel Coppieters, a Brethren missionary, was bringing a carload of young people to Asbestos for a Youth Rally when he saw our church all lit up. He continued right past it because he thought it looked too large, at least for those days, to be an Evangelical French Church.

*The Asbestos-Danville Church*

### A Fourth Blessing – God Gives Additional Growth

Marcel Cotnoir had been transferred to Asbestos by his employer months before we arrived. He and his wife, Verna, were a godsend because it meant we had one family with which to begin the new church. They were a help in the work and became close friends. Marcel's sister, Marguerite, and her husband, Armand (Jack) Boucher, followed them about four years later. Besides these two families, every member in the church in the first six years was reached with the gospel by the ministry of believers in the congregation; they were subsequently baptized there as well.

The first of an influx of believers from the outside was a young teenager. We learned that Ginette Paillé had quit school and was doing housework for a living. In view of this, we invited her to our home. In our conversation, we asked if she would like to continue her studies and Ginette replied enthusiastically that she would like that very much. We proposed that she could live with us and attend the local English high school, as there was no French Protestant high school in the entire southeast region of Quebec, but only if her parents would agree with the arrangement. Both Ginette and her parents accepted our offer. The newly named manager of Household Finance Corporation in Asbestos, and his wife, were the next to arrive. As mature Christians, they helped in many areas of the work, including our radio broadcast. Then help came from Ontario. A young university student had been assigned several three-month periods working for the Canadian Johns-Manville Company to gain experience for his engineering degree. These three-month stints not only helped him acquire a degree, but also a wife. When they had both finished hteir studies, it was my privilege to marry Ginette Paillé and David Bailey in Asbestos.

There were several young people in the Paillé family and that helped our youth group to grow. Marcel and Odile Tétreault, a young married couple, moved to Asbestos as well and helped with the youth ministry. Marcel was a businessman and Odile, a new convert, was blessed with a fine voice, which she used for the Lord. Odile's mother and family followed the Tétreaults to Asbestos, and her mother and several family members came to the Lord. Over the years, I baptized members representing three generations of the Tétreault/Lapointe families.

### Fifth Blessing – Help from Ontario

One person came to Asbestos in 1964 who left his mark in French-speaking Quebec for years afterward. I'm speaking, of course, of Alan Johnston. He was a medical student who had already told the Lord that he would go into missionary service if it were His will. Before returning to university in the fall, he vacationed at Muskoka Baptist Conference. Alan's roommate was a recent convert from Quebec and his incessant talk about his native province turned Alan off to the point of not wanting to hear the word Quebec ever again.

*Alan Johnston*

Back at university, Alan was anxious to get home the weekend of the Annual Missionary Conference at his home church, Calvary Baptist in Oshawa. Normally there was a Saturday morning class, but for the only time that year this class was cancelled. He was delighted and thought perhaps God's hand was on it, because he was now free to attend the men's breakfast, which was always a high point in the conference. When he picked up the conference pamphlet after arriving home, he discovered the speaker would be a missionary from Quebec!

That morning God not only spoke to Alan Johnston but to several young men. They came to see me after the program and said they wanted to come to Quebec for a weekend to help us. Some had a little high school French, but I wondered what I would ever do with fifteen to twenty young people for a weekend, and actually tried to discourage them from coming. The next day, after the morning service, they came back and insisted that they believed the Lord wanted them go to Quebec. This time I told them to give me a little time to think and pray about it and we would discuss it further after the evening service.

By that time, I had a plan.

> "Come down," I said, "but you'll be looking after yourselves. There's a place behind the church where you can camp and use our facilities and those of the church. If there are any of you who sing, perhaps you could sing for our congregation, but it would be good to choose hymns that exist in French so our folks can follow in their hymnbooks. If you'd like to give your testimonies, I will translate for you. I'll also translate for those of our people who might want to speak with you but who don't speak English.

I went on to explain that there were several villages around Asbestos, and that I would choose one that had never been evangelized where they could distribute French gospel literature. I warned them of possible opposition and made it clear that if someone said, "*Va-t-en*" (Get out of here) they should leave immediately! I left them with the latter part of verse 58 of 1 Corinthians 15, which reads, " ... you know that your labor in the Lord is not in vain."

The young men did come and were thrilled with their weekend. The French Christians, most of whom were new Christians, were encouraged and edified by their zeal and their testimonies. On two other occasions, they returned to distribute the good news to those villages that had never heard. Dr. Johnston accompanied them on at least one of these excursions and several from this group did eventually go into missionary work around the world. Others were pillars in their churches and witnesses in their communities and places of employment.

On one occasion, we had arranged for Alan Johnston to visit the local doctor who was the company doctor for the Canadian Johns-Manville Company, while also managing his own private practice. About a year later, this doctor came to see us. He had a piece of confidential information that he wanted to share with us, which was that he would be leaving Asbestos to continue his studies. His desire was to have someone take his place with the company and take over his private practice; specifically, someone with our convictions! He asked us to contact our friend to see if he would consider coming. We were delighted to carry through on his request.

Alan Johnston was surprised to receive my phone call, and even more so at the contents of my message. He explained that he was in an internship and that he'd recently signed a contract for a second year. He said the doctor in charge of the program was a hard man and was not easily swayed, but we agreed to pray, realizing that if this was the Lord's will, he would certainly open the door.

After taking a deep breath, he headed for the office of the doctor in charge, who happened to be absent. His replacement was a man of more understanding. He listened intently as Alan explained the opportunity before him and asked if he could be released from his contract. The doctor replied that if he was convinced that this is what he wanted, and no one was pressuring him, he figured it was a good opportunity. This was encouraging and seemed to indicate that the Lord might be opening the door for him to make Quebec his mission field. However, the doctor in charge still had to be consulted. He was ushered into his office by the secretary and began to explain the offer he'd received. In response to his request to be released from the contract, the doctor took the contract, held it up, and ripped it in two. Dr. Alan Johnston was on his way to Quebec!

To have such a prominent professional man in a lowly French Baptist Church in Quebec wasn't an everyday occurence. He was a great asset and the church appreciated his leadership, but it wasn't easy for him to take over the practice when most of the patients were French-speaking. One day he asked a well-known professional neighbor for advice in view of his work, being English-speaking in a French province. The neighbor replied, "You don't have anything to fear. If you were a Jehovah's Witness or a member of the French Baptist Church you might have reason to be concerned, but you'll be fine!" Dr. Johnston could have left the conversation there and hidden his membership in the beleaguered French Baptist Church, but he didn't. Instead, he said, "I'm a member of the French Baptist

Church." I'm sure this neighbor was embarrassed and possibly thought, "If Dr. Johnston is a member of that church and he's not ashamed to let it be known, maybe the negative things we're hearing about the Baptists aren't true."

Dr. Johnston came to Quebec a bachelor, but God blessed him with a helpmate, Janet Wright, a Christian from a fine Christian home and a member of a Brethren Assembly in Toronto. She had also studied medicine and had earned a B.Sc. in nursing; she had been active in Christian students' groups while on campus. All of this considered, we were sure that God brought them together. I had the privilege of being the emcee at their wedding reception.

***Alan and Janet Johnston***

Janet and Alan spent several productive years in Asbestos, both professionally and in their commitment to the work of the Lord. Dr. Johnston was called on to counsel many in Christian circles, not only in Asbestos but also throughout the province. He was also an avid soul winner. Since there was a change coming in his work situation, the Johnstons sought God's will for future service. They were led to Sherbrooke at a favorable time because the Sherbrooke church, under the leadership of Pastor Jacques Alexanian, had just begun a campus ministry at a French college and university. They prepared a drop-in centre in the basement of their home where students could meet for Bible study, prayer, fellowship, and fun. That year twenty-five students received Christ as Saviour and were baptized. They became members of the Sherbrooke church, or sister churches in their hometowns. The Johnstons were active in other aspects of church ministry, as we will note later.

After several years of fruitful service, they moved to Orleans, a vibrant, progressive French suburb of Ottawa. There they became members of Église Baptiste Évangélique de Gatineau, on the Quebec side of the Ottawa River, and also served on the Church Board. Alan's commitment to the local church and to counseling and caring for many pastors and their families has left an indelible mark upon the French work. They have three grown children – Daniel, Louise and Carolyn. The adventures of a group of young people became a blessing that culminated in an enduring blessing for the French work of the Lord in Quebec.

### A Sixth Blessing – The Gospel on the Airwaves

The Lord opened the door for us to have a radio broadcast on the Victoriaville station, CFDA. As I became acquainted with the manager of the station, he told me that there were only eight non-Catholics in that area and they were there because of business. The seeds for this radio broadcast were sown on a hill outside of the village of Wotton, about 12 kilometers (7 miles) from Asbestos. Through experience, I had discovered that it wasn't profitable to visit people in town during the warm summer months. French Canadians are known for sitting on their porches in the nice weather, often on a rocking chair or a swing. I was becoming very well known in town, and if I were seen visiting with someone and sharing the gospel, that person, or family, would be harassed and I'd lose the contact. It was hard enough to be harassed and ostracized when one became an evangelical Christian, but to receive this treatment even before taking an open stand was too much to expect of most contacts. After losing some promising prospects because of this, I decided to visit in the rural areas during the summer months.

One day while eating my supper along the highway at the summit of a large hill, and before starting an evening of door-to-door evangelism, I looked out over Mont Ham in the direction of Victoriaville, about 40 kilometers (24 miles) away, and Quebec City, at about 125 kilometers (75 miles) and I knew there wasn't one evangelical church in all that territory. Door-to-door visiting was a slow but effective, and often the only, means of evangelizing. As I sat there, I began to reason that most of the people between where I was parked and Quebec City would never be saved. Furthermore, they would never even hear the gospel as written in the Bible. As the tears ran down my cheeks, I said, "Lord, unless you do something they will never hear your good news, let alone accept it!"

Shortly after this episode, we had a visit from two pastors from Ontario. It was our desire that they'd see not only Asbestos but also Victoriaville, a city where we envisioned starting a daughter church. Driving around the city we came across the radio station. I suggested that we stop and see if they would sell us radio time for a weekly gospel program. Before leaving the building, we had signed a contract, and would begin our broadcasts in the near future, but we had no money, no team, and no program. With the help of these two Ontario pastors, the news was spread concerning the opportunity to preach the gospel on-air in an area where the nearest evangelical church was 44 kilometers (26 miles) away.

By this time, Marcel Cotnoir had been transferred by his company to Shawinigan, a town 90 kilometers (54 miles) from Victoriaville. Marcel was blessed with a rich tenor voice, and in spite of the distance, he agreed to help us with music for our weekly programs, which helped tremendously. At this time, there was no bridge over the St. Lawrence River and a ferry was necessary to make the crossing. On his way home, sometimes a fog would settle over the river, so dense that he would have to wait in his car up to four hours before it was clear and safe to cross. A bridge was built at Trois-Rivières in 1968, but at that time the ferry was the only means of crossing. Many others helped with music, including Janet Johnston, Lionel Gosselin, and Jeanine Coté.

In each recording session, four half-hour programs were recorded. When there was an error, or if a segment wasn't satisfactory, the tape was stopped, backed up to a suitable place and we started over. One evening there was a blip and the technician stopped the recording. The technician's hand was in the air, and everyone in the studio knew the moment it was lowered we were supposed to begin, and Marcel was responsible for opening with a prayer. When the technician lowered his hand, nothing happened. We all looked at Marcel only to see him battling for composure. "Look, fellows," he said, "I can start anything else on the program on a dime, but please don't ask me to do that for prayer." We understood, and it was one of the good laughs we had in recording programs.

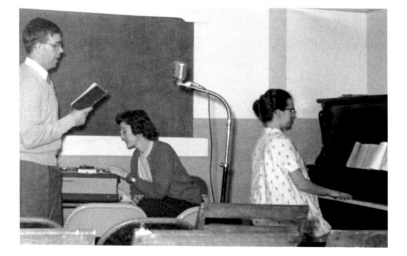

*Recording for radio: Marcel and Verna Cotnoir,*
*and Betty Keefe at piano*

During the construction of the Asbestos church, I happened to pass by a small manufacturing plant between Asbestos and Victoriaville that made excellent windows and doors. I entered to see what could be done for us. This plant eventually got the contract for our church, and the second time I went to see the owner I took advantage of the situation to witness to him. He looked at me and informed me that after my first visit he had told his wife that the man they listened to on CFDA was in the shop that day. This man lived in the area I'd felt burdened for when I was parked along the road at the top of the hill near Wotton. God had begun to answer prayers for that area, and the radio broadcast was one of the blessings that God afforded us according to his promise in James 5:10,11.

Another occasion to share the gospel over CFDA came when I was invited to take part in an interview between a Protestant minister and a Catholic priest concerning our beliefs. This came about because of changes in the Catholic Church before and during the Vatican II Council. John L. McKenzie, a Notre Dame University professor of theology, noted these changes and wrote, "There was scarcely any period in the history of the Catholic Church when its future was more difficult to predict than now."[6] An illustration that he gave of this was, "The Roman Church has made its first gesture of reconciliation toward the Protestant churches since the Reformation."[7]

Based on these new attitudes in the Catholic Church, the radio station in Victoriaville thought it would be good to have an interview between a Protestant pastor and a Catholic priest during the ecumenical week. The only Protestant minister they knew was myself, and only because of our broadcast. Also, the Asbestos church was the closest one, at only 40 kilometers (24 miles) away. I knew the concept of ecumenicity was as important to the Catholic Church then as it is now, so I didn't accept to participate with closed eyes. A well-known Canadian Catholic theologian and sociologist, Gregory Baum, wrote in his book *That They May be One,* "The last end of ecumenism is the return of separated Christians to the Church of Christ, that is, to the Roman Catholic Church; about this there can be neither doubt nor difficulty in the mind of a Catholic."[8] We'll treat this subject later when the Vatican II Council and its influence on Quebec are dealt with, but for the present we can underline the fact that I did not participate to further the cause of ecumenicity, but rather to further the preaching of the Word of God.

The young priest who shared time on the broadcast with me was very friendly. After we had finished, I suggested that we go to the restaurant and have a coffee together. We enjoyed further discussion, and I was surprised by the extent liberal theology had entered the Catholic seminary in Nicolet, a conservative Catholic area in a very conservative Catholic province. Interestingly enough, the only subject he said he wouldn't discuss with me was justification by faith. Evidently, he knew that this doctrine didn't correspond with what he'd been taught and he did not have the answers. It's hard to fathom how, only a few years prior to this broadcast, another missionary and I had been arrested and put into prison for distributing French New Testaments in Asbestos.

### Seventh Blessing – A Young Missionary

God continued to save people and one rich blessing was the salvation of a woman who is now in good health and over eighty years of age. Gabriel Cotnoir made this contact. He and Nita replaced us during the summer months of 1957. The years of stress had taken their toll on Betty's health, and her doctor and the French Mission Board encouraged us to take two months' vacation. Sometimes I would be late getting home as when I had a good contact. I knew that after my visit relatives and friends would harass them. As well, if the priest learned of my visit, he'd prohibit them from having further visits with me. In view of this, I took all the time I could to answer questions, and I would mark where in the Bible they could find answers to their questions. If I happened to knock on a door when visitors were present, there would be twice as many questions. In any case, we were so well known in the town, it seemed folk were glad to have me there to see how I would answer their questions.

*Gabriel and Nita Cotnoir, and Wanda*

Because there had been kidnappings, threats and manhandling of the early missionaries, Betty was concerned when I went out alone each evening, sometimes getting home late. One day in her personal devotions she read in Psalm 4:8, "I will lie down and sleep in peace, for you alone, O Lord, make me dwell in safety." She also reasoned that if something did happen to me and she had stayed up worrying, she wouldn't be in a good state to face a bad situation. Therefore, each evening, if I was not yet home, she would go to bed and sleep in peace, knowing the Lord was looking after her husband.

It was at this point that Gabriel and Nita came and took over responsibilities in Asbestos. I had asked him to visit the village of Kingsey Falls, 20 kilometers (12 miles) from Asbestos, that I had not yet visited. He covered the village door-to-door, and the best contact he made was a young widow by the name of Mme Alice Bernier.

She was in her early thirties and had lost her husband in a work-related accident in the factory where he was employed. He left her with five children – four daughters and one son – between the ages of ten months and nine-years-old. The son was the middle child. The Christians visited her for five years, and the men helped her by replacing the floor on her large veranda. She was open to the gospel but didn't seem to grasp the biblical truth that salvation is by grace through faith. One day when Jeanne Gosselin was visiting her, she encouraged Mme Bernier to read the Epistle to the Romans, and every time she came to the word justified or justice, to replace it with the words 'pardoned from all sin.' We had been studying Romans at the church, and Jeanne decided to use what she was learning to testify to this woman. Mme Bernier followed Jeanne's instructions and the Holy Spirit enlightened her; she believed in Jesus and was justified, declared pardoned from all sin (Romans 3:22-24).

Her life changed, and fellowship with the Christians was a great help to her. A young widow in poor health with five children to raise needs help and fellowship. I drove out to get her oldest children for the youth meetings every Saturday night. There was no local bus service, so other Christians helped with the transportation on occasion. One day when I was tired of spending so much time in the car while picking folks up for the meetings, I asked God to make my Volkswagen Beetle into a chapel. Two of the older Bernier children, much later on in life, reminded me of the good and profitable times we had discussing questions and seeing biblical answers in my car on the way to the meetings.

**Rescuing the Widows and the Poor**

One night one of the girls called us on a neighbor's phone. She had left her house through a window and her message was, "Mr. Keefe, come quickly. All the relatives are here with the priest and they want to take us away from mother. They say she's had a nervous breakdown and that's why she changed her religion. They say she's not capable of caring for us."

I immediately called on three men from the church who lived nearby to accompany me. I knew it was urgent from the tone of the daughter's call. I didn't think of it at the time, but I had called three of the huskiest men in the church! When we arrived at the home, all the relatives were seated in a big circle. French-Canadian houses in the 1960s, especially country houses, always had a huge kitchen because they had big families and the kitchen was the place to gather. The only unoccupied seat was next to the parish priest. As I sat down, he got up, saying, "I have a big day tomorrow. I must leave now."

It really upset me, seeing this young widow alone, facing fifteen to twenty adults and the parish priest, her children banished to another room. The children could hear the plan to take them from their mother and break up the family by placing them with relatives they barely knew. Whether the priest approved of this plan or not we don't know, but when he started to get up I took him by the sleeve and pulled him back to his chair, telling him that he must stay until the situation was settled. Mme Bernier said she was very capable of taking care of her family. She also confirmed that her decision to leave the Catholic Church was based on the Bible, which she had been reading for the past five years. She also told them that they hadn't shown any great interest in her when she first lost her husband and was in need of their help. She continued, saying her decision wasn't due to a mental breakdown but came from convictions based on the Word of God. Betty and I, along with Lionel and Jeanne Gosselin, had the joy of visiting Mme Bernier in recent years. She is now over eighty years-old but as keen as ever. Bible plaques grace the walls of her apartment, and among her reading material was her Bible and Christian literature. She is an active member of l'Église Baptiste Évangélique de Victoriaville, where her son is a deacon, and a daughter who lives in Victoriaville attends the church with their mother. This event shows how, even in the 1960s, the Catholic Church still had a grip on many of its followers.

Another anecdote that comes to mind concerns a woman who lived in Asbestos whose husband was unfortunately an alcoholic. He had a good job with a good salary, but most of his pay was spent on alcohol. Their home was nice and modern but was only partially finished. She and her children were clothed with hand-me-downs or whatever was given to her from St. Vincent de Paul, a Catholic charity. This woman was reading the New Testament and liked what she was reading, but she had a problem; she was dependent upon Catholic charities and social welfare, which were totally managed by the Catholic Church in the 60s. Her husband forbade her to go to the Baptist Church. One day I saw her on the front lawn, so I stopped to see if she was still reading her New Testament. I quoted Proverbs 29:25. She questioned, "Does the Bible really say that? Where does it say that?" I could see that she was greatly moved when I showed her the verse in the Bible, but our hands were tied, and so were hers. The Christians wanted to help but were kept from doing so. When we left Asbestos, there had been no change in her situation. We could only put her in God's hands.

Some years later, possibly twenty or even more, I was in Asbestos and there was a family that had come to the Lord who lived close to this woman's home. I described her and her family to the woman who lived close by, and told of the burden we had for the wife and mother in particular, and wondered if things had changed. The Christian woman said, "Don't worry, Mr. Keefe. The situation in the home has not changed. Poverty is still there and she is forbidden to attend church with us, but every Thursday that woman comes to my home and we have Bible study and prayer together. She is saved." What a relief this was for Betty and me after all the years away from Asbestos and wondering what became of that woman. Jesus is building her a home in heaven, and, in one sense, she is no longer poor. People who are really poor are those who live in luxurious homes and have money for the luxuries of this world, but who don't know Jesus as their personal Saviour and don't have a heavenly home. Jesus said to his disciples, "In my Father's house are many rooms … I am going there to prepare a place for you … I am the way and the truth and the life. No one comes to the Father except through me" (John 14:2,6). Only those who turn from sin and trust in Jesus, who died for our sins, will be able to enter heaven; they are rich.

## A Funeral That Touched the Whole Town

What took place in Asbestos is typical of what was being experienced in all evangelical churches in the 50s and 60s. Before leaving Asbestos, we experienced an event that was the greatest single breakthrough for the gospel in eleven years of ministry. One might wonder how this event, which was the sendoff of Rosaire Gosselin to his heavenly home, could glorify God to such a great extent. This man was on the elder/pastor team and the man whose conversion caused the Catholic Church to bring Les Messagers Catholiques to Asbestos.

It began when the telephone rang early Saturday morning. Mme Gosselin was on the line and told me that her husband had passed away in his sleep. I hurried over and arrived before the body was taken away. Mme Gosselin was alone, as her sons were already at the funeral home making the necessary arrangements. In the typical French-Canadian fashion of those days, a Fuller Brush salesman knocked on the door, opened it, and walked, in humming a tune. Mme Gosselin said to him, "I cannot sing like that this morning. There has been a great tragedy in our home. Rosaire passed away in his sleep. We are waiting for the undertaker." The salesman was speechless and tried to excuse himself. Mme Gosselin broke in on his effort to speak and said, "Don't feel badly for coming at this moment. Perhaps God wanted me to talk to you about the gospel. Ninety-nine percent of the wives in Quebec in my position would not know where their husbands are, but because Rosaire put his faith in Jesus Christ for his salvation, I know he is in heaven with his Saviour." She went on to explain the gospel to him.

The Gosselin sons returned to the house, where the discussion continued concerning the details of the funeral. The funeral director knew it wouldn't be a typical Catholic funeral, so he assured the sons that he would do whatever the family desired. In the first place, evangelical Christians don't light candles to indicate prayers being offered for the deceased. The candle stands were not removed; rather, they were converted! The Christians loaned their Scripture plaques for the occasion. Rather than a semicircle of candles, there was a semicircle of Bible verses around the casket. It was God's light of his Word – the true light.

Another question was what M. Gosselin would have in his hands? Catholics usually hold a rosary, but this man of God had abandoned this mode of prayer when he learned to communicate directly with his heavenly Father. One son said, "If he has nothing in his hands, people will say he died an atheist. Why not put his Bible in his hands?" Why not, indeed! The family agreed that this was a good idea.

The funeral director related some amazing information as Lionel and I spoke with him in his office. He began by saying:

When I was putting your father's Bible in his hands, it fell on the floor and opened. I noted that he had underlined passages in it. I said to myself that if Rosaire underlined something, it must be because it's worth reading. So I sat down and read all the passages that he had underlined. Despite my academic background, that was the first time I had read the Bible.

He went on to say that roughly thirteen hundred people had visited the salon, partly out of respect for the deceased and partly because they were curious to see an evangelical Christian's funeral. (Mme Gosselin stayed beside the casket and witnessed to as many as possible about eternal life through repentance of sin and faith in Jesus Christ.)

Then the director said, "I had another visitor early this morning. He lives across the street and he has been watching the steady stream of people enter the funeral home." Lionel questioned, "You mean the parish priest came to see my father?" "No, Lionel. He didn't come to see your father; he came to see me. He said that he wanted me to move your father to a Protestant funeral home in Danville, the neighboring town. I told him that Rosaire Gosselin is here; he is here to stay. I explained that I had taken an oath to console people when they were bereaved, and not add to their grief." It was courageous for a businessman of that era to stand up to his priest.

Our church building was under construction at this time, and the interior wasn't yet finished. One of the sons who didn't even attend our church said that he knew his father would haved liked his service to be in the Baptist Church. Consequently, men in the church got busy and, although they didn't completely finish the interior, made it more presentable. The local branch of the Legion loaned us sufficient chairs. I had prayed in French at their Armistice Service each year and they were glad to return the favor.

However, there was another problem. On the way to the church, I looked at the mirror of the funeral director's vehicle and saw the long line of cars following us. I reasoned that there wouldn't be enough place in the church to receive everybody. The funeral director assured me that I needed not worry because most of those following would stay in their cars during the service, since it was a sin to go into a Protestant church. However, not one person remained in their car. Everyone went in to the service. The two assistants, after placing the coffin, would wait in their car, because Catholic services were always similar and they knew about what time to re-enter the church. However, when they got to the door, and a young couple began to sing a hymn of hope and consolation, the two men turned around and stayed inside for the remainder of the service. By this time, it was standing room only, but that didn't deter them, as they'd never before witnessed a funeral like this one. M. Gosselin's testimony was read, hymns were sung, and other pastors took part, including Walter Angst, president of l'Institut Biblique Béthel. It wasn't a somber service, but a victory because Jesus, who raised himself from the grave, had received M. Gosselin's spirit, and one day he will raise his body (1 Corinthians 15:42-44).

As we left the building, the funeral director pointed to his heart and said, "You have something that touches us right here." An aunt of M. Gosselin said to M. Gosselin's brother, who was in the robes of his teaching order, "That was terrible. No Mass. No statues. The building is not even finished. It was terrible." The teaching brother replied, "True, my aunt. They don't have those things, but what they do have gets right down into the depths of your soul."

The pallbearers were friends of M. Gosselin and had worked with him at the mine. One of our Christians had suggested that unsaved friends of the deceased be asked to serve as pallbearers, so that they would hear his testimony. When these men returned to the mine, they were surrounded by other workers asking many questions. One who had acted as pallbearer said, "Go and see what we saw today and you will never throw another stone (figurative) at the Baptists."

Mme Gosselin outlived her husband by 19 years, and she was one of the most dedicated and persistent witnesses of the Lord that I've ever known. When she was in her 70s she still made several visits a week. In her last days in hospital she said to her daughter-in-law, "Jeanne, I am weak and too frail to carry on. I want to go to my heavenly home. I have evangelized everyone who has come near me in the hospital. I have witnessed to those who do the cleaning, serve the meals, and the nurses and doctors. My work on earth is accomplished. I am ready to go to the home Jesus is preparing for me."

So much more could be said of what God did in Asbestos, and other similar towns and cities in Quebec, through the testimony of evangelical Christians, but we will limit ourselves to what has been said in these pages. Needless to say, it was very difficult for us to leave the Asbestos church. We saw people suffer in their stand for Christ and we went through many trials together. Our resignation wasn't read from the pulpit. Rather, I began Monday morning and visited every family in the church to tell them personally about God's call to another city. Each family was asked to keep what I had said confidential until everyone had been made aware of the situation. Over the years as we have gone back, generally to preach, nearly every time new Christians have come to me and asked if I remembered visiting them. I had visited every house in Asbestos and in the surrounding villages and rural districts. As it was difficult for Paul to leave Ephesus (Acts 20:36,37), so it was difficult for us, but contrary to Paul's situation, we could still go back to revisit the people of Asbestos. It has been thrilling to see God's hand at work during difficult times and good times. We have recently been invited to join in the activities as the church should have never existed–at least from the unsaved judge's point of view–celebrated their 50th anniversary.

(Endnotes)
1    John A. Hardon, Abridged editor of *the Modern Catholic Dictionary* (Toronto: Doubleday, Imprimatur Joseph A O'Keefe, Vicar General, Archdiocese of New York, Dec. 13, 1979), p. 343.
2    Richard P. McBrien, *Catholic Theology*, Vol. II, p. 802.
3    M.E. Osterhaven, *Views of Lord's Supper*, in Walter A. Alwell (Editor), *Evangelical Dictionary of Theology* (Grand Rapids, MI: Baker Book House, 1984), p. 653.
4    M.E. Osterhaven, *Views of Lord's Supper*, p. 653.
5    Mason Wade, *The French Canadians 1760 – 1945* (Toronto MacMillan, 1955).
6    John L. McKenzie, *The Roman Catholic Church* (New York: Doubleday, Imprimatur Joseph P. O'Brian, Victor General, S.T.P. Archdiocese of New York, May 14, 1939), p. 327.
7    John L. McKenzie, *The Roman Catholic Church*, p. 332.
8    Gregory Baum, *The Church in Quebec*, (Ottawa: Novalis, St. Paul's University, 1992), p. 18-19.

# Chapter 6

# *School Daze for French Protestants*

## Introduction

As you read this heading, you will think we should go back to school to learn how to spell the word "days." You will see that school was a "daze" in those days for French Protestants.

It's unbelievable and astonishing that the Huguenots, a group of French colonists from France, were deprived of public education in New France for more than 150 years from the very beginning of the colony. Then after the Quebec Act, under British and Canadian rule from 1769 to 1964, they were deprived again of a French Protestant public education. The public school system under the Catholic Church was not a great success, even for Catholic children, "…in 1790, hardly 4,000 people out of 1,140,000 in Quebec could read and write." [1]

*La Société des Missions de Lausanne*, Switzerland, sent Henri Olivier and his wife as their first missionaries to Canada in 1834. When the Oliviers saw the illiteracy that existed in French speaking Quebec they thought offering free schooling for the children could be a way to reach people with the Gospel. Mme Feller was also well known in Lausanne for her ministry to the poor, prisoners, and the sick. Henri Olivier had been Mme Feller's pastor and "Mme Feller corresponded by mail with Mme Olivier who informed her of the difficulties in the Canadian mission."[2] Poor health, persecution and the Quebec winters caused the Oliviers to return to Switzerland after three years of successful ministry, but not before sowing the seed of French schools for children as a means of evangelism in the mind of Mrs. Henriette Feller.

Following the death of her husband, "Louis Feller, commandant de la Garde-Police de Lausanne,"[3] Mme Feller came to Quebec in 1835 accompanied by a young student, Louis Roussy. When she began to put this school program into action it stirred up hostile persecution from the catholic clergy. Nevertheless, she continued teaching school in the morning and visiting in the afternoon. The model of the French church providing a school for children as a means to have contact with French Canadians was used in the nineteenth century, but not in the twentieth century when French Catholic schools became more numerous.

**Our First 20th century missionary**

Wilfred Wellington and his wife Edna were our first missionaries. They served under the Regular Baptist Churches, which later amalgamated with the Independent Baptists in 1953 to form the Fellowship of Evangelical Baptist Churches in Canada. The Wellingtons' years of service in Quebec began with a visit to the province, where a friendly priest showed them through a cathedral. When they came to the altar the priest explained that Christ was offered on the altar in the mass and how it was a very solemn service. Mr. Wellington corrected him and said that Jesus Christ died once for all for our sins and cried out on the cross, "It is finished." He is now seated at the right hand of God, interceding for us and does not need to be offered again on the altar. The priest became very serious and said, "Don't teach any of our people."[4]

Upon his return to Ontario, Wilfred Wellington began to pray earnestly that God would send a missionary to Quebec to reach French Canadians with the New Testament message of the Gospel.

God answered his prayers and did send a missionary to Quebec. This missionary was Wilfred Wellington himself! Pastor and Mrs. Wellington arrived in Val d'Or, Quebec on October 30, 1938.

*Wilfred and Edna Wellington, with Murray Heron,*
*at rally in Timmins, Ontario, 1947*

*Wilfred and Edna Wellington1947*

*Wilfred and Edna Wellington, Malartic, 1953*

All our missionaries, as well as those of the Brethren and Pentecostals, were faced with the task of educating the children of new converts. The Wellingtons thought they had a solution for a family that lived a great distance from town. They would attend the Catholic school and ask to be exempted from religious teaching and visits to the Catholic Church for mass and confession. The parents wrote a letter to the local school board asking that their children, whose parents were no longer Catholic, be excused from Roman Catholic teaching. They were perfectly within their rights but the children "were dismissed from school at the insistence of the priest."[5] This cost the children an entire year of school before educational authorities demanded their re-admittance.

Another situation developed in a large mining town that had an English Protestant school board. Since Protestant French schools were non-existent before the arrival of missionaries, the children often had to be sent to an English Protestant school, learn English, and complete their education in English. In this town, however, the French children were only permitted to attend the English school if they spoke English fluently. Those recently converted French Protestants who were not fluent in English were therefore expelled from the French Catholic school and refused entrance to the English Protestant school. All this despite the fact the parents were Canadian citizens and paid school taxes; the English school board knew they were acting contrary to the law.[6] Their excuse was, "the claim of the (Catholic) bishop that if a child has been christened (baptized) Catholic he is Catholic for life."[7] Therefore, the children who were baptized Catholic were still considered Catholic despite the parents' abjuration from the Catholic religion to follow the Gospel. The children of school age, with hardly any exceptions, wanted to follow their parents and the truth they had found in the Scriptures. This extortion of a child's liberty at the time of birth, or shortly thereafter, may be a Catholic doctrine but it is surely not the position of Protestant theology. The Protestant school board should have come to the rescue of their fellow French Protestants.

## A Protestant French School in the Noranda Baptist Church

Another case is recorded by Murray Heron. It moved the Noranda Baptist Church, and the missionaries, to establish a private French Protestant school. He explained the problem,

> One Christian family that we knew continued to send their three school-aged girls to the Catholic-run public school. One day the students were asked to write out the commandments of the Lord as homework. When their parents heard about the assignment, the father promptly took out his Bible and had his daughters copy out the Ten Commandments word for word from Exodus 20:1-17. At school the next day, the girls handed in their

homework. The nun teaching the class wanted to know where they had found the commandments because they differed from the official Catholic catechism. The girls explained that they had copied them precisely as they were written in the Bible. Then without hesitation, the teacher closed their books, told them to go home and never come back to school. A few days later this Christian family received word from the government that their family allowance benefits were being discontinued because their children no longer attended school.[8]

Murray heard about this when the confused parents came to see him, asking for advice.

Out of compassion and concern, a French school was established in response to the urgent need. Following are the names, from the earliest to the last, of the young women who taught in the school: Annette (Trudel) Gariepy, Margaret (Campbell) Heron, Mildred (Ford) Stallmach, Josie Bury, Helen (Hall) Hamelin.

*Blanche Phillips and Mildred (Ford) Stallmach*

Mildred Stallmach, in a recorded interview, explained how the Christian school operated. First of all it was a faith venture. Murray Heron told her, "We will pay you $25.00 a week if the money is available." There were other missionaries scattered across Northwestern Quebec as well, so the money was equally distributed according to whether the teacher was single or married and whether there were children in the family. It must be said that for someone like Mildred Stallmach–who had taught for five years in the Ontario public school system and who had just graduated from Toronto Baptist Seminary with a L.Th. degree–it wasn't the pay and benefits that drew her to this school. It was her love for Christ and French Canadians, and children in particular. Years later, she applied for her teacher's pension but she wasn't credited for the three years she taught in Noranda. She said, however, that during those years, "No one ever went hungry." They trusted in Jesus' promise and obeyed His Word. Jesus counseled his disciples, "Do not worry saying 'what shall we eat, what shall we drink, what shall we wear...' Your heavenly Father knows that you need them. But seek first his kingdom and his righteousness and all these things will be given unto you as well." (Matthew 6:31-33).

The enrolment in the Noranda French Protestant school was twenty-eight students in different grades. Fortunately Mildred Stallmach had taught in a multi-class situation in Ontario, but a problem existed in that these children were French and could not speak English. Although she had studied French in high school and at seminary, the accent and vocabulary of French students were different to what she had been accustomed and it took about three months for her to become familiar with Quebec French.

Textbooks for French Protestants were non-existent. Teachers had to translate English textbooks and write the translation on the blackboard. Sometimes they used the French Catholic textbooks, but they were saturated (both the text and the pictures) with Catholic doctrine, so once again the teachers were obliged to select material and write it on the blackboard.

One day, a lawyer who was a French Canadian Jehovah's Witness, came to see Mildred with two of his children. The oldest was nine years old and had never been to school. He asked her if she would accept these children as pupils. She talked this over with Pastor Murray Heron. His response was, "Well, Mildred. You know best. You already have twenty-eight students in several different age brackets, so I will leave the decision up to you." Mildred told us that her heart went out to those children of Jehovah's Witnesses' parents and said to herself, "Every child deserves an education, whatever the religion of his parents." She then told the lawyer that she would accept his children but stated that her curriculum contained Bible teaching and stories. The lawyer agreed to these conditions and sent the children to the Baptist day school.

## French Catholic Colonies Provided by the Quebec Government

One of the families, whose children attended this school in Noranda, was the Vézina family. Their three daughters, Huguette, Denise and Rolande, were pupils. There weren't many young believers at that time and they had few outlets and activities for their Christian life. Christian camps were just beginning and the English Brethren lent their camp at Wallace Lake, on the American border near Sherbrooke, to the French speaking Baptist and Brethren young people. They got together for one week each summer. The fledgling Baptist and Brethren groups were glad to cooperate in giving the young people a camp together. Brethren and Baptists eventually developed their own camps to respond to the needs and programs of each group.

Huguette learned about the *Institut Biblique Béthel* from Réjeanne Trudel, a young Christian who attended the La Sarre church and their day school. They later enrolled together. Bethel was also one of the few outlets for Bible education in Quebec. Béthel was started in 1948 by Dorothy Kenyon along with Arthur Hill, a medical doctor and elder among the Brethren, and others. The following year, Baptist pastor Walter Angst of Emmaus Bible

School in Lausanne, Switzerland, joined Miss Kenyon, and a three-year Bible program was inaugurated. He was director of the school for its first 21 years.

*Réjeanne Trudel, around 1950*

Mention has been made in a previous chapter that these two young ladies, Huguette Vézina and Réjeanne Trudel, visited Jeanne Gosselin, with my wife Betty, the day Jeanne made a decision for the Lord. This was during a practical Bible School work assignment in the Asbestos Baptist Church.

The Vézina family was living in a colony. The colonies were districts in Northern Quebec where a village was established in virgin forest, and parcels of land were given to families who were willing to settle there. Each colony had a priest who decided who could or could not be granted a parcel of land. Each colonist was obliged to agree to help pay for the building and maintenance of a Catholic Church for that particular colony. Mr. Wellington reported that, "Thus numerous little colonies, begun from public funds," were, "entirely controlled by the Roman Catholic Church."[9]

Wilfred Wellington reports an example of how the Roman Catholic Church controlled these colonies:

These poor undertrodden people expressed enthusiasm for the New Testament and its message. Eagerly did they invite Gospel meetings into their homes. Frequent calls were made and evidently enjoyed. Then came the thundering threats of the papal despot. Their land would be forfeited if they continued to receive us. They must burn their New Testaments or be eternally damned. This double threat – material and spiritual – drove the blinded slaves to a resistance of the truth.[10]

The Vézina family had to endure similar threats.

In order to get first-hand knowledge of the colonies, I contacted Huguette Vézina by phone. She is now married to Claude Matthieu, a pastor working with Transport for Christ, a ministry that reaches both French and English drivers on their drive across Quebec. One of their daughters, Linda, is married to a pastor, Toe-Blake Roy. Huguette shared how her father received a New Testament and how it became known to their priest. Although it was another two years before M. Vézina understood the Gospel message and had the courage to repent and trust in Christ and take an open stand, the persecution began when he dared to have a New Testament and refused to destroy it. About five months after his conversion Mme Vézina also received Jesus as her Savior and Lord and received the gift of eternal life by faith in Christ. Subsequently persecution intensified.

Huguette further explained:

> There was only one store in the colony and the priest forced the
> store manager to limit the things that my parents could buy. Life
> had already become difficult, but to limit us to buying only the
> stark necessities of life made things that much more difficult.
> Then the priest refused to bless my father's animals. This didn't
> bother my father because he now trusted in the Lord, and not
> in superstition. Unfortunately, the other farmers in the colony
> were superstitious and they refused to buy animals that were
> not blessed by the priest. Furthermore, the priest informed the
> government representative that my parents were no longer
> Catholics and government grants that had been given to farmers
> who excelled in their work, or for new projects, were now
> withheld. He endured this for five years after his conversion and
> then decided to sell his farm that he had worked so laboriously
> to carve out of the forest. No one would buy it because it had
> not been blessed by a priest. He finally gave it to a relative in
> the colony and received nothing in return. The family left the
> colony with their clothes and a few pieces of furniture after
> seven arduous years.[11]

By the grace of God, and trusting in his promises, M. Vézina
had persevered. Surely the gospel of Matthew 5:11-12 applied to
these courageous believers, "Blessed are you when people insult
you, persecute you and falsely say all kinds of evil against you
because of me. Rejoice and be glad, because great is your reward
in heaven, for in the same way they persecuted the prophets who
were before you."

This family had yet another burden to bear. Their daughters
were obliged to attend the Catholic school, study the catechism,
and go to mass and confession. Furthermore, the children were
persecuted even though they had not personally made a decision
to trust and follow Christ, nor had they talked about the Gospel to
other students. In fact, at that time, Huguette was quite impressed by

the nuns and had a growing desire to become a nun. Nevertheless, the Vézina sisters were forbidden by the authorities to mix with the other girls at school. They were ordered to arrive either fifteen minutes before the other students or fifteen minutes later than the others, according to the directives of their teachers and at recess they were obliged to keep to themselves.

After seven years of persecution the Vézina family decided it was time to live a normal life and put their girls in a Christian school. They moved to Noranda and enrolled their children in the Baptist French day school where Huguette and Denise were in grade seven and Rolande was in grade two. During that year, Huguette and Denise received Jesus as Savior and after 50 years they still have their hands on the plough (Luke 9:36) and "their eyes fixed upon Jesus" (Hebrews 12:2). These girls admitted that the lack of textbooks and having several different grades in the same classroom made learning somewhat difficult. "On the other hand," Huguette said, "we were welcomed and loved and we sang hymns at school and at church, something we couldn't do in the Catholic school."[12] Furthermore, their teacher, Mildred (Ford) Stallmach, taught them life's most important lesson; she led them to faith in Jesus Christ.

### Young Ladies Filled a Dangerous and Pressing Need

Mildred's sister Blanche was asked to respond to an urgent need in the school at La Sarre. The beginning of the school year was upon them and they were still without a teacher for their one-room school. The school year for fourteen children hung in the balance, as well as the testimony and credibility of the French church and school. Pastor Les Barnhart contacted Blanche, who left her teaching post in Ontario in order to meet the need at La Sarre. It's helpful to know the background of the church in La Sarre to better understand the conditions under which she served.

The church at La Sarre began in the lumber camps where many French Canadians in Northwestern Quebec worked during the winter season. Wilfred Wellington joined with H.K. McLennan of the Shantymen's Christian Association in order to visit lumber camps, conduct evening meetings for the men, and leave literature with an offer for a New Testament. On one trip they were pressed for time so they decided to leave booklets at a small camp and continue on to a large camp for a service. As the Lord often does, He touched the heart of a man in the smaller camp, not the larger one. This man from the La Sarre area requested a New Testament by mail. La Sarre was one hundred and 30 kilometers (78 miles) from Wilfred Wellington's home in Val-d'Or. Other men from this area also requested New Testaments. For two years Wilfred Wellington and François-Xavier Trudel visited and spent hours in the homes of these contacts. Mr. Wellington remarked, "The unstinted hospitality, which so often characterizes French Canadians, was offered to us."[13] On one occasion, on a very cold northern Canada night, these men had been offered a bed in a house heated by a wood-burning stove. The big dog jumped up on their bed and they promptly chased him away. In the middle of the night, as the wood fire extinguished itself, they coaxed the dog back up on the foot of their bed to keep their feet warm!

Two years after the first visits, God began to save people and transform lives. A man who "had been a dreadful slave of drink … was tormented by another season of debauchery, which generally lasted for days, and sick at heart, he cried to God for deliverance."[14] He had read in his New Testament how Jesus delivered the demoniac in Mark 5:1-20, and he admitted that his demon was alcohol. God answered his prayer. He was not yet converted but at a special Easter service, where a French Canadian gave his testimony and was baptized, this poor man grasped the message of the Gospel and was saved. Another new convert lost his employment through the efforts of the priest. He was a millwright but after being dismissed, no one dared to hire him. He moved to La Sarre where he found work and other believers. There was also a woman who had become bitter with an unforgiving spirit against someone who had wronged her in the past. Even when she was in the hospital, dangerously ill, and the Catholic priest having heard her confession, "…she was unwilling, even at that critical hour, to forgive her enemy."[15] But later, as Mr. Wellington related, "Her heart was broken when she heard of the infinite sacrifice of the Saviour, who bled for his enemies. She became a forgiving and radiant Christian."[16]

Many others confessed Christ openly in the La Sarre area. There was need for help and it came from an unexpected source. Mr. Wellington reported,

> The one mining camp, in this large agricultural section, because of its pathetic need called for some immediate effort. In the summer of 1945, Miss Margaret McCreadie, a seminary student of winsome personality, came to our assistance here. Entering that field, she served Christ among the children for several months. An opportunity was opened, which she immediately seized. Six miles from the village was a friendly family whose children were receiving no education. Being a capable schoolteacher, she daily ministered to those boys and girls and to the neighbors' children who willingly came. A little private school was provided in the large front room of the home, being furnished with benches and rough tables. Several children, as well as the mother of the family professed Christ that summer.[17]

**At Last a French Canadian School!**

The work in La Sarre progressed so well that François-Xavier Trudel, from Val d'Or, who had made many trips to the area, became convinced that God wanted him to move there. Pastor Wellington describes "a joyous occasion, when on the 18th of November, 1946, this group of Christians met to form themselves into a New Testament church ... Brother Trudel was officially requested by the congregation to become its first pastor."[18] This was our first French-only Baptist Church in Quebec.

*The La Sarre Church*

The perennial dilemma for French missionaries showed itself again. With the success in evangelism in La Sarre, Wilfred Wellington stated, "…one great problem had to be faced in this connection – that of a school."[19] Margaret McCreadie was the logical candidate. She not only succeeded in teaching but also in evangelism. "Some of the timid contacts, interested but undecided, were encouraged to break with Rome"[20] through her spiritual fervor.

*Margaret McCreadie teaching in La Sarre*

There was no Protestant School Board in existence for many miles. This was a blessing as it gave the La Sarre Christians the privilege of creating their own local Protestant French School Board, and in return benefit from receiving their share of school taxes. The church continued to grow and spread the Gospel, in the same fashion as the Thessalonian Christians, as the local believers zealously shared what Christ had done for them, "they turned from idols to serve the living and true God, and to wait for his Son from heaven" (1 Thessalonians 1:9,10).

Put yourself, for a moment, in the place of the children of French converts. At La Sarre there were fifteen or more children in a small one-room school, six miles from the town. These children knew their parents had gone through persecution and had even witnessed the malicious burning of the house of one of the converts.[21] Two of the fathers had been jailed for taking part in an open-air gospel service. They were a marked people, and if their children went to a French catholic school they could, at worst, be in danger, or at the very least teased and harassed. Thus, parents and children were happy when Blanche Ford arrived. It was a mammoth task for her as she had studied French in high school, but this was not sufficient for the task at hand. Her first contact with French people in Quebec was to accompany a French Canadian teenager on the train from Montreal to Noranda. It was a long, slow trip in those days and she and the unilingual French Canadian found it very difficult to communicate with one another. It would have been helpful if Blanche had had the opportunity to take a yearlong course at the Institut Biblique Béthel or at a French university. Because of the urgency at La Sarre this was not possible because school was due to start in a few weeks. She began her school year but admitted that it took her about three months before she could communicate fluently with the students.

The school building was built on land donated by Alphonse Cloutier. He lived a half mile from the school. The building itself was divided into two sections. One side was the classroom and the other provided a kitchen and bedroom for the teacher. It was heated by a round potbelly wood-burning stove in the classroom, and by a wood-burning stove in the kitchen. The fires in the stoves would inevitably go out during the night and it was her lot to light both of them again in the morning. Blanche admits that she's still not very adept at lighting a wood fire. This was just one more difficulty faced in rural areas during that time, especially during the bitterly cold northern Quebec winters.

I enquired as to whether she had been nervous staying alone in the schoolhouse, especially in view of past persecution in that area. She answered that she had been lonely, rather than frightened. At first, she was apprehensive, but when she found out that the strange noise she was hearing during the night were sheep rubbing against the building, she had peace of mind! She explained the cause of her loneliness:

The school was situated six miles from the village and there was no public transportation and no mail delivery. She got into the village only on special occasions and would receive her mail at that time. Dinner and supper were graciously provided in the Trudel house, which was situated about two hundred feet from the school. Telephones were rare, and she did not receive or make any long distance calls to family or friends during the time spent in this area. On three occasions she was able to spend a weekend with the other missionaries in Noranda.[22]

Because Blanche was willing to make this sacrifice, fifteen French Canadian children completed a year's schooling and the testimony of the La Sarre Baptist Church was maintained. If after encouraging people to follow the Word of God, rather than church tradition, the La Sarre believers had been unable to provide schooling for their children, their credibility would have been tarnished.

## The Price of Following Jesus

Teaching wasn't all these young ladies had to do. As missionaries, they had extra-curricular activities, such as taking children on picnics or directing sports events. They also made visits and took part in open-air meetings. When Blanche went to La Sarre, she didn't expect to experience what happened in the open-air meetings in that town. However, she joined the meetings and participated by playing her accordion.

Many French people were interested in the Gospel and would have desired to attend a Protestant church, but this was forbidden as they had been taught that it would be a sin to do so. One rumor that circulated was that a Catholic entering a Protestant church would be required to step on a crucifix. How does one reach those people who are held in fear and forbidden to read the Bible or enter a Protestant church? In the 1950s and 60s, in my personal experience, there were countless cases where I had given a Protestant New Testament, or sold a Catholic New Testament at cost, only to have them destroyed by the order of the priests. The French believers did what Jesus did; they went out in the open air and preached the Gospel. But the results of French open-air meetings were very different from the meetings held by English-speaking churches.

Several books and the Christian Brethren magazine *News of Quebec* have preserved for history the price paid by French pastors and missionaries and ordinary French Canadians who dared to follow the word of God in the years from 1930 to 1960. Others had paid the price in the centuries before this. The editor of *News of Quebec* stated well the basis of this conflict. He wrote, "In Quebec... for some 333 years (from 1627-1960) every effort possible was made to keep the word of God away from people." The Catholic Church was the source of this censure of God's word. We are told in the past, "God spoke to our forefathers through the prophets... but in these last days he has spoken by his Son" (Hebrews 1:2). The apostles were glad when the people read the Scriptures or the Bible. In the Acts of the Apostles, we are shown that the ordinary

Christian is to read the Bible to make sure what is being taught from the pulpit is in accord with it. Paul and his assistant Silas, said "the Bereans were of more noble character than the Thessalonians; for they received the message (of Paul and Silas) with great eagerness and examined the Scriptures every day to see if what Paul said was true" (Acts 17:11). The Evangelicals see nothing better than having the people listen to them, and then, examine to see if it is in accord with the Bible. Jesus said to his Father, "your Word is true" (John 17:17). The Apostle John in his Gospel, the last Gospel to be written, writes, "Jesus said, I tell you the truth, whoever hears *my Word* and believes him that sent me has eternal life, and will not be condemned, but has crossed from death to life. I tell you the truth…" (John 5:24).

In a different situation, missionary Weldon Clark, in Chomedy (north of Montreal), also wanted to tell people about the wonderful gift that God wants to give by faith in Jesus, through his death and resurrection. He often chatted of these things with his landlord. He tells us in his book how he became friendly with him, but there was one thing he could not grasp, that we are saved by faith alone, and not by works. "That," he said, "was impossible!"

One day, Mr. L. said to Weldon, "I am not able to reply to your scripture verses, but I know someone who can. Would you come with me some evening to see a Jesuit? Weldon agreed. When they were received and taken into his office, the priest immediately mounted his defense.

Now, Mr. Clark, you have probably come here this evening with a good knowledge of your Bible and able to quote many verses. I am not greatly familiar with certain texts that you may quote. I shall not try to answer, verse for verse, since it is not important to me. In the Roman Catholic Church system, we do not count upon the present Bible as our final and only source of revelation. On equal footing with the Bible, and having equal authority, we have tradition, that which has been passed down to us. There are also the dogmas of the church. It is like a continuing source of revelation from God through the Pope and Archbishops.[23]

Like the Pharisees in Jesus time, the Catholic Church stands upon its own tradition, rather than the word of God.

Jesus replied, "Isaiah was right when he prophesied about you hypocrites, as it is written: 'These people honor me with their lips, but their hearts are far from me. They worship me in vain; their teachings are but rules taught by men.' You have let go of the commands of God and are holding on to the traditions of men." And he said to them, "You have a fine way of setting aside the commands of God in order to observe your own traditions!" (Mark 7:6-9)

Jesus paid with his life for the truth as well as for our salvation.

The next few pages will show how when believers encouraged people to read the Bible to see if what they said was true, they were often met with violence and fallacious talk. Opponents would sometimes destroy or throw away the very book used to verify truth.

Persecution took many forms. While the pastor was the main target of abuse, the ordinary French Canadian evangelical Christian was also ill treated, and Christian women were the targets of fire crackers, garbage and vile language. Here are examples of how the persecutions were reported in newspapers.

### Evangelists Jailed

*Some of those jailed in 1950 - Leslie Barnhart, Maurice Boillat, Alphonse Cloutier, Lloyd Carr, and Noël Rossignol*

La Sarre, Que., July 24—Five Baptist evangelists were showered with eggs, potatoes and rubbish, beaten and finally jailed. In a mob scene involving 250 residents of this northwest Quebec village Saturday night. Today the five were awaiting trial on charges of illegal assembly.

The Baptists, victims of the riot—although seemingly willing victims—were charged with creating it when they would not obey police orders to halt their meeting. Even as police questioned them, their beating by town residents continued, without police interference as far as could be seen.

Jailed under section 87 of the Criminal Code were Leslie H. Barnhart, 37, pastor of the Bonne Nouvelle Baptist Church, four miles east of La Sarre; Maurice Boillat, 24, professor of French at the Central Baptist Seminary, St. George St., Toronto; Lloyd Carr, 20, a student at the seminary; Alphonse Cloutier, 40, La Sarre, farmer, and Noël Rossignol, 35, La Sarre, welder."[24]

Also attacked but not jailed were Howard Killick, 20, of Essex, a student at the Toronto Seminary; Mrs. Rossignol, Mrs. B. Cloutier, Mrs. Barnhart, Annette Trudel and Blanche Ford.[25]

The town authorities had hoped that the jailing of the local pastors and two key members of the local church would end the Baptist's zeal to spread the Gospel. The opposite took place. On July 28, 1950, headlines of the Rouyn-Noranda Press proclaimed:

La Sarre Council Asks Provincial Police Aid—Mayor is Bedridden after Baptist Brawl. The mayor was unconscious for 24 hours and still is too sick to receive visitors…Mayor Martel sustained an attack of angina pectoris after receiving many telegrams of protest from various parts of Quebec and Ontario regarding the treatment of the small group of Baptists who, Saturday evening, were buffeted by an angry crowd of at least 300 people on La Sarre's main street.[26]

**Pastor's life endangered**

On August 21, *The Toronto Telegram* printed a detailed account of another conflict in La Sarre under the headline: 'Mob Baptist Group, Hurl Firecrackers as PC (police constable) Stands By.'

A Baptist revival meeting was violently broken up by a mob … that had swollen to nearly 200 people, with the violent elements jostling the Baptists and elderly persons standing on the sidewalks, laughing and jeering.

Suddenly there was a splutter of red flame and firecrackers began to explode around the Baptists' feet. Then the crowd started to hurl the crackers straight at Mr. Barnhart. They exploded in his face and bounced off his clothes.

The blue haze from the fireworks that were cracking like machine-guns covered the crowd. Suddenly Mr. Barnhart's hymnbook was snatched from his hand and sent hurtling over the crowd where it was trampled in the dirt.

A gang of youths charged the Baptist minister and sent him staggering. More firecrackers blazed red in the dusk. The crowd yelled and hooted with delight as a half-drunk lumberjack grabbed the small preacher by the shirt front and yelled abuse in his face.

In desperation, Mr. Barnhart called off the meeting and tried to get back to his car through the jostling crowd. Youths seized the bumpers of the car and rocked it from side to side and up and down. Every time he tried to back out they pushed the car against the curb.

Mrs. Barnhart got out and appealed to the crowd to let them go, but she was greeted with screams and abuse. Then someone let the air out of one of the back tires. Mr. Barnhart got out to try and fix it and firecrackers were thrown into his face as he bent over the wheel. The jack was kicked away from under the car and the pastor's hand was crushed between the tire and the fender. Although the town council of La Sarre promised the evangelists protection, the town's six-foot constable, Edward Carpentier, did not appear until nearly ten o'clock, when the preacher was still trying to get away.

Mr. Barnhart put his head inside the trunk of the car to get at some tools and the catch was knocked free so that the trunk cover crashed down on the back of his head.

White and shaken, the Baptist minister held his head for a moment while the crowd roared with laughter. The policeman stood by Mr. Barnhart's side and laughed with the crowd.

At about 10:30 p.m. Mr. Barnhart gave up trying to fix the tire, and his wife managed to get to a taxi stand. The minister worked his way through the crowd and half fell, half crawled into the cab.

As this reporter left town, a rock crashed against the side of the truck.

"Go back to Ontario!" someone shouted. "You won't put our pictures in the papers."

Yet the Lord stood by his people and strengthened their faith in the midst of this trial.[27]

---

The women who took part in the open-air meeting were not spared. Their nylon stockings were burned full of holes from the firecrackers, and the accordion that Blanche Ford used to accompany the singing was subject to the same treatment and the same results. It too was burned full of holes. When young women accepted to teach in these fledgling schools they experienced the truth of the words of Jesus, "If they have persecuted me they will persecute you also" (John 15:20).

Further solemn news followed. The Toronto Star of August 3, 1950 reported the death of the mayor of La Sarre:

F.X. Martel, first mayor of the town of La Sarre, seized with a heart attack last week, died at his home here today. Mr. Martel suffered a seizure after having received a number of telegrams and other messages from different points in Ontario and Quebec denouncing treatment of Baptist church members near La Sarre … From the time he suffered the attack which most people believe was brought on by worry over the Baptist incident in which he had taken a leading part, little hope was held for his recovery.[28]

These messages of concern about the riot were coming from Catholics as well as Protestants.

The town officials had a change of heart and one wonders if they saw the hand of God in what took place with the mayor's death. Murray Heron gives the following account,

A few days later the town council of La Sarre phoned our lawyer in Rouyn to arrange an urgent meeting. They hired a taxi and the entire town council travelled 55 miles to meet us at our lawyer's office.

We were taken aback by what we heard. They deeply regretted the arrests and shoddy treatment our men had received in the past weeks. They wanted the prisoners released immediately and were withdrawing all charges against them. In addition, they granted us permission to preach and promised police protection to prevent further ill treatment from the public in La Sarre.[29]

### Jean (John) Hamelin

Jean and Helen Hamelin were pastoring a church in Malartic. After having twice visited all the town of Malartic door-to-door offering French New Testaments, Jean felt he must go to others who had never heard the Gospel or even seen a New Testament. So he went to St. Maurice, a farming area in the shadow of the Amos Catholic

Cathedral where years before the priest in the Cathedral had said to Wilfred Wellington, "Don't teach any of my people."[30]

*Jean Hamelin doing door-to-door visitations in Abitibi*

*Jean and Helen Hamelin*

God, who by the Holy Spirit had guided Jean Hamelin, blessed his ministry in the rural area and three families placed their faith in Jesus Christ. When the Catholic Church became aware of this, the children were expelled from school. What could be done? The Bouffard family alone had ten children. Large families were common in Quebec in that era and together those three families had twelve school-aged children.

Helen Hamelin, already busy with the responsibilities of a pastor's wife and young children of her own, took over the task of teaching all 12 children even though the families lived 50 kilometers (30 miles) from the Hamelin home. She had taken the one-year French language course for missionaries at Institut Biblique Béthel, and she was fluent in French. Josie Bury upon hearing about this came to the rescue of overworked Helen Hamelin and took over as teacher for these children.

## Josie Bury

Josie Bury is the daughter of Polish immigrants, who grew up in Noranda, Quebec where she and her siblings were saved through the Salvation Army Sunday School. Later they began to attend the English Baptist Church and their parents joined them. The parents, far removed from their families in Poland and living in a Northern Quebec mining town, had turned to alcohol to help them cope with the loneliness they endured. Through the testimony and preaching of the church, they not only found a Saviour who saved and delivered them from their enslavement to alcohol, but they found a family in the church and gained many friends. Their daughter, Josie, was a teacher under the English Protestant School Commission and taught in Noranda and, for a period of time, in Lennoxville, Quebec. When she heard of Helen Hamelin's efforts to teach school 50 kilometers (30 miles) from her home she took over the teaching, became a blessing to a dozen French children and a model and encouragement to their parents, not to mention a relief for Helen.

This entire venture was the result of a team effort and came with a price. Jean Hamelin persevered courageously in door-to-door visitation despite persecution; Helen Hamelin willingly took charge of the school despite her own heavy schedule; and Josie Bury sacrificed a stable and well-salaried teaching position to go, by faith, to teach in a small school with no building and no French text books for French Protestant children. These families showed great courage in that after coming to the knowledge of salvation, they did not fear the wrath of the Catholic Church, which, with the backing of the Quebec government ruled the district, and in reality, the entire Province of Quebec.

*Teacher Josie Bury with French language day school students in*
*Noranda Baptist Church*

## Fernand St-Louis

In September 1947, in another part of Quebec, school doors opened for another school year. This was a Catholic school and a teaching brother, dressed in his cassock, stood before his class with a stern expression on his face. His voice thundered, "The Protestants have entered our area. Some people have changed their religion and I want to warn you that we will not tolerate any heresy in this class, or anyone who cares to differ with the teaching of the Catholic Church or our catechism."[31] At this pronouncement, a young lad trembled in his seat. His parents had been renounced by the priest from the pulpit of the church, which was in the same parish as the school. They had recently been branded as heretics. The boy had not only been a good student, but he was a member of the "Croissée", an organization similar to the Scouts except with a strong religious emphasis. Members wore white uniforms with a cross on them, and they took part in parades and other religious activities. The "Croissée" had religious studies, besides the regular catechism, which everyone studied. Fernand even dreamed of becoming a priest some day. But on that September day, did that teaching brother know this student had become a "heretic," and one who followed the Bible rather than the Pope?

Fernand arrived home that day in tears. Mr. and Mrs. St-Louis didn't have to be told what had happened. How could he return to school under the gaze and discipline of this stern teaching brother who had warned the class that he would not tolerate anyone who strayed from Catholic doctrine? Would Fernand be allowed to attend the catholic school? It wasn't only at school that he faced persecution; he even had to be protected by an adult when he went to the corner store.

Mr. and Mrs. St-Louis were the first converts from Catholicism to the Gospel in the whole St- Maurice River Valley. What would they do for the education of Fernand and his sister? Two other families converted after the St-Louis family faced this same problem. Mr. St-Louis and evangelist Paul Boeda, along with

Fernand, went to visit the principal of the Trois-Rivières English Protestant School to see if Fernand, his sister, and the children of the other two families could attend the school. The principal asked Fernand in French if he could speak any English. Fernand said that they studied a little English at his previous school and repeated a few sentences such as, "open the door," and "feed the dog." The principal wasn't able to hold back his laughter and said, "That is enough Fernand. If the others do as well as you have, you're all accepted as pupils at the Trois-Rivières Protestant School." What a wonderful answer they received, but the school also presented a challenge for the children and parents alike. For the children it meant learning a new language and being taught in it; for the parents and the missionaries it meant these children would be anglicized.

## Girardville

Girardville, in the Lac Saint-Jean area, was the first French Protestant School to receive a grant from the English Protestant School Commission. There had been some division in the parish between the visiting priest and some of the parishioners about the location of a new church building. The parishioners did something untold of in Quebec: they sought a Protestant minister! Richard Strout describes what happened,

> The work of the Christian Brethren in Girardville was born over a difference between
>
> the leadership and the lay people regarding a decision taken in 1932 to build a church four miles from the location of the original little chapel. To reverse this decision, several parishioners decided to contact Protestant ministers, hoping to frighten the clergy and to encourage them to give them their own priest.
>
> An ad was placed in *Le Soleil* (The Sun), a daily French newspaper, requesting a reply from a French Protestant minister but there was no response. Later, after receiving some

Evangelical tracts in the mail, the people wrote to the address at the back of the tracts- 'Centre of Life and Liberty' in Montreal, requesting a Protestant minister. At last, in March, 1933 John Spreeman and Noah Gratton arrive by train in Girardville. The next day they preached the Gospel in the little Catholic Chapel. After a certain time, they were forbidden to preach. Nevertheless before the departure of the missionaries, the wife of the Mayor was converted to Christ. When the two preachers returned in the summer, several of the villagers had been converted although others were fiercely opposed to the Gospel.

In order to oppose this Evangelical work, the Mayor, Pierre Doucet, (who was later also converted) and other citizens, at the instigation of the priest, drove Mr. Spreeman and Mr. Gratton out of town. About twenty men put them in the box of a truck and drove them to the Police Station in Saint-Félicien, 30 miles away. Despite the threats of their abductors, the evangelists, without money, returned the next morning to Girardville. They had found a man willing to drive them there for five dollars that they promised to pay on arrival. The Christians who had gathered in prayer for their safety, received them with tears of joy.

The truth of the Gospel, and the testimony of these preachers who refused to sue their abductors because of their Christian convictions, deeply impressed the people of Girardville and several were converted as a result.

Their testimony continues to this day despite the work of the enemy. For 17 years, three different priests celebrated a special mass on February 11th in the hope of expelling Protestants from the area.[32]

The children were also caught in the crossfire. When they went to school, the teacher would ask each one if he/she had been to mass on Sunday. If a child responded negatively, they were asked to give the reason. The children of believers would reply that their parents no longer believed in the mass, or a similar response. On the spot, before all the other children, the child was told to gather his/her belongings and leave. One can only imagine the trauma this caused primary school children.

There was no Protestant school in the area, not even an English language school. The French believers wrote to the English Protestant School Commission in Quebec City and for the first time since its establishment, some 70 years earlier, the English Protestant School Commission gave a grant to a French Protestant school.

Leila Boyd, a young bilingual English woman who had just graduated from Teacher's College, had a burden for French Canadians. She later married W.S.Whitcombe, a professor at Toronto Baptist Seminary who was credited with casting the vision for French Canadian evangelism in our Baptist churches. She offered her services to the Girardville Assembly and they readily accepted.

*The Girardville School*

Mr. Lessard, a French Canadian Protestant and school inspector, was sent to look over the situation. Miss Boyd was on site and already teaching. Mr. Lessard was so excited that at last a French Protestant School had been recognized and supported by the Protestant School Commission more than 60 years after the commission was formed. Miss Boyd taught there for three years.

Leila studied under Professor W.S. Whitcombe after completion of her three-year stint in Girardville. The Timmins Baptist Church then hired her as deaconess with an emphasis on youth work. It was during W.S. Whitcombe's visits to the Timmins Church that he became impressed with her as a person and with the ministry in which she was so ably engaged. When I spoke with her, she laughed about how the Professor surprised her with his proposal. He asked, "Could I have your hand? I have something for you." She thought he had bought her a pair of gloves and replied, "I just bought a new pair of gloves." He opened his hand and showed her a beautiful engagement ring that Mr. Remous, a jeweller in the Timmins Church, had prepared for him. After their marriage, they served together for many years in Toronto Baptist Seminary and later in Central Baptist Seminary. They also served in different pastorates, but their hearts were never far away from French evangelism. Later W.S. Whitcombe was able to teach French courses at our seminary, SEMBEQ.

Mgr. De Laval, Bishop of Quebec in the 1600s, prohibited non-Catholic French schools. The Girardville School was the first French non-catholic public school in nearly 300 years! The grant wasn't very large, only $300.00 per year, which included part of the teacher's salary. Fortunately, God sent her further support through His faithful children.

However, the Protestant School Commission was ready to support French Protestant schools only if, in their judgment, they were warranted. This means that if there was a local English Protestant School, the French parents would be obliged to send their children to that English school.

212     God in the Midst of the Events that Shook Quebec

Blanche (Ford) Phillips confirmed that a similar situation existed in La Sarre when the French Protestant School started in 1946, in a district where no local Protestant School Board existed. The Christians at the La Sarre Baptist Church gave their school taxes to the local Protestant School Board, which was made up of French Christians elected to form a French Protestant School Board. She recalls the visit of an inspector of the Protestant School Commission who managed to get a taxi from La Sarre to go inspect the French Protestant School. His taxi was a small Bombardier vehicle, somewhere between a car and a bus, that traveled on rubber treads and could go over snow easily, both on and off the road. Transportation was provided only one way, however, so the inspector had to walk six miles back to La Sarre in winter weather, which he did amicably. He was very pleased with the French school and the local Board.

Another case was in the Asbestos-Danville area where we were living at the time, and where a number of French Canadian families had come to the Lord. I approached the principal of the Protestant School and explained the plight of our French Protestants. Many of the children of our church members were already attending that school out of necessity. He had arranged a meeting between the Regional superintendent of the Protestant School Board, himself, and myself. We considered the problem and it was concluded that if we could find a qualified French Protestant teacher they would consider working with us in establishing a French section in their Regional School Program. The problem was all the trained French-speaking teachers were Catholics because colleges and universities, which trained French teachers in that era, were all French Catholic institutions. We did find an English Christian teacher who spoke French, who seriously considered coming to our area, but after much prayer she didn't believe it was the Lord's will for her. This reveals the difficulty French Protestant minorities faced. The principal agreed that if no French teacher could be found, his school would continue to receive the children of French Protestants. However, he made it clear that the children would be anglicized as soon as possible so that they might get along with their studies and be prepared for life. The word *anglicize* and not *teach them to speak English* still echoes in my mind 50 years later.

It would seem that the best solution for French Protestants would have been to let their children attend French Catholic schools, but grant them exemption from Catholic religious studies and practice. As well, they should have had the liberty to attend without harassment. This would have been an occasion to teach both Catholic and Protestant children to practice the words of Jesus, "So in everything, do to others what you would have them do unto you… and be at peace with each other" (Matthew 7:12; Mark 9:50). This would have taught both Catholic and Protestant students to love, rather than hate, without surrendering their personal convictions, yet to be ready to do so if one discovered his convictions and Scripture did not agree.

I was in elementary school, grade six, when Italy entered the Second World War on the side of the Nazis. There was an Italian girl in our class who didn't attend school the day following Italy's declaration. The teacher wisely told us not to harass that student but to show love and consideration toward her. I've never forgotten the girl, who wasn't one of the most popular nor most beautiful girls in the class. The understanding and amicable reaction of the students, thanks to the wise counsel of the teacher, made this girl feel wanted and loved. This same openness and respect should have been offered to French Protestants in Quebec.

**French Schools in Montreal**

W.H. Frey wrote an interesting article concerning a successful effort to have French schools under the Greater Montreal Protestant School Board. The revival of the 19th century had produced French day schools, and some boarding schools, that were supported by Protestant churches. One such school survived the decline of Protestant French churches, the school of Pointe-aux-Trembles. Unfortunately this school found it difficult to pay adequate salaries to the teachers in order to keep the school open.

All French Protestant ministers of Greater Montreal then urged the Protestant School Board to take over the educational program. Peace Centennial School made room for the first 46 French-speaking pupils. By 1957, their number had risen to 250, and 100 more were added each year. Mr. Frey had the privilege two years ago, of joining the Greater Montreal School Board and urged them to start a second school, which would be nearer Verdun and the west of Montreal. This request was granted and Victoria School, near the Forum, made room for French pupils. Peace Centennial has now 530 pupils, and Victoria about 180. There is a possibility of the School Board opening a third school on the East side of Montreal. For the time being, buses are sent daily by the School Board to bring in the children from all parts of the city to the elementary schools.

In addition to this, and in response to the energetic request of the French-speaking ministers, the School Board started a French High School. In 1961 they started Grade VIII, in 1962 Grades VIII and IX, in 1963 Grades VIII, IX, and X. and in June 1965 the students should be able to write the examination papers for-entrance to a university.

The French High School is held in Baron Byng School, with 86 students. That school was chosen for its greater laboratory facilities.

Still another wonderful progress is the opening, this year, of a French Normal School at McDonald College, which is part of McGill University. Unfortunately, of the two students that applied, only one actually attends, and special arrangements had to be made by the Faculty to make it possible for this lonely hero to continue his studies there. It is to be hoped that in the ensuing years more future Protestant teachers will avail themselves of this fine opportunity of getting their teacher's certificate. [33]

**Unexpected Acts of Compassion in Noranda and Saint-Valère**

This severe persecution was general in every area evangelized, but in some places in the late 1950s and early 60s a change began to take place. Not all Catholics agreed with the persecution of Protestant believers. Murray Heron reports a touching situation:

> During this period Mr. and Mrs. Hould, who had 13 children, came to know the Lord and He accomplished a wonderful work of transformation in their lives. Immediately after their conversion, they realized it would be unwise for their children to continue attending [the Catholic] public school. Our school was in operation and ready to receive them, but they faced a costly transportation problem because they lived some distance from the church and had previously had free school transportation for their children.

> The father, Robert Hould, worked at the local copper mine and his large family already stretched his financial resources to the limit. City bus fare for his school-aged children was an added cost that he could not afford, but he was convinced he had to make this sacrifice for his family. A few months after the Hould children joined our school, I received a telephone call from the secretary of the Roman Catholic School Board. He was aware that the Houlds were attending our school and paying for their own transportation. He announced that although the school commission could not furnish a school bus for the children, they would provide city bus tickets for the whole family. I was simply to make a list of the children who needed transportation and they would supply enough tickets to last until the end of the school year.

> God's timing was impeccable. Just a week before this unexpected telephone call, the Hould family had felt convicted to give 10 percent of their income to the Lord's work. They had just learned about the blessing of giving to the church and this was an extremely big step of faith for them. They took it after considerable soul-searching and despite the limits of their personal finances. When they learned of God's gracious provision of school transportation for their children, they were

overwhelmed with gratitude as this represented a larger amount than their offering.[34]

That was a most unusual occurence for that era, and especially so in that it was initiated by the Secretary of the Catholic School Board. The Secretary was only doing what he should have done, however, because the French Christians continued to pay school taxes, which couldn't be transferred to the private school of the Noranda Church. Their school taxes were being allotted to the Catholic School Commission. Later on, if a child of a French believer attended the English school, their taxes were transferred from the Catholic School Commission to the Protestant School Commission.

There were other cases when leniency was shown. Let us consider the Elphège Paillé family where the parents and some of the family members had trusted in Christ as Saviour. They lived in the small village of St-Valère, situated about 50 kilometers northeast of Asbestos. We had begun to take steps to establish a church in Victoriaville, 11 kilometers (seven miles) from St-Valère. It was then that I made contact with the Elphège Paillé family and visited them from time to time for a Bible study. When the effort to start a church in Victoriaville began officially under the leadership of Gabriel Cotnoir, they were the first and only Christian family to stand with us. In fact, they were identified as the only born-again believers in the entire area. The closest evangelical churches were Drummondville and Asbestos, both about 45 kilometers (27 miles), away in different directions. There were nine children in the family, six girls and three boys. We have kept contact with the family over the past 45 years and one of the daughters, Solange, a zealous Christian, lives close to us. I asked her to describe her experience of being educated in the French Catholic public school system.

Since the family lived 45 kilometers from the nearest Protestant school, which was English, their children had no choice but to attend the local Catholic public school. Solange (Paillé) Lapointe (now an adult) not only granted an interview, but she contacted other members of the family to have their opinions on the questions at hand. The members of the family were all in agreement that each one of them had been accepted into the Catholic school and had been exempted from catechism and attending religious services. Solange did say jokingly that it was difficult to concentrate on reading a book when the other 30 pupils were being taught the catechism aloud in the same room. The other members of the family found it difficult to be called "Protestant" or "Heretic." The word Protestant was derogatory among French Catholics at that time. What hurt Solange the most was when her best friend's mother realized she was an evangelical Christian, not a Catholic, and she forbade her daughter to have any contact with Solange. This friend was not even allowed to talk to her.

Solange's research revealed something that the children of French Canadian Evangelicals often underwent. Her sister, Ginette didn't find attending the Catholic school a major problem, but it was how they were ostracized that was hardest to take. The following anecdote reveals the unhealthy state of a province with an exclusive religious monopoly.

Elphège and Jeanne d'Arc Paillé had his parents living with them. When Elphège and Jeanne d'Arc became Christians and left the Catholic Church, his parents were furious. Moreover, other family members stopped visiting, which cut off all contact for the elderly couple as well. Other farmers in their district and close neighbors also stopped visiting them. French Canadians are known for being extroverted and family-oriented. The Paillé family's highlight of the week was when aunts, uncles, and cousins filled their farmhouse for an afternoon together and a meal. Now it was empty every Sunday afternoon. Even the neighbors stopped dropping in for friendly visits. The priest was supreme in the parish and if he said parishioners were not to visit a certain family, or if he announced from the pulpit that there were heretics now in the parish (sometimes naming the family), it took a very courageous person to go against the priest's warning.

Had there been another family of born-again Christians nearby in their district they could have visited one another. Even better, if there had been an evangelical church within driving distance, its members would've become their new family. That need was only fulfilled nearly 10 years later. The Christians did have rallies besides their regular meetings, and when there was a Quebecois cultural outing for Catholics, evangelical churches would arrange an activity as well so that those who were ostracized would have somewhere to go.

### The Réveillon

A case in point was the annual "Réveillon." This was a Christmas gathering for families. Christmas Eve began with the midnight mass, which everyone attended in that era. The families then gathered in one of the homes. With their typically large families sometimes it was necessary to rent a hall. The children received their presents at this time, and it was followed by a sumptuous feast. The partying continued until the early morning hours.

Out of necessity, our church in Asbestos arranged to have a "Réveillon" at church every year on Christmas Eve. This included a special service with carol singing, and a message, followed by a buffet with all the traditional French Canadian treats. Christians would often give testimonies of how Christmas was different for them since the new birth had transformed their lives. The worship does not stop at the scene of Bethlehem but goes beyond to Jesus' teaching and miracles, to the cross, and the empty tomb. The meal was followed by a time of fellowship with one another or the playing of games as late as everyone cared to do so. This made it difficult for English-speaking missionaries

> because generally we also had the traditional Christmas Day festivities with our own families and friends. Although we were nearly all young couples, before the day was finished it became very clear that it wasn't easy to burn the candle at both ends!

It was the sacrifice of the French Canadian believers of the 50s and 60s that laid an evangelical foundation in Quebec. They were lonely, persecuted, deprived of their school rights, ostracized, and considered as second-class citizens to be shunned and feared. Sometimes they suffered the loss of employment or, if they had their own business, certainly the loss of some customers. Through faith, they weathered the storms and were given the courage to face each new threat that came their way. Today in every area, and even beyond the frontier of Quebec where there is a French population, French Canadian born-again Christians can find fellowship. It must be emphasized, however, that the need is still great and the school situation is only partially settled, because the school system is now secular with an anti-religious slant.

**The consequences to believers and their families**

Evangelism brought new people to Jesus, but it also brought opposition and suffering for Christ's name. I remember the words of Lionel Gosselin about the day he was saved. He was among the first fruits in his city and he knew that to follow Christ would cause opposition. He struggled for months and then one day God spoke to him in a miraculous way, and he couldn't resist any longer. He began to read the Gospel of John, at the same time telling the Lord that he believed in Jesus. Coming upon the verse found in John 16:2-3 he read, "They will put you out of the synagogue; in fact, a time is coming when anyone who kills you will think he is offering a service to God. They will do such things because they have not known the Father or me." He stopped there and prayed, "Thank you, Lord, for these verses. Now I know why I will suffer." But, perhaps the most heart-breaking suffering was on the part of the new converts' children and their school experiences, as we have already made clear. Lionel Gosselin's children had to attend an English school because they had no other options.

Blanche (Ford) Phillips, who was one of the teachers in those early days of persecution in the 1950s observed, "Perhaps the worst persecution was the expulsion of children from the public French-Catholic school system. French schools had to be provided, and the onus was on the evangelical churches. English-speaking young women, with a limited knowledge of French and no adequate textbooks, did their utmost to take up the challenge."[35] Blanche also spoke of another type of punishment for children who didn't go to mass on Sunday because their parents took them to the Baptist church. They were put in the corner of the classroom to wear a dunce hat and the other children were allowed to call them names and throw things at them.

### Was the Absence of French Schools for French Protestants an Oversight or Willful Denial of their Rights?

To answer that question we must go back in history. The French Protestants from France were the Huguenots, or sometimes called Calvinists. They were the French arm of the Protestant Reformation of the sixteenth century. "The Huguenots were persecuted, suffered torture and martyrdom in France which led to wars of self-protection."[36] In New France, however, anyone studying the beginning of the colony would have agreed with Jean-Louis Lalonde who described the colonization (1524-1627) as, "*Un bel espoir de cohabitation*"[37] ("The beautiful hope of living together") between Catholics and Huguenots. A monument in Quebec City, facing the Château Frontenac notes that the city of Quebec was founded in 1608 and the first priests to settle there were the Récollets in 1615. There was peace between the Récollets and the Huguenots.

The situation began to change with the arrival of the Jesuit Mission in 1625. Charles Lalemant, Superior of the Jesuit Mission in New France, according to the book *The Jesuit Missions,* "… had no sooner landed on the shores of New France that he became convinced that the mission (i.e. Jesuit) and colony itself were doomed unless there should be a radical change in government."[38] After this statement some of the problems were enumerated then the author concluded with these words, "But the gravest evil, in Lalemant's mind, was the presence of so many Huguenots."[39] These ominous words were to play out their threat in the near future when in 1659, Mgr. François de Montmorency Laval came to New France, "…having been named by Rome as Victor Apostolic of New France, at the instigation of the Jesuits." [40] The Jesuit order was getting a commanding hold upon New France and the severity of their order, and Laval's own character, were disclosed by a decree in 1664. The decree "required all Protestant parents to have their children baptised in the Catholic faith on the day of their birth. This ordinance also stated that those newborns had to depend on catholic institutions for their future education." [41] This was the beginning of three centuries of untold misery for French Protestant families and a denial of their rights.

One event that gave the Protestants liberty was the removal of the Jesuits. Their seminary became a barracks for the British soldiers and their property was appropriated. The priests had come mainly from France and they were no longer allowed to bring in Jesuits, Récollets, or Sulpicians. Soon there were no more Jesuits coming to Canada and the last Jesuits died here. This removed the source of persecution for Protestants.

In the *Treaty of Paris*, three years after to fall of Quebec, the King of England stipulated through his representative that his new Catholic subjects would be free to observe and practise their religion according to the Roman Catholic rite, as long as they observed the laws of Great Britain.[42]

Despite the context of the *Traité de Paris*, the English still wanted to assimilate the French Canadians. It was difficult for the English to see their new colony in North America speaking another language. An unusual message was sent to Governor Murray,

> The tenor of the drastic new program of government has been admirably summed up thus, 'an old French colony was to be remade into an English colony.' English laws and English courts were established; and provision was made for a large influx of British settlers, drawn either from old soldiers or from the crowded American colonies to the south. Assimilation was to be the order of the day; lands were set aside for the support of Protestant clergymen and schoolmasters, "To the End that the Church of England may be established both in Principle and Practice, and that the said Inhabitants may by Degrees be induced to embrace the Protestant Religion, and their Children be brought up in the Principles of it." The governor was even urged to report "by what other Means the Protestant religion may be promoted."[43]

Murray, the military governor of Quebec soon after General Wolfe's victory resisted this plan from England because he knew it was impossible and "because of the sympathy he had formed for the French" (Wade, p. 54). To further orders he replied, "I cannot be the instrument of destroying, perhaps, the best and bravest race on the Globe."[44]

### Two School Boards

In 1869, Premier Boucher of Boucherville abolished the ministry of public instruction and introduced two committees, one for Catholics and one Protestants. It was a step forward for English Protestants but "for French Protestants, there was no place"[45]

The decision to make two school boards didn't affect the French Protestants as much in the 19th century as it did in the 20th because most French Protestants Churches in the 19th century

(Congregationalists, Presbyterians, Anglicans, and, Baptists) had their own French schools and colleges. It was the French Protestants of the twentieth century who experienced difficulties. They had to begin from zero to establish their churches and their schools.

This was a victory for the Ultramontanes among the Catholics and the proof of is made clear from the following quotation: "Monsignor Adelard Langevin rejoiced to see several of our statesmen so disposed to recognize and respect the rights of the church in matters of education." [46]

---

**Ultramontanism**

Ultramontanism meant centralization of the church under absolute papal authority, coupled by independence of the Roman Church from state control and, where possible, subordination of the state and the rest of society to papal Catholic dogmatic and moral principles. The term, used pejoratively since the seventeenth century, implied attachment to Rome, 'i.e. beyond the mountains, (the Alps).[47]

Richard Lougheed, a Canadian author and resident of Quebec, observes, "In Quebec, this term designated the Catholics who were fiercely loyal to papal directives." [48]

As an example, Bishop Bourget was an ultramontane priest involved in what was called a political "Holy War" in Quebec. In a circular he sent to clergymen, he stated, "I am very happy to see the formation of a group which is heartily attached to the teachings of the Holy See, which approves all that the Pope approves and condemns all that the Pope condemns." [49]

It should be no surprise that Sir Charles-Eugene Boucher of Boucherville, "…formed the new provincial government and was supported by clerical influence in the 1875 election."[50] This situation gave a school commission to English Protestants and another to French Catholics, both heavily directed by the Catholic clergy, but as previously stated, absolutely nothing for French Protestants! In the mind of the Catholic Church, the only real French "*Québecois*" (Quebeckers) were French Catholics. The slogan of French Quebec was "*Notre foi, notre langue, notre patrie*" (Our faith, our language, our homeland.) The three went together and were indivisible. It seemed inconceivable for many that a French Canadian would not be Catholic. As late as the 1950s and 60s new converts reported being treated as *"turncoats"* or "traitors*"* to their country because they had changed their religion

When the minister of the Quebec government affirmed that, "Les Catholiques et les Protestants ont donc deux comités qui s'occuperont des droits respectifs des différentes nationalités," ("Catholics and Protestants therefore have two Commissions which will deal with the respective rights of the different nationalities,")[51] it was a *coup d'état* in favor of the Catholic Church and a death knell for French Protestant schools. It extended the 1664 ordinance of Mgr. de Laval, which required all Protestant parents to have their children baptised in the Catholic faith and have them attend Catholic schools.[52] With the fall of New France, the first part of this decree regarding the parents lost its force, but not the latter part. The Ultramontanism of the Quebec Catholic Church took care of that.

The French Canadian Protestants had two choices: either send their children to English Protestant school, if one existed in the area, or go to Catholic public school. In most cases attending the Catholic schools was nearly impossible. On the other hand, for these children to attend English Protestant school would mean the death of possible a future for French Evangelical churches, since these schools anglicized children as quickly as possible so they could get on with their education.

## Liberalism and Anglicization

What were the causes of the rapid decline in the number of French Evangelical Churches in the latter part of the 19th century and the beginning of the 20th? It was partly due to Anglicization, whereby the children of French Protestants had to attend English Protestant schools. There was also persecution and emigration to English Canada and/or the United States due to the lack of work in Quebec, especially for French evangelicals. However, one of the major causes was liberalism. Liberal theology holds that the Bible is not the inspired Word of God, and shouldn't be taken literally. It casts doubt on major biblical beliefs such as the virgin birth of Christ, his resurrection, and deity. It also undermines the biblical view of salvation, relying too much on human nature instead of trusting on the finished work of Christ on the cross. One could conclude that Anglicization attacked the second generation of French Protestants, while liberal theology affected the main Protestant denominations, who reduced their evangelism and missionary efforts following the tide of rationalism coming out of Germany.

Richard Strout said emphatically, "Some churches that had not wavered under persecution succumbed to the changes brought in by modernist Protestant theology."[53] David Dobson attested to "... the devastating impact of liberal theology on Protestant evangelism during this period."[54] John Gilmour, a Baptist leader and former director of Institut Feller said, "Liberal theology, the vehicle of the modernist movement, profoundly affected Protestants."[55]

To evangelize effectively one must be totally convinced that the Bible is verbally inspired by the Holy Spirit (2 Timothy 3:16), and any teaching contrary to the cardinal doctrines of the Bible must be confronted and declared false (Galatians 1:6-11; 2 Corinthians 11:1-6; Philippians 1:6; Isaiah 8:20). Paul's words in Galatians 1:8,11 settle this question once for all:

> But even if we or an angel from heaven should preach a gospel other than the one we preached to you, let him be eternally condemned! ... I want you to know, brothers, that the gospel I preached is not

something that man made up. I did not receive it from any man, nor was I taught it; rather, I received it by revelation from Jesus Christ.

As the mainline Protestant churches moved to a social Gospel, rather than a redemptive Gospel based upon the death and resurrection of Christ, the need to evangelize French Canadian Catholics, or English Protestants for that matter, subsided in the mind of those swayed by liberal theology. Neither did they see the need for French Protestant schools. The English Protestant School Commission was in a quandary about what to do with these small groups of French Protestants scattered across the province. Nominal Protestants didn't understand why French Canadians, who were enlightened by the reading of the New Testament, were ready to abjure from the Roman Catholic Church, which was thought to be the church of the "Québécois." Because they didn't see the need for French Protestant schools, they integrated the French Canadians believers in the English schools, thereby encouraging Anglicization. Anglicization, in turn, didn't contribute to the continued growth of French churches.

Access to education was a real challenge for new believers in those early years. Courageous men, women, and children had to face hardship and opposition, but they eventually broke new ground in obtaining education for French Canadian Protestants.

(Endnotes)
1   Jean-Louis Lalonde, *Les loups dans la bergerie, Les Protestants de la langue française au Québec, 1534-2000* (Montréal: Fides, 2002), p. 59.
2   Jean-Louis Lalonde, *Les loups dans la bergerie*, p. 110.
3   R.P. Duclos, *Histoire du Protestantisme français au Canada et aux États-Unis*, Vol.1 (Montréal: Librairie Évangélique, 1913), p. 109.
4   Wilfred Wellington, *Rome's Challenge Accepted – Ten Years with the Gospel in Northern Quebec*, (Published by the author, 1949), p. 7.
5   Wilfred Wellington, *Rome's Challenge Accepted*, p. 30.
6   Wilfred Wellington, *Rome's Challenge Accepted*, p. 30.
7   Wilfred Wellington, *Rome's Challenge Accepted*, p. 30.
8   Murray Heron, *Footsteps Across* Quebec (Dundas, Ontario: Joshua Press, 1999), p. 82.
9   Wilfred Wellington, *Rome's Challenge Accepted*, p. 36.
10  Wilfred Wellington, *Rome's Challenge Accepted*, p. 36.
11  Ernest Keefe, telephone call with Huguette Vézina, Fall 2007.
12  Ernest Keefe, telephone call with Huguette Vézina, Fall 2007.
13  Murray Heron, *Footsteps Across Quebec*, pp. 81-82.
14  Wilfred Wellington, *Rome's Challenge Accepted*, p. 62.
15  Wilfred Wellington, *Rome's Challenge Accepted*, p. 62.
16  Wilfred Wellington, *Rome's Challenge Accepted*, p. 62.
17  Wilfred Wellington, *Rome's Challenge Accepted*, p. 60.
18  Wilfred Wellington, *Rome's Challenge Accepted*, p. 66.
19  Wilfred Wellington, *Rome's Challenge Accepted*, p. 64.
20  Wilfred Wellington, *Rome's Challenge Accepted*, p. 65.
21  Wilfred Wellington, *Rome's Challenge Accepted*, p. 60.
22  Ernie & Betty Keefe, interview with William & Blanche Phillips, May. 2005
23  Weldon Clark, *Sowers of the Seed, The Life and Ministry of Mr. And Mrs. Weldon Clark* (Printed in Canada by Copy Xpress, 1372 des Récollets, Trois-Rivières, Québec, Canada), p. 93.
24  Don Delaplant, journalist, "La Sarre", July 24, 1948.
25  Don Delaplant, journalist, "La Sarre", July 24, 1948.
26  Murray Heron, *Footsteps Across Quebec*, p. 57.
27  Murray Heron, *Footsteps Across Quebec*, p. 59-60.
28  Murray Heron, *Footsteps Across Quebec*, p. 57-58.
29  Murray Heron, *Footsteps Across Quebec*, p. 58.
30  Wilfred. Wellington, *Rome's Challenge Accepted*, p. 7.
31  Ernest Keefe, taken from a telephone interview with Fernand St-Louis, Jan. 9th, 2006.
32  Richard Strout, from a letter sent to Ernest Keefe, 2005.
33  William Frey, *The Evangelical Baptist*, March 1965.
34  Murray Heron, *Footprints across Quebec*, p. 83-84.
35  Ernie & Betty Keefe, interview with Blanche Phillips, May 2000.
36  A. Vulliet, *Scènes de la Révocation de l'Édit de Nantes – 1685* (Lausanne: Georges Bridel, Éditeur), 1885.
37  Jean-Louis Lalonde, *Des loups dans la bergerie*, (Éditions Fides 2002), p. 27.
38  Thomas Guthrie Marquis, *The Jesuit Missions – Chronicles of Canada*, Volume 4, (Toronto: University of Toronto Press) p. 29.
39  Thomas Guthrie Marquis, *The Jesuit Missions*, p. 29.
40  Mason Wade, *The French Canadians*, 1760-1945, (Toronto: The MacMillan Company of Canada Limited, 1956), p. 37.

41   Michel Gaudette, *Guerres de religion d'ici : catholicisme et protestantisme face à l'histoire* (Trois-Rivières, Québec: Éditions Souffle de vent, 2001), p. 23.

42   Duclos, *Histoire du Protestantisme français au Canada et aux États-Unis*, Vol. 1, p. 49.

43   Mason Wade, *The French Canadians*, p. 54.

44   Mason Wade, *The French Canadians*, p. 56.

45   Lalonde, *Des loups dans la bergerie*, p. 148.

46   Lalonde, *Des loups dans la bergerie*, p. 150.

47   C.T.McIntire, *The New International Dictionary of the Christian Church*, General Editor J.D. Douglas, (Grand Rapids, Michigan: Zondervan Publishing House) p. 993.

48   Richard Lougheed, *La Conversion controversée de Charles Chiniquy*, (Québec: La Clairière) p. 24.

49   Mason Wade, *The French Canadians*, p. 356.

50   Mason Wade, *The French Canadians*, p. 155.

51   Jean-Louis Lalonde, *Des loups dans la bergerie*, p. 148.

52   Michel Gaudette, *Guerres de religion*, p. 23.

53   Richard Strout, *The Latter years of the Board of French Evangelization of the Presbyterian Church of Canada 1885-1912* (Master thesis, Bishops University, Lennoxville, Quebec, 1986).

54   David Dobson, *A Legacy of Suffering – The Persecution of French Protestants 1837-1960*, (Presented to Dr. Bruce L. Guenther, A.C.T.S. Seminary, British Columbia), p. 20.

55   John S. Gilmoure, quoted by Roland Grimard , *Le principe indigne et la Mission de la Grande Ligne 1834-1970* (Thesis presented to La Faculté de Théologie Évangélique, Montréal, QC, 1988), Annexe B. viii.

# Chapter 7

# *Name Calling*
# *And The Results*

### Duplessis Offensive on "Communism"

In Quebec, Catholicism had long been intimately linked to politics. In 1923, Premier Taschereau pointed out what he called, "the miracle of the French and Catholic survival on this part of the continent."[1]

Fifteen years later in front of the Hôtel du Gouverneur, decorated in papal colors, the then, "Premier Duplessis expressed his delight concerning a demonstration of faith that happened in Quebec, which he called the "the cradle of the French and Canadian Christian civilization."[2]

But not all was well, because "more and more the clergy and the traditional elite of Quebec were fearing the infiltration of communism and socialism." [3]

This fear, however, wasn't limited to the clergy and the elite. "The editor of the women's page of the *Action Catholique* magazine denounced the 'rage of communism,' which was the cause of new bathing suits, movies advocating divorce, and the defiance of women toward religious authority." [4]

This fear reached the highest echelon of the Catholic Church. Cardinal Villeneuve of Quebec City was the author of a brochure entitled, *La Menace du Communisme au Canada* (The Menace of Communism in Canada). It's easy to believe Michel Gaudette's statement that, "The thinking at that time, was that being associated with communism was a public scandal."[5]

## Duplessis, the Man

Former Premier, René Levesque, said of Duplessis:

> He was himself insensitive to money, but he knew its power. He was a spender only when he had to counteract or put down those infamous unions and progressives, especially the intellectuals [...] Others were purely and simply 'communists,' capable of blowing up the Trois-Rivières bridge, or tarnishing our reputation. [6]

Nevertheless, he was sincere in what he did for "my province," as he called the Province of Quebec. An example of his tenacity was his challenging of the Federal Government on the distribution of money gathered from taxes. This dispute between the Federal Government and the province still is still active today. As the other provinces let the Federal Government gather income taxes, Duplessis resisted the centralization efforts of the Federal Government that came after the Second World War. "Duplessis alone refused to yield. On the contrary, in 1954–a fundamental date in Quebec's evolution–he dared to establish a provincial income tax (which forced the Federal Government to diminish its own taxation by 10%)."[7]

Duplessis' persistence and abusiveness were carried over to his battles against communism. The unions were one of his main targets. His policies and repressive laws resulted in union demonstrations before the parliament buildings in Quebec City.

One of the first public manifestations of that kind was in reaction, in 1953, to Bills 19 and 20, which led to the removal of accreditation of supposedly 'communist' unions (the definition of the word 'communist' being so flexible that it could apply to any union judged too militant), and public service unions on strike. [8]

Duplessis' press conferences were unique, especially if he was confronted. The 1949 strike at the Canadian Johns-Manville Asbestos mine challenged him, or at least his position, on that matter. The strike stretched on for 145 days. It cost millions of dollars to the company, the government, and the union. It was also marked by vicious riots that, on several occasions, nearly resulted in the death of strikers and members of the police force. The strike brought the Catholic Church and the union into confrontation, and the settlement wasn't completely to Duplessis' liking. He called the strikers communists to their faces, and openly blamed the strike on communistic leaders of the union.

In one press conference with Duplessis, journalist Pierre Laporte arrived late and attempted to slip in unseen. His late arrival did not go unnoticed by Duplessis, who openly mocked him, "Well! If it isn't Mr. Laporte, the brilliant young journalist from *Le Devoir.* What good wind blows you here, my dear Laporte? The wind of insolence and poor interpretation of the facts, I suppose?" [9]

After regaining his composure the young journalist replied, "I come here simply to get information on the strike in Asbestos, Sir." [10]

Duplessis, taken aback a little by the young journalist, attacked the newspaper itself, "As long as *Le Devoir* is what it is, a newspaper advocating communist ideas, a newspaper encouraging breaking the law, a newspaper which for some months has demonstrated total dishonesty towards my government, its journalists will be very out of place at my press conferences." [11]

Laporte responded by accusing Duplessis of going too far and not respecting freedom of the press. Once again Duplessis showed his authoritarian character and thundered, "I respect the liberty of the press but not the license of the press. It is I who direct things here, Laporte. 'La porte' (the door), your name is appropriate, take the door and get out. (Speaking to his bodyguard, Jacques, he says, 'Put that man out of here, immediately.' Laporte leaves and the Chief carries on, satisfied with his tirade." [12]

Duplessis went a step further in an exchange of words with another journalist, Jean Thivierge. Thivierge questioned the settlement of the Asbestos strike and the fact that Antonio Barrette claimed that the settlement was equitable for both sides–the Canadian Johns-Manville Company and the union. Addressing the Premier Maurice Duplessis and speaking about the settlement, he brought to his attention the fact that, "Madam Casgrain of the C.C.F. (socialist) party is not in agreement with the procedures that you have adopted." [13]

Duplessis didn't even let him finish before beginning another tirade, "Let's see, Sir! How can a communist be in agreement with my politics?" [14]

Jean Thivierge looked Duplessis in the face and fearlessly stated, "...even so, Sir, Madam Casgrain has declared correctly that in your attacking the rights of the people, it is you who are encouraging communism." [15]

That was too much for the Premier and he lost his composure and yelled at this journalist, "Thivierge, because you have posed the most idiotic question that I have ever heard, I have the pleasure of informing you that you are invited to leave here immediately! He makes a sign with his head to his bodyguard, Jacques! (Thivierge leaves)." [16]

## Premier Duplessis, Mgr Charbonneau, and the Asbestos strike

Duplessis didn't stop there; he had the archbishop of Montreal, the largest diocese in Canada and the spiritual home of one-third of the population of Quebec, removed from office by Pius XII! Why did he do it? How did he do it?

Mrs. Renaude Lapointe, an experienced journalist, traveled from Montreal to Vancouver, to Spain, and to the Vatican to consult with numerous newspapers, domestic and international, in an effort to break the silence around what was called "the painful event of Mgr Charbonneau's resignation and the circumstances that led to it." Her book was entitled *L'Histoire bouleversante de Mgr Charbonneau* ("Mgr Charbonneau's Upsetting Story").

The preface of Mrs. Lapointe's book describes Monsignor Charbonneau as being "the clear-sighted, dynamic and impetuous leader belonging to the segment of Quebec society which wanted French Canada to be more open to social reforms. But Maurice Duplessis had sworn that he would ruin him. He was the sacrificial victim... the victim of his social environment." [17]

We shall compare Mgr Charbonneau and Premier Maurice Duplessis in their character and their ambitions. Mgr Charbonneau was born and raised in Hearst, a small town 200 miles south of James Bay, situated along Highway 11, Ontario's most northerly highway. His father had cut a farm out of the bush. Duplessis once called Mgr Charbonneau a lumberjack from Ontario. But this lumberjack had studied in Quebec for eight years, held three earned doctorates and taught philosophy at the University of Montreal, where he was prefect. He grew up in the pluralistic province of Ontario, and during his years in Quebec he was a passionate man who was counted among those Quebeckers who were concerned about social issues. "Wholehearted, impulsive, generous, he profoundly felt the social problems of the time and he wanted with all his might to repair what Pius XI had called, 'the scandal of the 19th century; that is to say, the loss to the church of the working class." [18]

In his efforts to right the wrongs of society, however, we discovered that he could be violent, "he had at certain times limited control of his outbursts, with his words." [19]

As for Premier Maurice Duplessis, he too could be violent while defending his cause. His cause, however, was the opposite of Mgr Charbonneau's. "Politicians, like Maurice Duplessis, wanted to give the Quebec people the image of a population submissive to its bosses and a source of docile laborers on whom one could rely." [20]

Regarding paternalism and corporatism in industrial relations, Duplessis favored paternalism, as one can extrapolate from the following memo:

The employers must direct their industries with justice, integrity, and goodness but as leaders. The workers, in turn, must know how to obey orders, performing their tasks to the best of their abilities. They must also be just, honest, and good. The unions in turn must protect their members but not by advising them that the bosses are the enemy, and not by intimidating those who do not wish to become union members. [21]

Due to the Asbestos strike, the smoldering fire between these two men, Premier Duplessis and Mgr Charbonneau, became a raging inferno. Mgr Charbonneau had already taken the side of the strikers in the past, but this was different. It was a strike against the Canadian branch of a large American Company, Johns-Manville. The strike began on February 13, 1949, though the negotiations had begun on December 13, 1948. The strike lasted 140 days. It was violent and brutal.

Jean Marchand, secretary of the CTCC (*La Confédération des Travailleurs Catholiques du Canada,* "The Confederation of Catholic Laborers in Canada"*),* who was in Asbestos because of the strike, addressed the leaders of the local union:

My dear friends, I have nothing new of importance to tell you. You know, as do I, that negotiations with Johns-Mansville began on December 20th of last year. Today is February 13th and negotiations have come to an impasse. The company representatives have only offered us a salary increase of 5% and have refused to consider the totality of our union demands … $1.25 an hour, elimination of dust, the right to collective bargaining.[22]

The local union members were warned by Premier Duplessis, who was also in Asbestos at the time, that they must return to work the following day, otherwise he would bring in *scabs* to replace them and threatened that he would crush the union and, if necessary, jail the union leaders. He further affirmed that reinforcements for the police were already on their way.

The local chaplain of the union asked for permission to address the men. He said:

I would simply say this, 'A strike is a serious matter.' However, I want to tell you that if you vote to strike, I personally, your chaplain, and several members of the clergy across the province, will support you right to the end. (Here the workers applauded, showing their satisfaction.) One last recommendation: The company has begun to mail to you individually, letters whose sole purpose is to denigrate in your eyes, the union leaders of Asbestos. The company is also trying to make the outside world hostile to your strike by paying for full-page advertisements in newspapers. I beg of you all, never fall into their trap. Remain united and retain confidence in your leaders; it is the only way to win this strike. The company is going to do everything to divide you … I ask you, 'Let us remain united.'[23]

This was the first time the clergy had come out in such numbers to challenge the Duplessis government and support the strikers. This was the dawning of a new day in Quebec.

Asbestos, you recall, was where Wilson Ewin and I were arrested and jailed for selling Catholic New Testaments, in December of 1955. (We offered freely other New Testaments provided to us by the Scripture Gift Mission.) It was also where Betty and I established our first church, not fearing the judge's warning that we would be manhandled and arrested if we returned to preach the gospel. God had encouraged us with these words he said to Paul, "I am with you, and no one is going to attack and harm you, speak because I have many people in this city" (Acts 18:10).

Our arrival on the scene was six years after the strike, but folks still spoke often the suffering of the strikers and their families, how they lacked food and clothing, lost their cars and even in some cases, their homes. A farmer described to me how scabs were chased by strikers along the narrow gravel road in front of his farm at full speed. They were courageous men and women to challenge an authoritarian Premier like Duplessis and also a rich American conglomerate.

Robert Lacour-Gayet, in his book *Histoire du Canada,* described the Asbestos strike and Duplessis' role in it, as well as the reaction of Mgr Charbonneau and his subsequent exile:

Unionism, which did not exist before the war, was now in full expansion and was becoming aware of its strength: One noticed that from 1940 to 1950 strikes were three times more numerous than in the preceding decade. This action did not please a man as despotic as Duplessis, who saw communists and Marxists everywhere. Unions had to submit to a weeding-out process and violence became the reason for legal regulations. Nearly twenty years later, people have not forgotten the tragedy of Asbestos, a little mining town in the East of the province. The workers of the American company Johns-Manville had ceased work: their decision was declared illegal through a legal pretext. The union did not accept this judgment so the company decided to reopen its doors with new workers. The strikers became obstinate, the police intervened: scenes of brutality took place, which raised the indignation of the Archbishop of Montreal, Mgr Charbonneau. Duplessis, who was used to more flexibility from the Hierarchy, was at first frustrated but did not become intimidated. [24]

Mgr Charbonneau was president of the Episcopal Commission, which handled social questions for the Catholic Church. He "approved the document of the Episcopal Commission called *Secourons les travailleurs de l'amiante* (Let Us Help the Asbestos Workers) and announced an offering for the families in need." [25] This declaration was the basis of Mgr Charbonneau's memorable and passionate sermon from the pulpit of Notre-Dame Cathedral. It was in part caused by a desperate visit from the chaplain of the Asbestos union, accompanied by a very concerned taxi driver who had brought him. Here is part of the pleading that took place just before the sermon. They told of the arrival of strikebreakers, who had been brought in to take their jobs and how "hundreds of police had arrived from Sherbrooke to protect the strikebreakers.[26]

The police began to patrol the town looking for strikebreakers. All those who were found in the basement of the church were arrested, and then there were several who were beaten because they tried to escape by the Glebe House. The arrests continued all night. The next morning the Riot Act was read. [27]

The chaplain continued:

I know that the Mayor of Asbestos intends to lodge an official protest to the Provincial Chief of Police. The Minister of Labor declared yesterday that our refusal to resort to arbitration was illegal. Then the Commission of Labor Relations threatened to no longer recognize our union. Many people are very upset. If we no longer have a union, what are we going to do? It would be a state of abject poverty in Asbestos, Your Eminence. Merchants are refusing to sell to the strikers. All who are rich and influential have joined together to divide the union members. Mgr Charbonneau, you are our only hope…

Journalist Renaude Lapointe reports that Mgr Charbonneau:

… publicly took a position in favor of the workers in Notre Dame Cathedral in Montreal. He emphasized his strong words by pounding his fist on the aisles of the choir. 'The working class is a victim of a conspiracy which wants to crush it and when such a conspiracy exists, it is the duty of the Church to intervene. Our political leaders must pass labor laws of peace, of justice, and charity. We do not condone everything that the workers have done; there are failures on all sides. But our hearts are with the working people and we are organizing this collection to prevent little children from suffering from hunger.[28]

Premier Duplessis, however, had boasted to the representative of the Johns-Manville Company concerning his surefire method to end strikes in favor of his objectives. His method was completely contradictory to Mgr Charbonneau's. Duplessis explained his plan to the representative of the company:

I have an infallible blueprint to combat the strike. I begin by declaring the strike illegal. That is what I have just done. Next, I order my men to arrest all the union leaders and all the extremists. Naturally, I take care to protect the strikebreakers

[...] Finally, I sit down quietly and wait. When the strikers are dying of hunger, I announce my conditions. (He snaps his fingers.) I win, they lose. Child's play! There are not one hundred ways to save the province from an economic depression. It's that or nothing. [29]

These two powerful men, Duplessis and Mgr Charbonneau, crossed swords over the Asbestos strike. On one side was one of the Roman Catholic Church's most outspoken and controversial archbishops; on the other side was Premier Duplessis, "Those who knew him were unanimous. He was the most authoritarian man that there was." [30]

Duplessis warned Charbonneau, "We are able to force you to obey. For example! You are not the supreme authority of the Church, Monsignor Charbonneau. It is very easy to go to Rome today, and I maintain very good relations with the Vatican." [31]

First of all it must be emphasized that Premier Duplessis did in fact have continual contact with the Vatican and Pius XII. As well, he had an envoy named Dumont who had the ear of several cardinals. He wrote a 184 page document covering the Asbestos strike which was delivered to the Vatican by Mr. Dumont himself.[32] There were those, according to Dumont, who were accomplices of communist leaders because they used their influence to demolish the authority of the only Catholic government in North America.

A former professor at *Séminaire de Philosophie et de Théologie* in Montreal, Father Edouard Gouin, came to Canada for six months in 1948. He wrote, "The circumstances permitted me to realize that the actions and persistence of M. Maurice Duplessis indicated his ambition to subjugate the Canadian Church."[33]

He also revealed the character of Duplessis' envoy, Mr. Dumont, who, according to him, was probably a fascist. He had been condemned to death in France after the war, but managed to get to Canada with a false identity under the name of Dumont. He gained the confidence of the archdiocese and of Mr. Duplessis. He wrote, at Duplessis' demand, a document against Mgr Charbonneau, and delivered it to Rome.

Another document, 124 pages long, written by Mgr Courchesne, Bishop of Rimouski, directly attacked Mgr Charbonneau, declaring that his beliefs encouraged communism. Premier Duplessis prodded Mgr Courchesne to take it to the Vatican by means of a voyage paid for by the Quebec Government. To make an even better impression on the Vatican, he also sent Dr. Albini Paquette and Antonio Barrette, Ministers of Health and Labour respectively, on an all-expense-paid trip to the Vatican. Mgr Courchesne had compiled many criticisms against Mgr Charbonneau, such as his desire to deconfessionalize the Catholic Union and co-operatives. However, Mgr Charbonneau didn't want to do away with Catholic unions and co-operatives, but simply wanted to allow non-Catholics to become members. One of the members of the Asbestos church had been a union representative before making a profession of faith and joining the Baptist church. After joining the church he continued to hold this position. There was a meeting of union officers at which the Catholic Bishop was present. When the member in question shook hands with the Bishop rather than bowing before him and kissing his ring, this caused an uproar. Mgr Charbonneau simply wanted to avoid such situations.

Pius XII received these defamatory documents and demanded Mgr Charbonneau's resignation. Mgr Charbonneau already had an airline reservation to the Vatican, but Pius XII refused to receive him. He was condemned without a trial. "Pope Pius XII made his decision rapidly, personally and without the Consistory. He acted according to the procedure *"fondée sur la conscience bien informée."*[34] ("founded on a well-informed conscience"). On January 2nd, 1950, "Mgr Charbonneau received from the Secretary of State, of which the Pope was the chief, the order to resign. Sentence without appeal."[35] When Cardinal Cushing of Boston heard about Mgr Charbonneau's forced resignation he remarked, "This is the work of wicked men."[36]

These actions of Premier Duplessis caused people to ask, "Who is running the Catholic Church in Quebec?" He certainly controlled the majority of Bishops for they were:

> ... dependent on subsidies from the government. All had to march in line before the full parliament where he had them eating out of his hand. We know that he rewarded the most meek and obedient. In the camp of the rebels, Mgr Desranleau, for his part, was denied subsidies for three years and Mgr Charbonneau experienced a more stinging punishment. [37]

Mgr Charbonneau wasn't only deprived of his office; he was sent to Victoria, B.C., far away from Quebec, so friends or the press wouldn't be able to visit him. His departure wasn't worthy of an Archbishop, especially one who was supposedly ill and had given of himself beyond measure. Journalist Renaude Lapointe described his departure:

> At daybreak on January 31, 1950, he left without an escort, as he had come. He carried two suitcases and less than $70. Although warmly clothed, he was shivering. He had not slept for a month. An order had come from the Apostolic Delegation to the offices of Air Canada, 'Please treat this departure with the greatest discretion.' A black limousine with its drapes drawn was waiting for his Excellence. The representative from Air Canada was accompanying the chauffeur. With special permission, the limousine proceeded onto the tarmac right up to the stairway going into the North Star. Sixteen hours later, a door opened in front of the old Archbishop of Montreal, that of Mount St. Mary's Home for the Aged, in Victoria. [38]

This lengthy coverage of Premier Maurice Duplessis' reign, which historians named *la grande noirceur* (the Dark Age) was necessary to give the reader a comprehensive picture of what French

Canadians had to face when they chose to follow the Bible and therefore leave the tradition of Rome, and what the missionaries who gave them the Bible had to encounter. This also casts light on *"The Quiet Revolution,"* and how much it was needed.

### The Padlock Law

Of all the laws which Premier Duplessis passed in order to curb communism, and for that matter any issue in disagreement with the Catholic Church, there was one that stood out above all others. This law,

> ... called The Padlock Law, permitted the closing of every property where communism or bolchevism was being propagated. This certainly spared Quebec from the infection of ideas from the extreme left which were gaining ground in so many countries. The unreasonableness of this measure and the abuses that it produced said a lot for the politics that inspired it. [39]

This law further stated:

> If three or more people were gathered for a cause, other than one authorized by the state, police could enter the house, stop the meeting, arrest the leaders and padlock the door.[40]

Concerning the Padlock Law, Jean-Louis Lalonde noted in his book on French Protestants in Quebec, "the law applied to union militancy but also against certain Evangelical Protestants and against Jehovah's Witnesses. Certain priests, from their pulpits, associated Baptists with communists." [41]

The law did cause fear for anyone against whom it could be used. Following are a few examples of how communism was used against Evangelicals, and especially against Baptists.

Bill Phillips and his wife Blanche moved to Maniwaki to begin a church with a few believers who were the fruit of evangelism in Val-d'Or and Rouyn-Noranda. They were received in a way typical for the times. Here is Phillips' own description of their "Welcome Wagon."

When Blanche and I moved to Maniwaki in 1954, the priest announced in church that no one was allowed to rent or sell to the "communists" that had come to town. As often experienced elsewhere, God has a humorous way of changing the rough surf of opposition into a blessing. A taxi driver who was in conflict with his priest, heard of the declaration and came to see me. He offered to sell us a lot for half price [...] Soon after, a building bearing the name of *Maniwaki Baptist Church* appeared.[42]

In the southeastern part of the province, a foothold for the Evangelical Baptist Churches and other Evangelicals was being established. French-speaking Fellowship Baptist pastors started getting together for baptisms. They had no church buildings and, therefore, no baptisteries, so they gathered at the Sawyerville Baptist Church where their fledgling churches would sometimes baptize as many as 20 new believers at one time. Those were glorious times when suffering new believers discovered they weren't alone. The following is an account of what one family went through before their baptism:

These new Christians have already known persecution for the sake of the Lord. They had their home ransacked by the police, because the priest had reported that they had communist literature in their possession. The priest has also threatened to take away a girl adopted by them when they were Catholic.[43]

The strength of the Lord prevailed and they joyfully took their place with the other new believers, gave their testimony, and were baptized.

In Rouyn-Noranda, in the northwestern area of the province, close to the Ontario border, associating Baptists with communists took a different form, as reported by Pastor Murray Heron:

In the early 1950s, we learned that some of the mail we sent out was not always being delivered into the right hands [...] None of us knew what steps to take to correct this problem. We prayed and asked the Lord to intervene.

God's answer was not long in coming. Shortly after our meeting, Les Barnhart visited the post office in the village of St-Germain, near Noranda, where people had informed us they were not receiving our literature. The clerk in the post office admitted that she never distributed any mail coming from the Baptists, but had a 'special order' from the parish priest to give it to him.

The editor of a local journal was outraged. He decided to investigate this country parish and speak to the priest personally to verify these claims. The editor was a faithful Roman Catholic, but said he could not tolerate anyone violating the privacy of a Canadian citizen by tampering with his mail.

A few days later, the wires of the Canadian Press carried the news that a Quebec priest regularly destroyed Baptist mail. On August 4, 1951, *The Telegram* reported: 'Father Roy told a reporter the mail in question gave the people 'wrong ideas' and that he had been burning it for about three years...'

Another storm of protest swept across our country and Canada's Postmaster General sent in representatives to investigate. In a statement to the press, the Postmaster General said his department would do everything in their power to prevent a repetition of this incident...

The St-Germain postmaster resigned and charges were laid against the priest and the 16-year-old mail clerk involved. At their trial in September 1951, both pleaded guilty to tampering with the mail. Their lawyer asked the court to be lenient, arguing that Father Roy had no criminal intentions but acted to protect his parish from what he believed were "Communistic" attacks on the Roman Catholic Church.[44]

He was sentenced to a $100 fine or a month in jail. He paid the fine.

Leila Boyd, the first teacher in the new French Protestant Primary School at Girardville, had a harrowing experience on the train trip back from her teaching post. Young men, already intoxicated, were walking up and down the aisle. One of them identified her as the teacher of the new French Protestant School. In their view, anyone connected with the school would be a communist. They continued to circulate in the aisle and every time they passed her they would call her a "damn communist," as well as other inappropriate names. Their anger grew as time passed. Leila Boyd admitted that she had been very frightened. Accompanying her was a young student who had boarded with Christians in Girardville so that she might attend a French Protestant School. She was also petrified. They finally arrived at Chambord, much to their relief, and they boarded another train where they weren't recognized. These unruly young men, however, were just one example of the paranoia that existed at that time at all levels of society. Those who were called communists, or even said to be associated with communists, were often the objects of persecution from either personal or governmental sources. Evangelicals, especially Baptists, were counted among them.

Due to the large number of Evangelical churches that exist in Quebec today and the decline in attendance in Catholic churches to 15% or less in some parishes, one can be an Evangelical Christian in Quebec today without persecution. When we moved to Trois-Rivières in 1967, the situation was already opening up. We had subscribed to the local newspaper *Le Nouvelliste.* Over the course of our residence in that city I wrote several letters from the evangelical viewpoint to the editor; they were all published. This hadn't been the case ten years before. Here is a quotation from the *Le Nouvelliste* dated the 6th of March 1950, "We have also learned that [...] evangelical Christians have been receiving their funds from an organization in Belgium that is associated with a communist organization."[45] This article was like throwing an ignited match into a can of gasoline.

There had already been one serious incident in Shawinigan, a city situated only 34 kilometers (20 miles) from Trois-Rivières:

A group of citizens from Shawinigan expelled Monsieur Boeda from the city without violence on Saturday afternoon. They considered him to be a promoter and preacher of the Evangelical Christians and he was believed to be one of their Archbishops. This group of citizens made an appointment with Mr. Boeda, who left in a taxi with them. One of the group then explained the situation to him, then all accompanied him to the R.R. station in Three Rivers, where they put him on the train for Montreal, which was leaving at 3:40 pm.[46]

Dr. Arthur C. Hill, editor of *News of Quebec* (an evangelical news periodical printed in Quebec by the Christian Brethren), quoted a local newspaper that had reported:

On Saturday, March 4, Paul Boeda was kidnapped from Shawinigan Falls and sent off on the train to Montreal. A scurrilous attack against him was printed the next Monday in the local newspaper and he and his family were threatened with violence should they ever return to Shawinigan. A number of Christians from Sherbrooke, Drummondville and Montreal went up to Shawinigan to see the mayor and other authorities. However, no satisfaction was secured and no attempt was made to find and punish the kidnappers.[47]

Following this, the unidentified spokesman for the kidnappers placed this warning in the local newspaper:

By this gesture, he declared, we wish to teach a lesson to all others who ought to know that we have an organization powerful enough to dispatch from the city at the same time all the members or adherents (of the evangelical faith) with their families and their belongings. This can be done in a few hours and will be free of charge.[48]

After these warnings, the kidnapping of Paul Boeda, and accusations that evangelicals were being funded by a group in Belgium which had ties to communism, chaos broke out in Shawinigan. Michel Gaudette, a citizen of Trois-Rivières and missionary with the Salvation Army, describes the scene:

We are going to examine a recent event described in *Le Nouvelliste*. It concerns the holding of a prayer meeting in Shawinigan, organized by the Christian Assembly from Cap de la Madeleine. The journal describes a hostile and violent demonstration: 'A meeting of the Christian Assembly on 4th Street between Tamarac and Station Avenues, yesterday evening, caused a gathering of several hundred people opposite the building. This caused some damage when the demonstrators threw stones, at the building, breaking windows, let the air out of the tires of an automobile, and turned a car over on its side opposite the building.'[49]

I asked a person whose relatives were inside the small two-storey building how they felt inside during the riot. He told me they feared for their lives.

*News of Quebec* gave their account of what had taken place:

The sequel to all this was the riot on April 12th, when a crowd estimated at 2000, demonstrated for 3 hours against the Christians as they gathered in their little meeting place, and then finally wrecked the little hall entirely. Although police officers freely mixed with the crowd all this time, no restraint was placed upon the rioters and no arrests were made […] However, the press throughout Canada, and in many other places, took up the cudgels on behalf of the "Christian Brethren" in Shawinigan Falls and demanded some definite action. Finally, being pressed by local English Protestants to action, the mayor and council of Shawinigan agreed to pay the damages in the chapel and the car of one of the Christians amounting to $1412. To date no action has been taken against any of the rioters. It is probably significant, however, that shortly afterwards, the Chief of Police retired from duty, along with three of his men.[50]

One must conclude, however, that every effort to spread the gospel in Quebec was still being opposed.

Eileen Veals was visiting homes in Rouyn and giving out copies of the Gospel of John, when she was accosted by a priest who said she could no longer distribute this book. A few minutes later the police arrived and took her to the station. She was warned that she was transgressing the law and was threatened with arrest if she continued. Eileen had given out close to 100 Gospels of John in two weeks. Most people had eagerly received the Word, and very few had refused a copy. We felt a deep conviction that God wanted us to continue offering the message of life through the printed page, and chose to continue this ministry despite the opposition of the city bylaw. Eileen bravely resumed visitation the very next day.[51]

It should also be mentioned that the Provincial Film Board Censor for the Province of Quebec even banned a film on the life of Martin Luther.

## A Letter from Jail

Lorne Heron, pastor at Val-d'Or, spent a total of more than one year in jail for preaching the gospel in the open air. The words here are but a few thoughts taken from a letter he wrote from the Amos jail on July 17, 1951 to Bill Phillips.

Greetings from the cloistered walls of the Amos convent. 'Thanks be to God for His unspeakable gift.' How we do rejoice in Jesus our Savior. He who 'saved us from all sin and has raised us up together and made us sit together in heavenly places.' Thank you for your letter, Bill. The Lord is blessing in La Sarre ... open air ... door-to-door visitation ... conversions, etc ... When we compare Val-d'Or with La Sarre it makes us feel very small, as if we are doing nothing ... The battle here remains slow and hard. The field is too valuable to give an inch ... We have had times of blessing here ... Constantly we have preached and quite a few have listened with real interest to the gospel. Today I talked with a person for one hour. ... Perhaps the best news yet has been that of Mr. Matté. The morning guard had been visited at his home twice ... Mr. Matté admits he has been resisting the gospel. He went to church Sunday morning with his daughter, stayed for the evening service. He enjoyed it ... promised to be back ... pray for him.

What a day it will be when the noise of battle dies away. We will lift our Hallelujah songs of redemption unto the Lamb who is altogether worthy. We leave here on the 13th of August. Perhaps we will be heading back on the following Sunday. We hope it will not be necessary but are ready to do as He bids.

In this last part he speaks of preaching in the open air and the possibility that he could be arrested again. If he does not return, people will not hear the gospel. The Apostle Paul's words in his letter to the Philippians, in the first century, express Lorne Heron's thoughts in Quebec twenty centuries later:

> Now I want you to know, brothers, that what has happened to me has really served to advance the gospel. As a result, it has become clear throughout the whole palace guard and to everyone else that I am in chains for Christ. Because of my chains, most of the brothers in the Lord have been encouraged to speak the word of God more courageously and fearlessly (Philippians 1:12-14).

## Blessings During Persecution (1940-1959) The La Sarre Church – All French

The La Sarre church was a blessed exception. The church was totally French from the beginning; all the believers were French. When they organized into a church, they called the French-Canadian evangelist, Xavier Trudel, who had worked alongside Wilfred Wellington to evangelize the area, as their pastor. One can easily understand how a recent

*Xavier Trudel, La Sarre*

French-Canadian believer would feel more at home entering a French church. This holds true as well for evangelism. When a French Canadian who isn't an evangelical believer enters an evangelical church or meeting and notices that everyone is French Canadian like him, he realizes he can be both a French Canadian and an evangelical believer. The gospel is for all nations and all tongues and one must be careful to avoid giving the idea that it is a religion for English speakers. Furthermore, French evangelical churches have now exposed the lie that had existed for two centuries, "To become a Protestant is to become English and to be a traitor to his people."

### The Inception of a Fellowship French Mission Board

In 1950 there were three bilingual churches in the province and one unilingual French church in La Sarre. Unfortunately there was no Fellowship French Mission Board. Men like Dr. Whitcombe, Dr. John Armstrong, and Dr. John Boyd helped to raise money for work in French-speaking Quebec and some churches began on their own initiative to support individual missionaries to Quebec.

An example of the scarcity of workers is found in the case of Bill Phillips before the formation of the Fellowship of Evangelical Baptist Churches in Canada. He had an interview with Dr. J.F. Holliday, who at the time was Director of Home Missions of the Fellowship of Independent Baptist Churches. Bill Phillips wanted to go to Quebec to plant French language churches, but there were no funds available. Dr. Holliday shared Bill's burden for Quebec, as he was a native Quebecker – born and raised in Quebec and his forbearers were among "the pioneer settlers of Sept-Îles, Quebec."[52] All Dr. Holliday could do was to offer Phillips an English language pastorate in Ville-Émard in Montreal. He was able to study French and do some visitation on the side.

In the case of Murray Heron, he went to Noranda in 1947 to pastor the English language church (founded in 1930 by Stanley Wellington, a brother of pioneer French missionary Wilfred

Wellington). Murray Heron reached out to French people – some were saved and the church became bilingual. It retained this status until 1958, when French Canadians were able to have their own unilingual church.

A beautiful brick building in the heart of the twin cities of Rouyn-Noranda became available. It had been an Anglican Church, whose English-speaking congregation had dwindled, and the remaining few felt it was time to let a French-speaking group use the building. It far surpassed our expectations. The facilities came with oak pews, a complete basement, a kitchen, space for classrooms, and even a tall steeple tower with a bell.

The Anglican bishop gave us excellent terms and graciously allowed us to move in before we made our first payment. We had a great time of celebration with over 100 people gathered for the opening service. We joyfully rang the bell high up in the steeple to invite people to come and hear the Word of God.[53]

When the Fellowship of Independent Baptist Churches and the Union of Regular Baptist Churches amalgamated in 1953 to form the new Fellowship of Evangelical Baptist Churches in Canada, the goal was to establish a strong movement in order to take the gospel into all of Canada and to all the world. One of the tasks God had waiting for us was the evangelization of our fellow French Canadians. In the first year of the newly formed Fellowship, some "$6,000 was sent in, mostly designated support for individual missionaries."[54] The same year the Executive Council took a giant step forward when they "authorized support for Rev. Wm. Phillips to go to Maniwaki as a missionary."[55]

Dr. Watt wrote, "The developing attitude of the Fellowship to its responsibilities in the French work seemed to be manifested at the Annual Convention in 1956 when a budget of $24,000 was adopted for this work alone."[56] He further noted, "Each year the budget was raised a bit higher for the work and the number of missionaries. Seven workers were supported in 1957 but that number was climbing."[57] "The missionaries and the Executive could see the need for an all-out French language ministry and that was on its way."[58] It was getting more exciting all the time.

In 1963, I recall being invited to tour Western Canada, especially British Columbia, for an extended deputation trip. People were surprised when they heard of the persecution on the other side of Canada against those who preached or received the gospel. Tears often flowed as they heard of the conversions of French Canadians and how English-speaking North America, with its thousands of evangelical churches, had overlooked Quebec for most of its 350 year history. We told them how I heard French Christians in our French churches thanking English visitors for sending missionaries, otherwise they would still be in spiritual darkness.

Our itinerary included a presentation at British Columbia's Annual Convention. Something happened as the Spirit of God took over after the presentation of the need for reaching French Canada with the gospel. A senior pastor stood up; I believe it was Dr. J.B. Rowell of Central Baptist Church who, himself had striven to bring Roman Catholics to Christ and had written to expose the errors of Roman Catholic theology. He proposed an offering be taken immediately for the Fellowship work in French Canada. It was carried unanimously. In 50 years of attending Baptist Conventions, I believe that was the only time I have seen an impromptu offering proposed and accepted! The Holy Spirit was at work in our Fellowship and we are so grateful for the privilege we had to participate in reaching French Canada with the gospel.

It was all part of a movement toward a French Board in our Fellowship of churches. Every year, donations coming in for French work were increasing. In response to the need, a French worker was given a seat on the Fellowship Home Missions Board and I was privileged to be that worker. We were made to feel at home on the Home Missions board, but our two areas of work were as different as hockey and baseball. We needed a board that understood French work, the people, their culture, their needs, their religious background, and how they saw things.

Pastor E.S. Kerr of Snowdon Baptist Church in Montreal took a special interest in the French work. In 1956, he called the French workers for a conference graciously hosted by his church. As an English pastor in Montreal, he saw the difference between the English and French people. William Phillips wrote:

> We, the French workers requested Pastor Kerr, as a member of the Executive Council of the Fellowship, to present our request for a French Mission committee to the Executive Council. One of the most important dates in French Canada evangelism was November 28, 1958 when Dr Morley Hall, General Secretary of the Fellowship, announced the formation of a French Mission Committee."[59]

> Dr. E.S. Kerr, pastor of Snowdon Baptist Church in Montreal, became Chairman of the newly formed Fellowship French Mission Board. Other members included Dr. W.G. Brown, Rev. Lorne Heron, Rev. Ernest Keefe, Rev. W.H. Frey, Rev. Harold Hindry, Rev. D.A. Loveday and Rev. Jack Scott. These men met with the French missionaries in January of 1959 to confer together and discuss policies, practices and strategy for advance in a rapidly changing Quebec.[60]

**Growth in Number of Workers from 1950 to 1959**

Following is the roster of the churches and workers from 1950 to 1959:

> Wellingtons in Hull, the Keefes in Asbestos, the Ewins in Coaticook, the Methots in Lachute, the Phillips in Sept-Îles, the Hamelins in Malartic, the Freys in Verdun, the McKenzies

in Maniwaki, the Beaus in Longueuil, the (Ernest) Houles in St-Georges, the Flahauts in St-Jean d'Iberville, the (Gabriel) Cotnoirs in Victoriaville, the (Murray) Herons in Rouyn, the Carsons in Drummondville, the Cochranes in Sherbrooke, the Hurtubises in Valleyfield and the Killicks in Jean-Cote, Alberta. During the decade, buildings had been constructed or purchased in St-Georges, Maniwaki and Rouyn. Land was bought in Asbestos.[61]

Every one of these churches is a miracle in itself. Let me make you aware of just one of these.

## Our First Self-Supporting Church

Ernest Houle was a Quebec farmer and the most fervent Catholic in all his area. One thing bothered him. In his missal, which he used at the Catholic mass, there were prayers, rites of the mass, and quotations from Scripture. One quotation from the Bible, Gospel of John 1:12, bothered him especially. This text teaches that those who receive Jesus and believe in his name (i.e. his person) become children of God. He had always been taught that it was through baptism that one became a child of God. He put this aside as a mystery he didn't have the education or intelligence to understand. Christians, however, contacted him and showed him other verses that contradicted Catholic theology. He was used to following the Church's interpretation, instead of just following the Bible. Karl Rahner, one of the leading theologians of Catholic Church in the 20th century, claimed that when a Catholic, "opens the Scriptures, they are for him the Church's book; he receives them from the Church, and reads them with her interpretation [...] even when the Church's pronouncements, in their outward form of expression, seem to have a different ring about them from the words we can read directly in the New Testament."[62]

As Ernest Houle read the Bible, even if it was a Catholic Bible, he noticed it contradicted many of the teachings of the Catholic

Church. It bothered him. He couldn't set aside the Bible and accept the Church's teaching any longer. Jesus himself said, "If you hold to my teaching, you are really my disciples. Then you will know the truth, and the truth will set you free" (John 8:31,32). He and his wife continued to read the Bible and found the truth. God had spoken to them, not by the Church, but by his Son, as it's mentioned in Hebrews 1:2. Obeying the Scriptures, they trusted in Jesus alone for their salvation, "Salvation is found in no one else, for there is no other name under heaven given to men by which we must be saved" (Acts 4:12). This man, who used to be a fervent believer in the Church's doctrine, became even more fervent in showing the truth as revealed in the Bible.

Ernest Houle sold his farm and enrolled at Institut Biblique Béthel in Lennoxville, Quebec. Upon completion of Bible School studies he moved to St-Georges-de-Beauce. He purchased a two-storey home and added a third storey. Half of the first floor was turned into a chapel, and the second and third floors provided living quarters for the family. During construction and renovations on the house he told people about his plans to establish an Evangelical Baptist Church so people could know the truth of the Bible and be saved. There wasn't a single believer of the gospel in the town but he went ahead and announced the date when the first service would be held. He expected that no one from that area would attend, since he hadn't yet started to evangelize or visit people. Instead, he asked Wilson Ewin and me if we would be present for that first weekend. We were happy to accommodate him, so Saturday evening we had an open-air meeting on the front porch of his home, which also housed the chapel. However, as far as the eye could see, cars were lined up around his house. At first people were attentive as we sang hymns. Wilson Ewin accompanied on the accordion, and we took turns giving *"sermonettes."* Someone in the crowd decided to throw small stones at us. As the crowd became more excited, the stones increased in size and number and began to bounce off the house all around us. It was then that we decided to end the first Evangelical service in St-Georges-de-Beauce *ex abrupto!*

***Pasteur Ernest Houle***

Ernest Houle, one of the best door-to-door evangelists I have known in Quebec, began his work as an evangelist and persevered. People were saved, and before long, a church was built on the property next door to the Houle's home. The local newspaper, *Le Progrès de St-Georges* (The Progress of St. Georges), ran the following article in its column *Dans l'ombre de la Métropole* (In the Shadow of the Metropolis) on September 18, 1958:

A large number of curious people were walking along St. Wilfrid St. in the West side of town last Sunday. They were watching closely the goings and comings of the new converts of the Evangelical Baptist Church ... It was rumored that the Knights of Columbus were preparing an energetic counterattack as a result of the opening of this church. The Knights of Columbus has for its principal mission, the defense of the Catholic Church against its enemies. This will certainly be an opportune occasion for the K. of C. to show of what they are capable.[63]

As a result of its appearance in the newspaper, the Roman Church sent members of the Knights of Columbus and other Catholic groups to break up these services. The Houles were not discouraged by the opposition but kept preaching the word. The Holy Spirit worked, and the humanly impossible happened – several people trusted in Christ and left Catholic church tradition to follow Jesus Christ and his Word. Furthermore, these brave folk were ready to testify to their faith in the waters of baptism. Following is a partial account of the article describing this first baptismal service as it appeared in the *Fellowship Baptist* in May 1959:

The smoke of this battle cleared somewhat on the evening of March 28 to reveal the first true water baptism ever to take place in St. Georges. Catholic priests were furious. During the afternoon preceding the baptism they made every effort to stop the ceremony. First the homes of the candidates were visited by throngs of protesting relatives. Next came the mayor of the town to advise the new Christians of their future financial position as citizens in that area. He was followed by the chief of police, who spared no pains in warning these folk that he would be unable to assure them protection from bodily harm in the months ahead. Last of all came the candidates' former mediator between themselves and God – 'Monsieur le curé,' the local priest.

In spite of many tears, threats and other opposition, nine French Canadian adults joyfully obeyed their Lord in water baptism … Violence has followed and these brave folks need the prayers of God's people. Windows have been smashed and property damaged. However, the work of the Lord goes on. Pastor Houle has organized a church with fourteen charter members … The First Baptist Church of St-Georges is now a memorial to the promise of our Lord regarding His church – 'the gates of Hell shall not prevail against it.' To Him be all the honor and the glory.[64]

Forty years after these events, I had the privilege of speaking at the fortieth anniversary services of the church. Ernest Houle, the founding pastor, was too ill to attend, but the mayor of St-Georges and his wife were present. In his remarks to the church he thanked them for the testimony and good influence they had been in the community of St-Georges. The mayor was very friendly and he gave me a City of St-Georges lapel pin that I still treasure.

To add another postscript, the church at St-Georges opened a new, modern church building in 2006, situated on a hill overlooking the city. It measures 200 by 80 feet (66 by 26 meters) and can seat 500 people. Jesus said, "You did not choose me, but I chose you and appointed you to go and bear fruit – fruit that will last" (John 15:16). This is Jesus' work, not ours, and as a Fellowship of churches we should thank the Lord that when He began a work in Quebec, he gave us a part in it along with other Evangelical churches.

The St-Georges Church became our first self-supporting church and continued to grow. We should mention that in those years, soon after St-Georges, the Centrale Church in Montreal (now named Rosemont) also became self-supporting.

## Baptisms in the Eastern Counties

The decade of the 1950s began with riots and imprisonments, but in the 1959 report, the Chairman, Dr. Kerr wrote:

The Lord is beginning to glorify His name in an unusual way among the French people of Canada, thus answering the faithful prayers of many, and granting fruit to the laborious efforts of the Fellowship's French missionaries. We wish that it had been possible for all our English churches, for instance, to attend the all-French baptismal service at the Sawyerville Baptist Church on September 20 … nineteen French believers were immersed by three of our missionaries. Tears of joy and testimonies from redeemed people moved the hearts of all in an atmosphere of great expectancy and devotion.

The French missionaries who had begun to evangelize the southeastern counties of Quebec had no buildings, let alone baptisteries, but they did have converts! They asked the English Fellowship Baptist Church in the area for permission to use their building. It was noteworthy that French Canadians from our young French churches should be the guests in one of the oldest English Baptist Churches in Canada, with its unusual history. In 1794, a group of new converts contacted The American Baptists to see if they would send a pastor to conduct a baptismal service. The distance between Fairfax, Vermont and Sawyerville, Quebec was over 200 kilometers (120 miles) to be covered by horse. Leslie Tarr explains the rest of the story:

> Rev. Elisha Andres of Fairfax, Vermont, went north in the early winter months of 1794. He met with a number who desired baptism and conducted further gospel preaching meetings. The result? An outdoor baptism in the Canadian winter. The American Baptist pastor describes the event in the most matter-of-fact terms – 'The next day we repaired to the Lake, cut a hole in the ice, and fifteen of those happy and devoted disciples were, in the name of the Father, Son and Holy Ghost, immersed agreeable to the command of the divine Savior.'[65]

**This was the beginning of the Sawyerville Baptist Church.**

The French and English believers admired one another. The French admired the English because of their courageous beginning and that they were faithful to Jesus and his Word for nearly two centuries. (Today, Sawyerville Baptist Church has passed the two-century mark.) The French also admired the English for their hospitality. They not only gave the French believers the use of their building but also served them a sumptuous meal after the service. The English admired the French Christians because they knew the courage that it took for them to turn from church tradition to the Word of God and openly confess faith in Jesus Christ alone in a Catholic country. Those baptisms at Sawyerville taught French and English believers a deeper sense of the words, "You are all one in Christ Jesus" (Galatians 3:28). A new day had begun in Quebec.

One anecdote shows how this new day began. On a Sunday afternoon when we had a baptism, the large church parking lot was filled with cars and others lined the road around the church. On the following day, the owner of the largest grocery store in town met Pastor Oscar Cook, pastor at that time of the Sawyerville English Baptist Church, and asked him in broken English, "Do you give gold stamps?" (In a bid for business, it was common practice at that time for grocery stores to give out gold stamps that could be redeemed for small household appliances, etc.). Pastor Cook understood this pleasantry and went on to explain that these folk had come together to see 19 French Canadians – men and women – be baptized according to the teaching of the Bible, after having received Christ as Saviour. The light of a new day is shining ever brighter!

### The Spread of the Gospel
### Door-to-door Visitation and Literature

The report submitted by the seven men receiving direct grants in 1957 reported the following figures: distribution of 419 New Testaments, 17 Bibles, 1,123 Gospels, 12,895 tracts; 14,326 calls on new prospects, 43 confessions of faith, and 27 baptisms. What a year!

### The Air Waves

There was a breakthrough in radio and television. Wilfred Wellington first held broadcasts in English and French in Val-d'Or in 1939. I'll let him tell his own story:

At about this time a radio station was opened in Val-d'Or. Desiring to avail ourselves of every opportunity for witness, we secured, by God's providence, a quarter hour in English every Sunday, beginning December 27, 1939. A month later the program extended to a regular half-hour broadcast; half of the time being devoted to English and half to French ...

However, this could not go unchallenged by the powers of darkness. About a month later, an organized campaign to stop our program was begun by the local hierarchy. In spite of the fact – doubtless because of it – that the vast majority of listeners were highly appreciative; the people were told to register complaints ...

Because of such opposition I was asked to send my manuscripts of the previous Sunday to the CBC office for examination, and had to await its reply before continuing to broadcast.

In the meanwhile, word was received back from the CBC office in Toronto. Nothing had been found amiss in the examined manuscripts, but certain omissions were suggested for the sake of peace. I was told to submit the scripts regularly for local examination. A French Catholic was to judge them, deleting all that he thought might cause offense. Thus this station, owned by a Protestant, was selling to Rome full religious control. God overruled, much seed was sown (broadcast) and many requested New Testaments were mailed ...

On Sunday afternoon, November 8, 1942, the French-Canadian manager of the local station called to see me.

'I have complaints about your broadcasting', he said. 'That is strange,' I ventured. 'The public with whom I am widely in contact with has been expressing considerable appreciation. But who,' I asked, 'is complaining?' He evaded the question and simply queried, 'Why do you broadcast in French?' ...

Before leaving, he demanded copies of my manuscripts for the evening, promising to have them examined. On the same afternoon, a telegram arrived from him in which he said, 'Don't come down. I have cancelled your broadcast.' However we went, accompanied by two witnesses, asking if he would allow me to explain to my waiting audience why I was not permitted to preach. I was refused. Demanding kindly an explanation of his action, I was given none whatever. 'What did you find in my manuscripts contrary to regulations?' 'I have nothing to say,' was the only reply. A letter written to the nominally Protestant owner of the station yielded no satisfaction. The purport of his answer was simply, 'I will not discuss the justice of the matter. I must support my manager.' Thus the door was closed.[66]

While the Roman Catholic Church succeeded in keeping their members from hearing the gospel over the local station, other doors opened. I recall as a teenager in Timmins that Mr. Bauman, a French-Swiss member of the Timmins Baptist Church, with the encouragement of Dr. W.S. Whitcombe, had begun French gospel broadcasts there. Later, Murray Heron began broadcasting over Timmins, Kirkland Lake and Rouyn-Noranda. Murray Heron reports that, "by 1959 they had a half-hour air time ... from four stations – Rouyn, La Sarre, Val-d'Or and Amos."[67] Then, to put the cherry on the sundae as French Canadians would say, Murray Heron saw men erecting a high tower for a new TV station. He prayed:

'O Lord, make this towering antenna a pulpit upon which I may stand and tell all this needy area the good news of the gospel.' Within a few weeks my prayer was answered. Our half-hour program was called '*Sur les ailes de la foi*' (On Wings of Faith). It was aired during primetime on Saturday evening just prior to the hockey game.[68]

And it wasn't just any game; it was the beloved Montreal Canadians. God had opened the door that the enemy had temporarily closed, and he opened it to an even wider audience than before the attack.

*Dan Lesar*
*at CKVD-AM,*
*Val d'Or,*
*around 1960*

*TV program "On The Wings of Faith", Noranda, around 1965*

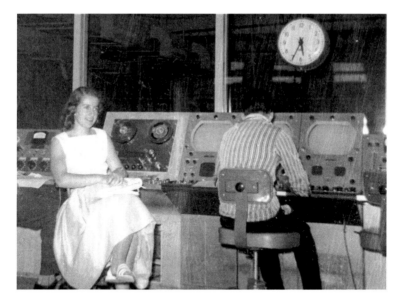

*Betty Casni in TV Studio, Noranda, around 1965*

## The Power of the Pen
## – Literature

A new chapter opened in our work of reaching Quebec with the arrival of the Freys from Switzerland, upon the invitation of the French Mission Board. Mr. Frey was an accomplished writer, and he put out an evangelical journal from his humble home and renovated garage/office in Verdun, Montreal. The journal, which served not only Quebec but also many of the world's French-speaking

*Le Phare, July 1963*

countries, was called *Le Phare* (The Lighthouse). In addition to *Le Phare*, a steady stream of tracts and booklets were printed. All articles appearing in the *Le Phare* had to pass his scrutiny. Jean Flahaut, Wilson Ewin and I wrote many articles and tracts. Some were written in view of current events and had only one printing, while others were printed and reprinted many times. Mr. Frey discussed each article with us, made corrections and prepared them for publication. Numerous other workers also submitted articles for publication. Wilson Ewin, in a very good article on the use of tracts, wrote, "Virtually all of the tracts are the product of his [Frey's] pen, although the actual composition was done by various workers."[69] Words from a Catholic Bishop are proof of their effectiveness:

A news item from *Le Citoyen* reports the concern of the Roman Catholic Bishop of Nicolet, Mgr A. Martin. He warns his people that the centers established in his diocese by the new sects and the victories won among the 'faithful' ought to open the eyes of the Priests concerning the ignorance of many of the faithful in the realm of faith. The new sects referred to include our evangelical Baptist missionaries.[70]

### Conversions

It would be interesting to meet two families who were transformed by the gospel in that period. Their testimonies appeared in the Evangelical Baptist.

Mr. Petit-Clerc had an accident which hospitalised him for two years, followed by convalescence. Mrs. Petit-Clerc had to start working to provide for her family; one woman for whom she worked was a Christian. She witnessed to Mrs. Petit-Clerc and suggested that her pastor could visit Mr. Petit-Clerc at the hospital. Mr. Petit-Clerc accepted and this lead to his salvation and that of many in his family. Below is the testimony of his son Fernand.

### I Wanted to be a Priest – God Wanted me to be a Pastor
### Fernand Petit-Clerc

*Pastors William-Henry Frey and Fernand Petit-Clerc*

I was born in Val D'Or, Que. in 1936, as the second child of a family of four. I had an older brother and a younger one, and my sister was the youngest. We were devoted Roman Catholics. Since my early age, I tried to be just before God and men in practicing my religion in all sincerity. It is because of His grace that today I can give an account of my conversion by faith in Christ, and of His call to serve Him.

Pastor S.F. Gillespie, with other Christians, came to our home for Bible studies. This caused a real revolution in our family! At first my mother, my older brother and I were opposed. But it was not long before my father was saved, then my mother and sister …

Each Sunday my parents, along with my younger brother and sister, were going to the French Baptist church while I was still attending the Roman Catholic Church. I couldn't believe that my family would be saved by leaving the only true apostolic church, as I had been taught. I was then an altar boy and very devoted to my religion. I had done penance, closed retreats, and never would I have missed church on Sunday morning and evening, or the first Friday of the month. I liked my priest and all the tracts and New Testaments that I found at home I would bring to him, but sometimes before doing so I would read them secretly. I was very surprised not to find anything wrong in them. But … the words of my catechism were strongly impregnated in my mind. 'Out of the Catholic church there is no salvation.'

For two years my parents kept asking me to go with them to their new church, but I always refused. I remember times when my parents would go to prayer meeting and I would ask them to drop me off at the theatre. They used to say: We will pray for you.

Their prayers were not in vain. On Christmas Eve 1951, my mother told me, "Why don't you come to church tonight, we are having a special Christmas meeting? Refreshments will be served and you will meet some pretty girls!"

I went along for these things, but once in the church, I forgot about refreshments and all the rest. I had never heard hymns sung with such fervor in my own language. Neither had I ever seen people with such conviction that I could not go back to the Roman Catholic church. I said to myself: These people have something that we do not have in our church and I must find it.

I bought myself a Bible which I read every morning, and asked God to show me the right way. I began attending the meetings of the Baptist church as regularly as I had attended the meetings in the R.C. church. But, what a miserable life I lived for several months! I had a hard time believing that all I had learned in the R.C. church was not true. Every Monday I attended Bible lessons given by Child Evangelism, and during the summer I went to Bethel Bible Camp. Finally I realized that the truth that I was searching for was in Jesus Christ. I gave myself entirely to Him, now knowing that no one else could save me. Ephesians 2:8-9 were the verses that the Holy Spirit used to enlighten me. I had always believed that by my penances, sacrifices and good works I would be saved. I received the joy of the Lord. I was now devouring the Word of God, which was entirely new to me.

It was at Easter 1953 that I was baptized, promising by the grace of God to be faithful to Christ. His grace has helped me to grow in Him.

Before my conversion, my desire was to become a R.C. priest. Once saved, the desire to know the Holy Scriptures better and to consecrate my life to His service was revived in me.

Shortly after we were married, Evelyn and I entered to *Institut Biblique Béthel* (Bethel Bible Institute) to prepare for the work of the Lord.

After graduating from Bethel, the Lord directed us to come and work with Pastor W.H. Frey in Montreal at the Église Baptiste Évangélique de Verdun."[71]

In his testimony Fernand mentioned his young sister. She studied at The Institute Feller, which was founded by Henriette Feller in a small log cabin in 1836. Today, Marianne Petit-Clerc is the official translator of our Fellowship French office in Montreal. She has translated many books from English to French, including James Dobson's books and other well-known authors. Along with her partner, Carole Silvera, they have written books for all ages and have their own publishing/editing company, Publications Vivantes, Éditions Bérékia. Marianne is in demand as a conference speaker and she has also translated courses given by visiting English-speaking professors at our French Seminary, SEMBEQ.

God turned the accident of Fernand's and Marianne's father, which seemed to be a terrible misfortune, into a wonderful blessing for the family and for countless others. While the Quiet Revolution was being written in Quebec's earthly history, God was writing his eternal history in heaven.

---

### From Rome to Christ – Peace Disturbed, Restored and Proclaimed

Jean-Louis Jacques

I was born in the province of Quebec to French Canadian parents. Together with other members of the family, I was faithful to my Church and ready to give my very life in service if necessary. I married a very religious woman who had spent some years in a convent. Together with our five children we moved to Florida in 1952. Our object was to obtain a better salary, more friends, and last but not least, to avoid the misery of Canadian winters. Our hope was realized and to complete our happiness several brothers, sisters and my parents moved to Florida.

Ten years later, a friend came to visit us from Canada. In the past years, we had spent countless evenings together in various nightclubs, dance hall and taverns. To my great surprise, he refused my offer of a glass of liquor with the words, "I have found something better." Frankly curious, I asked him to explain. "Well," he said, "I must know first whether you believe the Bible." To this question I replied yes, for I believed it to be the Word of God. He then proceeded to show me God's plan of salvation and the marvelous change that takes place in the believer's life. Heaven comes as a free gift according to what he read from his Bible.

Immediately, I was impressed. The difference I reasoned, between what I read and what I was taught, lay in the fact that my friend's Bible was false. I brought out my big Bible, which had only been used for the pictures it contained. Why read when we felt that the Church teaches us all that is necessary. I was quite shocked when I was shown that Ephesians 2:8 in my own Bible was the same as what I had read in the Protestant Bible. My wife who was listening stated quite bluntly, "We have our religion, we know that it's true and we don't wish to be bothered." She then put our friends out of the house. My wife knew I was impressed and determined to read my Bible, so she hid it. When I asked her for it she replied, "no, and there will be trouble if you speak to that friend again." Without saying a word I bought another Bible and hid it in my truck. Whenever the opportunity arose I would park in a hidden place and read it in secret.

My friend was building a new home and I consented to help. While I plastered, his wife followed me around with a Bible in her hand. As I moved from place to place she read from the Bible and asked me if I believed what it said. I was astonished, as formerly she would bring me liquor. Often I went to my truck to compare with my own Bible.

Sometime later my wife learned about these activities. She became furious, turned the children against me and encouraged by her own friends, began to seek a divorce. Because I read the Bible and believed its truth, my friends became my enemies and even my family turned against me. To add to my misery, the Scriptures convinced me that I was lost. All of my hopes of being saved by my Church were swept away. I had clung to the bishop's words at my confirmation. "If you wish to be saved, repeat five *Our Fathers*, five *Hail Marys* and five *Glory be to the Father* before going to sleep each night." But I thought about what Jesus said, "I am the way, the truth and the life: no man cometh unto the Father, but by me" (John 14:6). Furthermore, the Word of God said that Christ's death on the cross had atoned for all my sins; there was no penance to be done or purgatory for my soul. To have eternal life I needed only to put my trust in the blood of the Lord Jesus Christ.

One day, my brother came with a message from the whole family. Unless I abandoned my Bible reading and destroyed the Bible then all fellowship would end, my wife would obtain a divorce and that I would be placed in an asylum. Once again, the Bible brought a message to my heart, "He that loveth father or mother more than me is not worthy of me: and he that loveth son or daughter more than me is not worthy of me" (Matthew 10:37).

I went to bed that evening but not to sleep, for I had come to a crossroad. I was free to choose and choose I must. If I denied the Word of God to keep my family and worldly pleasures, I wouldn't be worthy of Christ. But if I was ready to sacrifice all and follow Christ, then I could be saved. That sleepless night decided my choice; I would follow Christ.

I was working for a Christian contractor who said to me next morning, "John what happened to you last night? You look awful." He then came to my problem with the words, "You don't know Christ as Savior, do you?" I told the whole story and revealed the torment within my soul. Bringing me to his car, he took a badly worn Bible from a tool box. Once again I heard the story of salvation in Christ. Upon admission of my desire to accept Christ, the contractor led me in a prayer during which both of us shed many tears.

There, parked in an old car on a Florida street, I gave my heart to Christ.

"God is faithful, who will not suffer you to be tempted above that ye are able." (1 Corinthians 10:13). Although my conversion was followed by real violence from my family, my newly found Savior proved to be a loving, merciful, and sovereign Lord, my wife's violent resistance to the gospel broke down, and the Holy Spirit revealed the truth of God's Word to her heart. Her conversion was followed by that of all our older children except one.

We completed our Bible training and there was no surprise to some that God called us to serve Him back in Quebec.[72]

## The Final Outcome of the Name-Calling Era

Duplessis, the clergy, and even some newspapers offered us a lot of opposition. First they depicted communism as evil, and then they connected it to unions, theaters, actors, and to groups they considered enemies, such as evangelicals. Baptists got more than fair share of accusations because they were one of the most active groups in the province. Despite this era of name-calling and persecution, the work of the gospel prevailed. The Evangelicals were not crushed. God was preparing his church for the revival that was to come.

(Endnotes)

1  Jean-Marie Lebel & Alain Roy, *Québec, 1900-2000 : le siècle d'une capitale* (Québec: Commission de la capitale nationale et Éditions Multi-Monde, 2000), p. 45.
2  Jean-Marie Lebel & Alain Roy, *Québec, 1900-2000: le siècle d'une capitale*, p. 45.
3  Jean-Marie Lebel & Alain Roy, *Québec, 1900-2000: le siècle d'une capitale*, p. 45.
4  Jean-Marie Lebel & Alain Roy, *Québec, 1900-2000: le siècle d'une capitale*, p. 45.
5  Michel Gaudette, *Guerres de religion d'ici : catholicisme et protestantisme face à l'histoire* (Trois-Rivières, Québec: Éditions Souffle de vent, 2001), p. 76.
6  Lacour-Gayet, *Histoire du Canada* (Paris: Fayard, 1966), p. 535.
7  Lacour-Gayet, *Histoire du Canada*, p. 537.
8  Jean-Marie Lebel & Alain Roy, *Québec, 1900-2000: le siècle d'une capitale*, p. 60.
9  John Thomas McDonough (translation and adaptation of *Charbonneau et le Chef*, from Paul Hébert & Pierre Morency), (Les Éditions LEMAG), p. 87.
10  McDonough, *Charbonneau et le Chef*, p. 87.
11  McDonough, *Charbonneau et le Chef*, p. 87.
12  McDonough, *Charbonneau et le Chef*, p. 87.
13  McDonough, *Charbonneau et le Chef*, p. 88.
14  McDonough, *Charbonneau et le Chef*, p. 88.
15  McDonough, *Charbonneau et le Chef*, p. 88.
16  Renaude Lapointe, *L'histoire bouleversante de Mgr Charbonneau* (Montréal: Les Éditions du jour, 1962), préface.
17  Renaude Lapointe, *L'histoire bouleversante de Mgr Charbonneau*, p. 67.
18  Renaude Lapointe, *L'histoire bouleversante de Mgr Charbonneau*, p. 67.
19  Renaude Lapointe, *L'histoire bouleversante de Mgr Charbonneau*, p. 67.
20  John A Dickinson - Brian Young, *Brève histoire socio-économique du Québec*, (Sillery, Québec Les Éditions du Septentrion) p. 325-326.
21  John A Dickinson - Brian Young, *Brève histoire socio-économique du Québec*, p. 303.
22  McDonough, *Charbonneau et le Chef*, p. 26.
23  McDonough, *Charbonneau et le Chef*, p. 27.
24  Lacour-Gayet, *Histoire du Canada*, p. 537.
25  Jean-Marie Lebel & Alain Roy, *Québec, 1900-2000: le siècle d'une capitale*, p. 60.
26  McDonough, *Charbonneau et le Chef*, p. 18.
27  McDonough, *Charbonneau et le Chef*, p. 61.
28  Renaude Lapointe, *L'histoire bouleversante de Mgr Charbonneau*, p. 55-56.
29  McDonough, *Charbonneau et le Chef*, p. 18.
30  McDonough, *Charbonneau et le Chef*, p. 77.
31  McDonough, *Charbonneau et le Chef*, p. 77.
32  Renaude Lapointe, *L'histoire bouleversante de Mgr Charbonneau*, p. 79.
33  Renaude Lapointe, *L'histoire bouleversante de Mgr Charbonneau*, p. 79.
34  Renaude Lapointe, *L'histoire bouleversante de Mgr Charbonneau*, p. 79.
35  Renaude Lapointe, *L'histoire bouleversante de Mgr Charbonneau*, p. 18.
36  Renaude Lapointe, *L'histoire bouleversante de Mgr Charbonneau*, p. 61.
37  Renaude Lapointe, *L'histoire bouleversante de Mgr Charbonneau*, p. 66.
38  Renaude Lapointe, *L'histoire bouleversante de Mgr Charbonneau*, pp. 90-95.
39  Lacour-Gayet, *Histoire du Canada*, p. 515.
40  William Phillips, *Modern Day Missionary Miracles*, Published by Fellowship French Missions, 7415, boul. Gouin, Montréal, H4K 1B8, 1998, p. 21.
41  Jean-Louis Lalonde, *Des loups dans la bergerie, Les Protestants de la langue française au Québec, 1534-2000*, (Montréal: Fides), p. 247.
42  William Phillips, *Modern Day Missionary Miracles*, p. 25.

43   Wilson Ewin, *The Evangelical Baptist Magazine*, Nov. 1959, p.8.
44   Murray Heron, *Footprints across Quebec* (Dundas, Ontario: Joshua Press, 1999), p. 62-64.
45   *Le Nouvelliste de Trois-Rivières*, March 6, 1950.
46   *Le Nouvelliste de Trois-Rivières*, July 19, 1950, p.72
47   Arthur C. Hill, M.D. editor, *News of Quebec*, Aug. 1950, p.2
48   *Le Nouvelliste*, March 6th, 1950, p.6.
49   Gaudette, *Guerres de religion d'ici*, p. 74.
50   Arthur C. Hill, M.D., *News of Quebec*, August 1950, p.2.
51   Murray Heron, *Footprints Across Quebec*, p. 36.
52   Richard Holliday, *Dr. J.F. Holliday, Fellowship Trail Blazer*, book two, compiled by Fred A Vaughan, (Belleville, Ontario: Guardian Books), p. 173.
53   Murray Heron, *Footprints Across Quebec*, p. 88.
54   J. H. Watt, *Our First Twenty-five Years* (A Fellowship Publication, 1978), p. 83.
55   Watt, *Our First Twenty-five Years*, p. 83.
56   Watt, *Our First Twenty-five Years*, p. 85.
57   Watt, *Our First Twenty-five Years*, p. 86.
58   Watt, *Our First Twenty-five Years*, p. 83.
59   William Phillips, *Modern Day Miracles*, p. 26.
60   William Phillips, *Modern Day Miracles*, p. 29.
61   William Phillips, *Modern Day Miracles*, p. 29.
62   Karl Rahner, *Mary Mother of the Lord, Theological Meditations* (Montreal: Palm Publishers, Imprimatur E. Morrogh Bernard Vic. Gen. Westmonasterii, die 30. Novembris, 1962), p. 21,22.
63   *Le Progrès de St-Georges.*
64   *Fellowship Baptist*, May 1959.
65   L.K. Tarr, *This Dominion, His Dominion* (Published by the Fellowship of Evangelical Baptist Churches in Canada), p.53.
66   Rev. and Mrs. Wilfred Wellington, *Rome's Challenge Accepted,* (Published by the author, 1949), p.12-13, 21-22.
67   Murray Heron, *Footprints Across Quebec*, p. 97.
68   Murray Heron, *Footprints Across Quebec*, p. 97.
69   Wilson Ewin, *Fellowship Baptist*, March 1959, p.3.
70   Ernie Keefe, *The Evangelical Baptist*, July-August 1959, p.11.
71   *Fellowship Baptist*, May 1996, pp. 4,22.
72   Jean-Louis Jacques, *The Evangelical Baptist*, Oct. 1966.

# Chapter 8

# *The Quiet Revolution –*
# *1960 to 1970*

## Historic Seeds of the Causes of the Quiet Revolution

Gregory Baum, eminent theologian and social scientist, professor at McGill University, affirmed that, "The decade of the 1960.s was marked by a momentous event that changed 300 years of Catholic exclusivity and control of French Canadians in Quebec."[1] Dr. Baum's statement, "300 years of Catholic exclusivity"[2] is true, but we must note that in the early days of New France there was another group of French descent. They were called Huguenots, or Calvinists, and were the French arm of the Protestant Reformation. Mason Wade and F.X. Garneau, elite writers of French Canadian History, note that the Huguenots "played a considerable part in New France"[3] in cooperation with the Catholics.

## The Role of the Huguenots

France sent forth its first explorer, Jacques Cartier, in 1534. In his first voyage he discovered the Gaspé Peninsula and in his second voyage he discovered the St. Lawrence River which he followed as far as Hochelaga (Montreal). The king and nobles were not satisfied with his second voyage. He was replaced as leader of the third voyage by a Huguenot, Jean Francois de La Roque, Sieur de Roberval. This voyage was France's first effort to establish a colony in the New World. The colony was established but scurvy took its toll and after one year the effort ended. Jean Francois de la Roque was not only a Huguenot but also an "adepte de la nouvelle théologie"[4] that is Calvinism.

A second effort to establish a colony took place in 1600. It was under the leadership of another Huguenot, Pierre Chauvin, a gentleman and marine captain from Dieppe,[5] He established a colony at Tadoussac "in the name of the King of kings and immediately proclaimed religious liberty"[6] despite the fact that other explorers planted a cross in the name of the king of France and limited religious practice to the Catholic Church. Because of the severe winter the colony was abandoned, but it provided useful knowledge for establishing future colonies. Both Catholics and Huguenots were employed in this effort.

Another effort where there was cooperation between the Catholics and Huguenots was the Caen Merchant Company[7] King Henry IV of France gave patents to Catholics and to Protestants alike.[8] Port Royal, situated in Acadia (now Nova Scotia) was the third effort to establish a colony by France. Henry IV appointed "a Calvinist, Pierre du Gua, gentleman of the king's chamber … viceroy and captain general by sea and by land (November 8, 1603) "[9] De Monts also received a 10 year monopoly in the fur trade and fishing.

He was also aided by a great team: Louis Hubert, the Paris apothecary and Huguenot; Marc Lescarbot, who was a lawyer, a poet, and an historian who wrote the first History of Canada (New France); and Poutrincourt, who shared the leadership of the colony and who was a well known Catholic politician. Unfortunately, jealous traders and a politician who had opposed appointments at the beginning, succeeded in having de Mont's patent and monopoly rescinded. This meant the income of the colony was also lost. This was a very successful colony in regard to agriculture and organization, and they even learned how to treat scurvy. When it had to be shut down, the nobleman and politician Poutrincourt wept and even Samuel de Champlain lamented the closing of this model colony that his friend De Monts had founded. Champlain cried out to God expressing his indignation at the whole thing[10]

After the revocation of his monopoly and the abandonment of the colony in Acadia, de Monts turned to the St. Lawrence River. He had traveled it, and had judged it would be a good place to begin a new colony. This was the beginning of New France.

F.X. Garneau described what took place in De Monts' life after he was forced to leave Acadia:

Having obtained from the king a renewal of his privilege for a year, Mr. De Monts took on Champlain as his lieutenant. In 1608, armed with his associates, two ships, one to trade at Tadoussac, and the other to carry colonists, he started a new settlement along the Saint Lawrence River.

Champlain arrived at Quebec City on July 3rd. He disembarked on the small piece of land where the lower city is situated today.[11]

Once again, for a fourth time, which covered all of France's efforts to begin a colony in the new world from 1540 to 1608, the effort was led by a Huguenot. Pierre Gua de Monts was a key player in this time of cooperation between Huguenots and Catholics. Professor J.P. Bosher underlined this by quoting from Jean Liebel's biography entitled "Jean-Pierre Dugua, sieur de Mons, fondateur de l'Acadie et du Québec" where it was stated that, "Catholic and Protestant 'entrepreneurs' collaborated over the quarter of a century that followed, thus founding New France. Among them, a noble of Huguenot religion, Pierre Du Gua de Monts ( - 1628) was known as a leader."[12]

In 2008, on the 400th anniversary of the City of Quebec, it was fitting that honor was paid to one that history has in general forgotten, one who was a Christian and a Huguenot. What better historian could we have to do this than Marcel Trudel, a former teacher at Harvard, Laval, and Carleton University (Ottawa), who published the monumental ten–volume "Histoire de la Nouvelle France." He portrays de Monts as follows:

> Du Gua de Monts has been unjustly forgotten. As the first colonizer of New France in the 17th century, he inaugurated a work that will never be abandoned. Port-Royal (1605-1606) remained, with reason, an illustration of an enthusiastic and happy period of history. The foundation of Acadia began with him, as does the return of France to the Saint Lawrence River. He is the one who sent, at his own cost, Champlain to build "l'Habitation" of Quebec and who assured its existence until 1612. Canadian history has shown itself to be very ungrateful to him. On a 1613 map, the Cap Diamant summit is named Du Gas, but this name was soon dropped; and there is no important geographical site to remind us today that de Monts was one of the founders of New France.[13]

It's of note that in front of the Quebec City's Château Frontenac there are two significant monuments. One recalls the founding of Quebec City in 1608 and the other the arrival of the first Catholic priests, the Récollets, in 1615. This order seems to fit in well with the collaboration between Catholics and Huguenots. The historian Robert Wilson noted that, "The Récollets encouraged intermingling of Indians and French and cooperation with the Huguenots in civil matters."[14] And so continues what Jean-Louis Lalonde entitles, "Un bel espoir de cohabitation"[15] (A good example of living together).

### The Catholic Church (Jesuits) Takes Control of New France

The 15th of June 1625 was a significant day for the colony of New France. On that morning a blunt-prowed, high-pooped vessel cast anchor before the little trading village that clustered about the base of the great cliff at Quebec. It was a ship belonging to the Caëns, and it came laden to the hatches with supplies for the colonists and goods for trade with the Indians. But, what was more important, it had as passengers the Jesuits.[16]

The Jesuits is a religious order founded to reform the Catholic Church and to counter the Protestant Reformers. According to their own history, they considered themselves, "aggressive and powerful, uncompromising opponents of Calvinism."[17] The Jesuits had been banished from France the 29th of December 1594, but reinstated under Henry IV by threats, if Henry IV did not allow them to return.[18] Neither Henry IV nor his confidant Sully wanted to have the Jesuits return to France even under the Pope's prodding! Henry IV explained to Sully:

> Of necessity … I must now do one of two things: admit the Jesuits purely and simply, relieve them from the defamation and insults with which they have been blasted, and put to the proof all their fine sentiments and excellent promises, or use against them all severities that can be imagined to keep them from ever coming near me and my dominions. In which latter case, there is no doubt it would be enough to reduce them to utter despair and to thoughts of attempting my life; which would render me miserable or listless, living constantly in suspicion of being poisoned or assassinated, for these gentry have communications and correspondence everywhere, and great dexterity in disposing men's minds as it seems good to them. … The king then called to remembrance the eight projected or attempted assassinations which, since the failure of John Châtel, from 1596 to 1603, had been, and clearly established to have been, directed against him.[19]

In view of the power and intrigue of the Jesuits, their arrival in Quebec was an ominous sign. Charles Lalemant, Superior of the Jesuits, upon his arrival surveyed the situation of the new colony and according to Marquis – "the greatest evil, in Lalemant's mind, was the presence of so many Huguenots."[20] At the same time:

> Complaints about the Huguenots reached the ear of Cardinal Richelieu, an advisor to King Louis XIII of France. He engineered the end of the Charter of Caën – which gave patents to develop New France to both Protestants (Huguenots) and Catholics alike – and the establishment of a totally Catholic company, *Les Cents Associés* (The One Hundred Associates). Jesuit history solemnly notes: 'that moment ended the régime of the Huguenot traders in Canada.' Thenceforth, whether for good or for evil, New France was to be Catholic.[21]

For the few Huguenots who remained in New France, another menace appeared on the horizon. Francois-Xavier de Montmorency-Laval (1623-1708) was established by the Vatican as the first Bishop of New France. He was ordained Bishop despite the Gallican government in France, which wanted the king of France to name the new Bishop. Secondly, there is a rule in the Jesuit Order that its members cannot become Bishops. The Jesuits wanted control of New France so they turned their back on the King and government of France and even transgressed one of their own rules to get it. Catholic historian Mason Wade asserted, "Ever since, French Canada has remained a stronghold of clericalism, and very conscious of its spiritual dependence upon the Holy See"[22] (i.e. The Vatican). Wade published his book in 1956, four years before the Quiet Revolution and, coincidentally, the year we began the church in Asbestos.

The Jesuits not only took power from the Huguenots but also "barred the Huguenots who had played a considerable part in New France."[23] In his first edition of his *History of Canada*, the honored French Historian F. X. Garneau, whose statue is on the lawn of the Quebec Parliament, expressed regrets that such steps were taken because they affected the prosperity of the country. He deplored the fact that the Huguenots were not tolerated or even encouraged.[24]

Mason Wade asserts, "The aim of the Jesuits was to establish in Canada the closed theocracy which they later achieved in Paraguay."[25]

As the Jesuits were aiming to make a totally French Catholic country out of New France, Louis XIV was also imposing the concept of an exclusive Roman Catholicism on France. In his intolerance he even revoked the Edict of Nantes, which gave French citizens, including the Huguenots specifically, religious freedom. The Edict of Nantes had been introduced by Henry IV and it had brought an end to decades of costly civil religious wars in France.

The poorer Huguenots in France fled and hid. Many were tortured and others suffered martyrdom. Others made it to the frontier of other European countries, while the richer Huguenots in La Rochelle took their skills in "the areas of agriculture, industry, banking and commerce"[26] to countries that opened their doors.

The Huguenots of La Rochelle were able to flee to countries such as Holland, England and the United States. New York, Louisiana, and New England received the Huguenots with open arms. New France by comparison had a population of about 10,000 people while one third of Manhattan's population were Huguenot refugees[27] and there were at least 5,000 Huguenots in New England.

The Jesuits, blinded by their aim to keep New France totally Catholic and under their control, had difficulty in interesting French Catholics to come to New France as colonists. Huguenots meanwhile were fleeing France by the thousands to escape the cruel persecution of Louis XIV. They were looking preferably for a French speaking country in which to settle with all their skills and experiences. The result was that Quebec had a population of only 7,000 Europeans while the first census in the United States in 1783, counted 100,000 French speaking people.[28]

It seems that, "it would have been better, in the interest of the colony, to reduce this exclusion to Catholics who emigrated little; it was a fatal blow to Canada by closing the entrance to the Huguenots in a formal manner by the act of establishment of the company of one hundred associates. "[29]

Today French Canadians work hard to keep their language and their culture. There are 7.5 million French Canadians in the north eastern corner of North America, with small pockets of French citizens in other parts of Canada.

Betty and I moved to Quebec in 1954. We learned French and most of our friends in Quebec are French. Though many of them are bilingual we make it a point to always speak French with them. Our four boys all learned French from their childhood and two of our grandchildren are in a French school. We can only imagine today what Canada would've beeen like and how large the pockets of French speakers in this corner of North America would be if the Huguenots had not been excluded. There would also have been religious freedom and the Bible wouldn't have been a forbidden book. This Catholic exclusivity helped bring on the Quiet Revolution. The Quiet Revolution ended the exclusivity of any religion and made Quebec a secular state.

Historian Baird summarized the folly of exclusiveness:

> In this prohibition, religious intolerance pronounced the downfall of the French colonial system in America. The exclusion of the Huguenots from New France was one of the most stupendous blunders that history records [...]. Industrious and thrifty, and anxious to make any sacrifice to enjoy the liberty of conscience denied them at home, they would have rejoiced to build up a French state in the New World.[30]

It seems ironic that in the 19th century thousands of French Canadians emigrated to states in New England to find employment in the industries which were in part owned and operated by the very French Huguenots Quebec barred from their Province. Further on we will see that the lack of industry, entrepreneurship, training in engineering, banking experience and mercantilism were the very things that 20th century men like René Lévesque pointed to as problems for which Quebec needed to find solutions. Two centuries before the Quiet Revolution, these things had been offered to them in French by the Huguenots. However, they weren't allowed to land in Quebec because of their Reformed Religion.

## The English Conquest

The English Conquest of Canada in the 18th century did not bring religious freedom to the French Protestants, nor did it help the French Canadians' need of industrialism, banking and commercial knowhow. In fact they exploited them.

As to religion the 1763 Paris Treaty stipulates that catholic rituals were permitted[31]

The King of England was ignorant of the Catholic domination of Quebec. Lacour-Goyet observed that with the Quebec Act of 1774 the catholic clergy gains a new vigor and authority over the French speaking population.[32] This was also the opinion of the Canadian Protestant historian, R.P. Duclos.

We have to measure the King of England's action against the French population of Quebec. Here is the division of the population at the time of the writing of the Traité de Paris:

One hundred thirty seigneurs, 100 gentlemen and bourgeois, 125 notable merchants, 25 legal authorities and lawyers (of whom several had belonged to the Superior Council), 25 to 30 doctors and surgeons, and nearly as many notaries remained in Quebec instead of returning to France as they were permitted to do by the peace treaty. The French soldiers and officials, and some hundred of the colonial noblesse, deprived of their old opportunities for soldiering and fur-trading, were the only portion of the elite to emigrate. The clergy remained at their posts, and since their position alone among the elite was not affected by the conquest, their prestige as leaders of the people was strongly reinforced. The great mass of the population, the habitants, were little disturbed by the change of rule.[33]

This is a good picture of Quebec in the 18th and 19th centuries; very few were educated. Against the background of the elite was a mass of gregarious, docile, hard working, family-centered farmers, deprived of education and the Bible and ruled by the clergy. When the Evangelical Swiss believers heard of this, they sent missionaries to Quebec to educate the children and to share the gospel with the population. They were treated without mercy by the Catholic Church. When North American churches such as the Presbyterian, Anglican, Methodists, and Baptists tried to enlighten the people, they received the same treatment. Despite the opposition, "in 1900, there [were] more than 100 French Protestant churches."[34]

The following are two anecdotes, one of a challenge and another of a victory:

At Roxton Pond, [...] the factory, owned by a Protestant, was given over to the Catholics who employed (from then on) only people from their religion. The other [factory] was moved to another village [...]; Halpenny deplores these circumstances which resulted in unemployment for his parishioners.[35]

There were also many victories from the hand of the Lord. The one that follows here concerned what was called, "The Community of Berea" because of its similarity to the believers in Acts 17:10-12 where the listeners "received the message with great eagerness and examined the Scriptures every day to see if what Paul said was true" (Acts 17:11).

A Bible, that a young man from Massachusetts gave to his mother and a New Testament that Mr. Roussy gave to the father of a family, became the means (of the beginnings of this community). The lady and the father, having spoken to each other, became convinced that these books showed the way to the knowledge of oneself and to salvation through Christ.

Wanting to know more about the mystery of godliness, the father traveled to the Grande Ligne Mission and stayed for three weeks. Having found what he was looking for, he returned in haste to inform the lady, explaining to her with much enthusiasm what the Lord had shown him. One of his sons, having heard what the traveler had to say, spoke to his neighbor, who spoke to another. Before long, everyone wanted to know more. In order to answer these legitimate questions it was decided to invite Mr. Roussy, who was delighted to come. Eight families immediately broke ties with Rome.

Occasional visits from Mr. Roussy, Mr. Cellier, and Mr. Normandeau, [...] helped this small group of believers to make rapid progress. During the summer a small school was started in a modest room made available to the missionaries by a converted family. Because progress continued, it was soon evident that it was necessary to think of building a suitable house (meeting house).[36]

## Immigration to the United States

Gaudette portrays a great number of such victories but he also reveals the reality of an important period of immigration to the United States. It was caused in great part by persecution and a lack of employment, especially for the French Protestants who were a minority in a Province controlled by the Catholic clergy. Gaudette points out that:

In 1892, there were 12,000 French Protestants in the Province of Quebec. It must be said that the French Canadian exodus to the industrialized centers of New England greatly affected the development of French Protestantism in Quebec. We are talking about 20,000 who emigrated to the United States![37]

It wasn't only French Protestants who suffered from the Jesuits and the Catholic Church. Their aim was to make Quebec exclusively Catholic and in doing so they shut thousands of industrious Huguenots out of the Province. Their wealth and their knowledge of industry provided, in great part, the very American industries that later drew French Canadians to the United States.

This immigration to the United States for employment astonished me and touched me emotionally. The experience of R.G. Letourneau is an example. As a young Christian I read about his exploits in industry and his unwavering Christian testimony. I was ignorant of the important role the Huguenots had played in France and the Western world since the Protestant Reformation. R. G. LeTourneau was a Christian who spoke openly of his faith in Jesus Christ. "His Christian commitment led to sponsoring many works, involving missions and education, including the LeTourneau College, a Christian liberal arts college, and a technical school in Longview Texas."[38] He also spoke of his Bible reading and prayer with his wife. He gave her credit for strengthening his faith when he was downcast. The following is a short resume of his background and his relationship with Quebec:

We come from a long line of ministers and missionaries on both sides of our family. My grandfather, Jean LeTourneau, was a Huguenot minister, sent with his bride, Marie Louise, from Lyons, France, to the Grande Ligne Mission in Quebec in the 1840s. From all accounts, he and his wife had a rough time. The Protestant Huguenots were no longer subjected to the fanatical persecutions of the 18th century, but neither were they made especially welcome. Added to that was the primitive housing and the long, fierce Canadian winters. For a young couple from southern France, the winters must have been pretty grim, but they stuck it out until my father was born on January 12, 1857, in St. Sebastian, Quebec. Then, both in bad health, they moved to Richford, Vermont, only five miles from the Canadian line. [...]

I never really knew my grandparents; my one recollection of my grandmother when she visited us in Duluth is that she was small and spoke only in French. But I have a great admiration for them.[39]

R.G. LeTourneau's dependence on God also helped him as a businessman. Once, in his own time of prayer, when he was on the brink of bankruptcy, God put in his mind the thought of putting rubber tires on large machinery in place of the metal rims like we see on tractors in farm museums. It was unheard of but he tried it and it was a success. Later all manufacturers followed suit. Although his competitors thought he was crazy, history proved that his inventive genius was decades ahead of its time.

His biography also recalls another of his accomplishments:

A few years ago I got an idea for an off-shore oil drilling rig. There's so much oil under the ocean that I thought I'd start a business of making sea-going platforms for the oil companies who would be drilling there.

But first comes the development cost before the business can start. In our engineering department we took all we had learned about making heavy-duty equipment, and all we had learned about electric motors, gears of all kinds, and special alloys to resist salt water corrosion. We worked months checking and double-checking our figures on stresses and strains, on hurricane winds and tidal waves, finding surprisingly little information on the latter two [...].

Maybe we were way off, and maybe we weren't. We sounded out some oil companies drilling off shore and got this answer, "Go ahead and build it. If it works, come see us again." Now it was up to me to decide whether to back our project with the real thing, at a cost of $3,000,000, or drop it with a loss of a quarter of a million in paper work and models. I happened to have the three million, but I wouldn't have it long if I was wrong.

We made a deal that I believe is unique for untested equipment running into so many million dollars. The Zapata Off-Shore Company of Houston, Texas, gave us the order for the platform, later christened in New Orleans as *Scorpion*. They would test it for us under actual operating conditions. If it worked as guaranteed, we were all in business [...].

It worked [...] We saw it as the only off-shore drilling rig on the Gulf Coast to take the full brunt of 1957's Hurricane Audrey and escape undamaged. Since then we've built a dozen more, and seen them towed to as far away as Arabia and Italy, and you can say we've started a business."[40]

This was only one of his many inventions. It is said of him:

R. G. LeTourneau was largely responsible for the invention and development of many types of earthmoving machines that are in wide use today. He designed and built machines using technology that was years, and sometimes decades, ahead of his time, and became recognized worldwide as a leader in the development and manufacture of heavy equipment. The use of rubber tires in earthmoving; numerous improvements relating to scrapers; the development of low pressure heavy-duty rubber tires; the two-wheeled tractor unit (Tournapull); electric wheel drive, and mobile offshore drilling platforms, are all attributed to R. G. LeTourneau's ingenuity. During his lifetime, he held hundreds of patents on inventions relating to earthmoving equipment, manufacturing processes and machine tools. His factories supplied 70 percent of all heavy earthmoving equipment used by the Allied armed forces during World War II. LeTourneau also pioneered numerous manufacturing processes and the development of specialized machine tools.[41]

Any French Canadian who loves his country and his language and who wishes to keep his culture, cannot help but be saddened that the Huguenots were barred from New France and discouraged from settling in Quebec even after the fall of New France to the English.

Canada could also have used some of the 100,000 industrious French people who were counted in the first census of the United States in 1783 as the Huguenot refugees who made up "one third of Manhattan (New York today) inhabitants in 1701."[42] It is no secret that wherever the Huguenot refugees settled, every country profited from their integrity, their workmanship in manufacturing, in banking, in commerce, in agriculture, and in entrepreneurship. Imagine what the Huguenot refugees would've contributed if they could have settled in Quebec City and Montreal.

**Change Appearing on the Horizon**

In his classic book *History of Christianity*, the late Yale professor and historian, Kenneth Scott Latourette, put his finger on the problem in Quebec when he asserted, "In few countries did the Roman Catholic Church have so firm a hold on all phases of the lives of its members as it did on the French in Canada."[43]

Feelings of revolt were growing against the controlling Church but also against the politicians closely linked to the Church and against the large American companies exploiting the uneducated workers of Quebec. In 1949 Mgr. Charbonneau, Archbishop of Canada's largest Archdiocese and Premier Maurice Duplessis, locked horns over the Asbestos mine strike and the social issues involved around it.

While visiting a farmer one day he told me how a car came down the narrow gravel road in front of his farm at full speed, full of men. About three minutes later, before the dust had settled, another car passed at full speed chasing the strikebreakers in the first car. Another time a lady told us how the wives and ladies in favor of the strikers stuck their hatpins into the strikebreakers and the provincial police who were protecting them. Mgr. Charbonneau was from Hearst, Ontario. He had a pluralistic view of religion and also differed from some Quebec Bishops on their conservative social positions.

One day, Betty and I noticed that the famous Quebec play, *Charbonneau et Le Chef*, was showing in Quebec City. Since moving to Asbestos we had heard so much about the strike and its influence on Quebec's modern history that we wanted to see it. The authors of the play and many others believed that this was the beginning of the Quiet Revolution.

The Quiet Revolution did not begin peacefully in 1960; it was born in violence in 1949 in the small town of Asbestos, 45 miles east of Montreal. There, on the morning of February 13, one of the most tragic conflicts of our union history broke out. The asbestos strike shook Quebeckers down to the roots of their identity and made them acutely aware that everything was not as good in the best of worlds.

### Dissensions Within the Catholic Church and Within the Government

In order to bring the strike to an end in favor of his position, Duplessis thought that the shortage of food and winter clothing, plus the lack of money to pay for mortgages and car loans, would bring the strikers to their knees. Mgr. Charbonneau claimed that the Catholic Church should help the needy whether they were Catholic or not. Pressured by the needs of the people, Mgr. Charbonneau exhorted the Catholics in his huge Montreal diocese to bring food and clothing to the strikers. This angered Duplessis and split the Bishops of the Catholic Church in Quebec.

The Union Nationale Party members also vowed to not let Premier Duplessis use them as docile underpaid workers to draw the large American companies to Quebec any longer. This was because the politicians were filling their pockets with perks given to them by the American companies. The working-class indeed had reason to doubt their politicians and the American companies, as a Royal Commission later revealed in 1961. The following is a report on the Commission's conclusions by an American publication:

> In 1961 a royal commission investigating the old Union Nationale government, which had held power for almost 16 years, estimated that the total shakedown of companies doing business with the provincial government during that period ran as high as $100 million paid in the form of 'salesmen's commissions' to party politicians. A Mr. Gérald Martineau, the party treasurer, testified that he had arranged over the years for the collection and distribution to the party faithful of these business kickbacks, but insisted that 'I continued a system that was in force since 1935 and perhaps before.' In addition, the party in power sold liquor licenses for fees, which, in Montreal, ran as high as $30,000. Provincial liquor police had the right to enter and search any premises without a warning.[44]

René Lévesque, who later became Prime Minister of Quebec, also claimed that the Quiet Revolution took place in the 1960s but it didn't start there. He said:

> The modern development of Quebec began with the Quiet Revolution, of which the Liberal Party was the means of evolution. But the Party did not invent it. This Quiet Revolution was a kind of explosion that led to a rebirth in Quebec in the field of education and social life. All of that progresses as we go along.[45]

He further explained that:

> The adjective 'quiet' was used to reassure people, because no revolution is really quiet. Even in 1960, there was a revolution in the true meaning of the word, because it involved a fundamental change. It all went quickly in Quebec and it went far. Our rural and clerical society literally fell apart! Things had been simmering since the end of World War II up to the 1960s. The lids, that had retained the steam for so long, blew up.[46]

In his fiery speech, Lévesque described some of those who were behind the cause of the Quiet Revolution. He claimed:

> Only a few short years ago, there were still men who said, 'We don't want too much education because it could spoil the people.' There are still priests and bishops in our own lifetime who consider themselves, after God, to be the masters of their diocese or parish. If one were to discuss with them subjects that have nothing to do with faith or dogma, one might be excommunicated. The same situation was found in politics: certain deputies, who were slaves of their party, saw themselves as kings of the district. All this is disappearing gradually and it's all for the better.[47]

### Resisting the Priests – The end of Large Families

Another thing that brought on the Quiet Revolution was the exhortations by the clergy that their parishioners have large families. It had been a lifesaver for the early colony in New France, but it became distressing and irritating in the technological 20th century.

In the late 1600s, Colbert, an aide to Louis XIV, came up with a means to increase the population that F. X. Garneau referred to as "its tiny population of 12,000 inhabitants."[48] Colbert's plan would increase the prosperity of New France and provide protection from the Iroquois and the growing English population to the South. Therefore:

> Colbert, through Talon, told the people of New France that their prosperity, their subsistence, and all that is dear to them depend upon a general resolution never to be departed from, to marry youths at 18 or 19 years and girls of 14 or 15. Early marriage and large families were rewarded by the state, while bachelorhood was penalized; and a paternalistic king sent over shiploads of his poor or orphaned wards, the 'filles du roi,' to provide wives for veterans of the Carignan-Salières Regiment, and for the older colonists who had remained single in a land where white women were still rare. Thus the French-Canadian tradition of early marriage and large families was established, a tradition which has been one of the strongest forces in the tenacious survival and remarkable increase of this ethnic group. Large families were, of course, assets in the expanding agricultural economy of New France, though liabilities in the mother country.[49]

These plans worked out well in the fur, agricultural, fishing and lumbering eras, and at the time of the English conquest, which "might well have meant the end of French Canada as a cultural unit in North America, and of the French Canadians as an ethnic group."[50] Rather than see the French population diminish however, the French, who possessed an "indomitable will to live, witnessed in the first decade after the conquest [...] the highest birthrate ever recorded for any white people."[51]

Upon arrival in Quebec in 1954, my wife and I saw a different picture. The number of children per family had decreased. Nonetheless, a farming family near where we lived was anxiously awaiting their 20th child! Most of our first converts came from large families and one elderly lady told us that her grandmother, even though she was married, was so young that she continued to play with other children in the yard. That day had passed but the clergy were still exhorting people to have lots children in order to maintain a strong Catholic Church in Protestant North America. People, however, had begun to resist the priests and were saying it was really not the business of the priests to say how many children they should have. Furthermore, the priests were celibate and didn't have the responsibility of taking care of children or providing the necessities of life for them.

Catholic couples would ask Protestant pastors about the celibacy of the priests and Biblical teaching on marriage. I recall one fine couple in their early thirties who already had two children. The doctor told them it would be too great a risk to the wife's life to have a third pregnancy. The wife in question had a brother who was a priest. He had told them that if it were the case, then they would have to live celibate for the rest of their lives. Would this not be enough to cause great resentment in this couple! I heard people say, "The priest doesn't have even one child and he wants us to have several." People in Quebec have so rebelled that they now have one of the lowest birth rates in the Western World.

In the book *Mes Pas Sur La Plage* author Anita DeMers recalls the encounter of the parish priest with her mother in the region of Lac Mégantic:

After the birth of Réal, my mother, then 42 years old, decided she had finished having children. She said 'I had fourteen pregnancies. I have done my part for the country. It is more than enough and reasonable.' When the parish priest learned this, he came home to exhort my mother: 'You must not stop the family otherwise you will be going to hell!' In those years the Church forbade women to limit births. In a surge of anger my mother said to the priest: 'If I go to the Devil, you will go there too!' The priest, disconcerted, got up, slammed the door and never again addressed my mother.

My mother knew that she should no longer have children. My father was no longer healthy enough to support the family. Many parenting responsibilities rested on Mom's shoulders. Her multiple pregnancies, my father's tuberculosis, the death of several children, famine, poverty, moving, construction, all of that had exhausted her. Her own health became more and more fragile with the problems of high blood pressure that the doctor had just diagnosed. In a moment of discouragement, she offered to give my little brother Réal for adoption. [52]

Another thing that was discussed was the marriage of priests. A professional man, whom I know well, told me that he was training for the priesthood in the 1960s. It was an era of change in the Catholic Church, and, like many other students, he was expecting that the Church would finally give priests the right to marry. But when the Vatican II Council did not permit the marriage of priests, he and many fellow students in his class dropped out of the course.

The question of money also caused resentment. The average French Canadian had a meager salary, yet the Catholic Church insisted on having large, luxurious churches, expensive presbyteries, and extravagant ceremonies. Historian Wade wrote that after the 1880s, "A disastrous venture, in a style foreign to Quebec's tradition, and an example of the 'Folie de grandeur' which was to burden many a small community with a cathedral rather than a church,"[53] came to pass. To pay for these buildings the Catholic Church had the right by Provincial law to impose a mortgage on the houses of parishioners whether they agreed to it or not.

A man who was converted to the gospel through our church in Trois-Rivières sent his abjuration form into the Catholic Church. Following this, he went to the church office and asked to have the mortgage which the church held on his house removed since he was no longer Catholic and had abjured from the Catholic Church. This seemed like a reasonable request. The Catholic Church refused to do so. Our member went to a lawyer who told him it was a legal mortgage in favor of the Catholic Church and when he bought his house and signed the deed for his home he also signed for the mortgage that the Catholic Church held on his house. He had to pay it.

Another irritation were the luxurious cars of the priests. One day some time into the Quiet Revolution, a journalist who had attacked me in his newspaper, showed two cars on an important page. One car was a Volkswagen Beatle and the other was a luxurious American built car. Under the Volkswagen he wrote 'pastor's car,' and under the luxurious car he wrote 'priest's car.' There was no further comment.

The Catholic Church in Quebec faced moral problems among its clergy, as did English Catholic and Protestant Churches outside of Quebec. In Quebec, the majority of these moral problems were in the Catholic Church. In Quebec, it seemed everyone had an anecdote about some priest's actions, actions that we won't mention here, although many were well documented.

When French Canadians began to read the New Testament for themselves or enquired of Evangelical Christians about the celibacy of priests, they were amazed at what Jesus and the Apostles taught about the subject. The Apostle Simon Peter was married because he had a mother-in-law (Matthew 8:14-15); in fact all the apostles were married except the Apostle Paul (1 Corinthians 9:1-4). The local pastors were also married (1 Corinthians 7:1,2; 1 Timothy 3:1-4; Titus 1:5-7) and it was an exception for pastors and deacons in the New Testament not to be married (1 Corinthians 9:1-4).

Matters such as these, though they didn't relate to salvation, caused French Canadians to read the New Testament to see if there were any other contradictions between the Bible and the teachings of the Catholic Church. This led many to learn that salvation was by grace through faith and not by works.

## The Need for Change in Education

The issue which was the principal cause of the Quiet Revolution, and which brought about the biggest change, was education. Parents complained that too much time was given to religious teaching and activities at the Church and not enough to prepare the student for the 20th century workplace.

In his book "Option Quebec," René Lévesque described the situation in the first half of the 20th century in these words:

> For too long a time we have disdained education. We are short of scholars, short of administrators and of qualified technicians. We are economically the colonists whose three meals a day depend too often on the initiative of the goodwill of foreign owners or employees.[54]

A visitor to Quebec in this period between 1900 to 1960 would discover that managers, administrators, engineers, foremen, etc. were all English speaking. The French Canadians "were woodcutters and water carriers," much like the submitted nations mentioned in Joshua 9:21.

## The Need for Change in Institutions

French and English Protestants were also perturbed by the questionable actions of the Catholic Church, even in hospitals. Following is one act that should have had all of Canada up in arms. Here is the incident as it appeared in the Canadian Baptist, October 1958.

### Senator Nicol's "Conversion"

Senator Jacob Nicol, millionaire, financier, lawyer, publisher and politician, died in Sherbrooke, Que. on Sept. 23, at the age of 82.

The senator was once a small-town farm boy from Roxton Pond, Quebec. He worked his way through college and law school and became publisher of four French-language newspapers, president of three insurance companies, director of five others, and vice-president of La Banque Canadienne Nationale. He was Crown Prosecutor in Sherbrooke and Liberal party organizer for the Eastern Townships by 1906 and in 1910 he founded the Sherbrooke daily La Tribune. He was Provincial Treasurer of Quebec in 1921, was appointed to the Legislative Council and became Speaker of the Upper House in 1930. In 1944 he was named to the Senate.

Jacob Nicol was born of Baptist parents. He grew up in a Baptist home, attended Feller College (a Protestant school) and was graduated with the degree of Bachelor of Arts from McMaster University (a Baptist institution) in 1900. In 1928 McMaster conferred on him the honorary LL.D. degree.

Throughout his life Senator Nicol was a staunch Protestant and a faithful member of Sherbrooke Baptist Church.

Two months before the Senator's death he was admitted to the Roman Catholic St. Vincent de Paul Hospital. He was suffering from a broken collar bone caused by a nighttime fall in his home.

While in the hospital, the Senator's pastor, Rev. F. C. Amery of Sherbrooke Baptist Church, visited regularly every second or third day. Prayers were offered and Scripture passages were read.

At the Senator's request the Baptist pastor arranged for him to have Holy Communion on August 28. Just before the communion service the Senator stated to his Baptist pastor that, should he not recover, he desired a funeral service to be conducted by his Baptist pastor and a Protestant undertaker. Toward the end of the communion service, the Senator, being under some sedation because of continuing pain, had to be roused. He continued to be kept under increasing sedation and in an oxygen tent. Imagine the shock to his Baptist pastor when informed that the Senator had voluntarily become a Roman Catholic the next day after the communion service!

The only witnesses to the Senator's "conversion" to Roman Catholicism, if he ever made such a decision, were members of the hospital staff – all Roman Catholics. The Senator's brothers and sisters and his nephew were as surprised and shocked as the Baptist pastor at the news that the Senator was reputed to have become a Roman Catholic. They were told nothing could be done, presumably because of the Senator's being now under heavy sedation and in a critical condition, until he recovered and was able to renounce his "conversion" to Roman Catholicism.

The Senator, who had lived his whole life as a staunch Protestant and as a faithful Baptist, was buried from the Roman Catholic St. Michel's Cathedral in Sherbrooke.

The Baptist pastor comforted the Senator's broken-hearted brothers and sisters and their families. The Senator had no children. His wife, the former Émilie Couture, who survives him, has been a patient in a Roman Catholic institution for the past five years.

If the Baptists of Sherbrooke were surprised and shocked at the Senator's reputed "conversion," it might be well to note, to the credit of a great many Roman Catholic lay people, that they were incensed concerning the whole affair. They felt it did not reflect well upon their church or its clergy.

The man who was sent to remove the Senator's grave stone from the Protestant cemetery to place it in the Roman Catholic cemetery said, "This ought never to be, the Senator was a Protestant all his life and he died a Protestant."

Our sympathy is extended to the Senator's family and to his friends in the Baptist church at Sherbrooke and the Baptist schools in which he had a life-long interest. We have nothing to say concerning the Roman Catholics of St. Vincent de Paul Hospital, except that it is not likely that they would have been so zealous to convert a dying Protestant, who was under heavy sedation, right after he had received communion from his own pastor, had he not been a man of such great prominence and such great wealth.[55]

The City of Sherbrooke, as well as the Nicol family and the Baptist Church, were shocked and heartbroken. But that day the Catholic Church lost its respectability in the minds of many of the citizens of Sherbrooke, both Catholic and Protestant. There had to be a change in Quebec and the day was very close.

At that time, the Catholic Church controlled most Quebec hospitals. Once our people became believers they were fearful to use these hospitals. They were afraid they would not be treated fairly because of their faith.

### The Quiet Revolution Arrives

"The decade of the 1960s was marked by a momentous event that changed 300 years of Catholic exclusivity and control of French Canadians in Quebec."[56]

Gregory Baum, Catholic theologian and university professor, summarized the Quiet Revolution in these words, "The Quiet Revolution produced an explosion in Quebec Society leading to rapid secularization. How and why did this take place?"[57]

Premier Duplessis died suddenly while on government business in Schefferville, a small village in Northern Quebec touching the Newfoundland-Labrador border. This is close to the famous Churchill Falls. Ironically this was in the District of Duplessis, which was named after him. His death, however, didn't create the Quiet Revolution; rather, it opened the door to it. Duplessis didn't create a society of Catholic exclusivity, which had already existed for over 300 years, but he did try to retain it.

The following is an explanation of what it meant to live under the Duplessis government and to be forced to obey the Catholic Church:

Premier Duplessis opposed the formation of unions. He rejected government involvement in public services, especially hydroelectric power. Because he vehemently opposed social change, he became the defender of the predominant Catholic ideology and repressed religious and secular minorities that threatened to undermine its spiritual sway. The convergence of these different trends gave the Catholic Church a power and a presence with few historical parallels in a largely industrialized society. With funds made available by the government, the church was responsible for the educational system from primary school to university, for hospitals and other health services and for assistance to the poor and destitute. Though church and state were legally separate, in actual fact the church was deeply involved in promoting and ordering social life and exercised considerable influence on government decisions, not least by being the principal source of the public ideology. In the mid-20th century this was an astonishing situation.[58]

**The Quiet Revolution Brings Freedom**

The following is the story of a poor lady with an alcoholic husband. Her children were poorly clothed and their house was still covered outside with black tar paper. I met her one day while I was doing door-to-door visitation. Sometime later I saw her in her front yard so I stopped and spoke to her about the gospel, because she was very concerned about her salvation.

I quoted a verse to her and it so touched her that she asked me to show it to her in the Bible. The lady then told me of her predicament. Since her husband was an alcoholic and squandered all their money, she was dependant on the government for social benefits. Since that wasn't enough to live on, she had to rely on the Saint Vincent de Paul Society and the Knights of Columbus for food and clothing. "These are both Catholic organizations," she said and "if I leave the Catholic Church these sources of help will likely be cut off. I cannot see my children suffer any more than they suffer now."

Our hands were also tied because her husband didn't want to have anything to do with us.

On a visit back to a previous pastorate I asked the current pastor if it would be fitting for me to visit a man whom I knew well. His entire family except him had come to the Lord since I had left town. As I drove over to his new address, I realized they didn't live too far from the unfortunate lady mentioned above. When I got to their home I was anxious about the poor lady who lived only about half a mile from them. I thought maybe they could help. I asked them if they were aware of this person. To my great surprise the mother in the house said, "Mr. Keefe, do not worry about her. Every Thursday she comes to my house for Bible study and prayer. She is saved now." How happy I was to know that she had been freed not only from earthly enemies but from spiritual enemies as well. She was now safe in the arms of Jesus and now the children had a Christian mother.

The man I had come to see, however, was not at home but his neighbor was still working on the barn while he was away getting supplies. I began to chat with this man and the Lord opened a door to share the gospel with him. The man I wanted to see was still not back so the neighbor decided to go home.

His home was next door and when he went in he said to his wife, "There was a friend of the Ringuettes here and he talked to me about the Bible. After what I heard I must get my Bible out, the one that I had in college and read it." His wife said, "I saw the man and I know who he is. He used to be the pastor here and he often visited my parents to talk to them about the gospel."

The next time I saw this couple was at the funeral of a Mr. Cotnoir. They came over and asked me, "Do you remember us?" I wasn't sure. Then she said, "You used to come to our farm to speak to my parents about the gospel. I was six years old but your visits made me think of God and I never forgot about it. Since you talked to my husband we have both trusted in Jesus Christ and are saved."

I said, "That's wonderful, and what about your parents?" She replied, "They both accepted the Lord some time later and my dad was persecuted for his witness. Towards the end of his life his family tried to force him to return to the Catholic Church but his faith in Jesus never wavered despite the effort to make him change."

### From Middle-Ages to the 20<sup>th</sup> Century

After the death of Premier Maurice Duplessis the Union National Party had to choose a new leader. Even before Premier Duplessis' death there had been dissention in his party. Paul Sauvé, who was popular with the people, was also the one cabinet member who stood up to Duplessis. He was already working for change and was known by the word "Désormais," (from now on), because he wanted to bring about change. Political slogans such as: 'It is time that things change,' 'now or never,' and 'Equality or Independence' were the order of the day. The people of Quebec believed Paul

Sauvé was the man to bring about this change so he was chosen to replace Maurice Duplessis. To the chagrin of Quebec's population, Paul Sauvé died after only three months in office. He was replaced by a compromise candidate, Antonio Barrette, a long time minister in the Duplessis government and a yes-man to Duplessis. He was considered incompetent and unpopular.

In the 1960 election Jean Lesage, a brilliant lawyer with political instincts, [59] opposed him. His theme for the election was "Maître Chez Nous" (Master in our own house). As well as being a good politician himself, he also had an excellent team, which included the then journalist René Lévesque, jurist Paul Gérin-Lajoie, and former liberal leader, Georges-Émile Lapalme. [60] René Lévesque ran in Laurier riding where the Union National Party threatened people who were openly in favor of Lévesque. On election night they stole many of the ballot boxes where they knew that polling station was voting in favor of Lévesque. Lévesque still won by a landslide!

On election night in 1960, Evangelical Christians were fastened to their televisions or radios to see the outcome, just as they were later during the kidnapping of Pierre Laporte and James Cross. They wondered and prayed that the la Grande Noirceur (The Dark Ages) of Duplessis would come to an end. The votes were being counted and the Liberals were ahead. René Lévesque was on the way to a landslide victory in the Laurier riding.

That memorable night, "after 18 years of quasi-tyrannical rule, Duplessis' Union Nationale Party fell, and Jean Lesage's Liberals swept to power. In one night the province moved from a Catholic religious society, in many ways a holdover from the Middle-Ages, to a modern society. Institutional and social changes took place rapidly once a secular government was in place. Catholicism was now in a minority position in Quebec. The Roman Catholic Church suffered an enormous loss in membership."[61]

René Lévesque victoriously exclaimed that the modern development of Quebec began with the Quiet Revolution. He describes it as "a kind of explosion that can lead to a renaissance of Quebec from the point of view of education, from the social point of view":[62]

## Educational Change

While different aspects of Quebec life were changed, historical writers and modern observers are in agreement that the educational system underwent the biggest upheaval. The system of education was so out of line with the 20th century that it had limited French Canadians to the positions of ordinary workmen, while most of the management, engineers, and even foremen were English-speakers.

A personal anecdote touching this question was when an Englishman from the local mine drove his Cadillac into our driveway, knocked on our door and asked Betty, my wife, if she would accept the position of bilingual secretary at the local mine office. Betty declined because the children were still small and she was needed in the Lord's work. Today in a similar situation there would be many French Canadian bilingual secretaries available.

The Lesage government put education high on its agenda. Paul Gérin-Lajoie wrote a book entitled "*Pourquoi le Bill 60*"? (Why Bill 60?).

They passed Bill 60, which laid out the new approach to education and why a change was needed. The "Collège Classique" (College of Classical Education) was the cornerstone of education where residents, that is to say boarders, spent most of their adolescent life firmly supervised by priests.[63]

Usually the upperclass of a society are free thinkers, but not in Quebec. That didn't happen until the 1960s and 70s.

The state was then taking over social matters and education passed from the church into the hands of the laity.

Léon Dion wrote in the preface of the book, "Pourquoi le Bill 60", the following:

In the ordinary exercise of his ministerial duties, Mr. Paul Gérin-Lajoie, the current Minister of Youth, has undertaken a tour of information and, let's say, education, in order to explain to the public the content of Bill 60, which provides, among other things, for the establishment of a Ministry of Education and Youth and a Higher Council for Education.[64]

Bill 60 as explained, set aside the Church's control over education. It didn't attack the Catholic Church; it simply put it aside and replaced it with a Ministry of Education and a Superior Council of Education. Gérin-Lajoie insisted upon a democratic school system. Such a system voted by the people was a message to the Catholic Church that her days of controlling Quebec's education were over.

He pointed out some of the errors of the past, such as building the education system upon a negative foundation rather than a positive, aggressive foundation:

We were French and Catholic: we had to avoid any intrusion of an English and Protestant power. At first, the survival was ensured by illiteracy, or rather the refusal to enter schools we had reason to fear.[65]

He then described the present Quebec of the Quiet Revolution, a Quebec that had survived and one that was ready to move forward. In his own powerful, uncanny way, he rallied the Province to a new future. He reminded Quebeckers of their exploits and exhorted them to move forward:

A hundred years later, French Canadians have survived and the world is aware of this feat. It is no longer foreigners who threaten this survival: it can only be our own failings. Dynamism, flexibility, imagination are today the main factors

of our survival. We have 'survived' enough. The time has come
to give a positive meaning to this survival, to fix a goal for it, to
justify it. In 1963, the nation is ready to give back a hundredfold
what it has received.[66]

He describes the way they were going to do it:

The French Canadians will demonstrate what they are: a fearful
people, or a democratic nation, capable of assuring freedom of
thought, capable of taking charge of their own destinies. By
setting up a school system, a society defines itself. In creating
a modern school system, French Canadians will show what
they are worth.[67]

The new school system was the cornerstone of the Quiet
Revolution, but other areas were touched as well. Jean-Marie Lebel
and Alain Roy stated:

The Quiet Revolution leads to a profound and necessary
transformation of the political and administrative apparatus of
the government of Quebec.

The Quiet Revolution entails a significant national and social
boom. Students, civil servants and state employees, as well
as various political and social groups come to Quebec to
proclaim their demands or protest against government decisions,
marching on Grande Allée and other arteries, and even before
the Hotel of the Government. [68]

They admitted, however, that, "It is the educational system that
is experiencing the most profound upheavals."[69]

This new approach in Quebec encouraged us to have pastors and churches who were filled with the Holy Spirit but who also knew their Bible and the world around them. This way it could be said of them what was said about Stephen, "… they could not stand up against his wisdom or the Spirit by which he spoke." (Acts 6:10).

## Casualties of the Quiet Revolution

Another piece of literature also contributed to the Quiet Revolution. It preceded the book *Pourquoi le Bill 60.* It began with a series of letters to *Le Devoir* newspaper under the pen name of Frère Untel (Brother So and So), a teaching brother who taught in a Catholic College. It criticized the present school system and it's teaching. In 1960, the book *Les Insolences de Frère Untel* (The Arrogances of Brother So and So) was published. It stirred up a lot of discussion in Quebec and became a bestseller. The copy in my library is from the seventeenth edition and was far from being the last print run.

Journalist Louise Coté concluded that Frère Untel, whose name was Brother Pierre-Jérôme, "had crystallized in 150 pages filled with humor and impatience all the weariness of a people suppressed by a paternalism filled with the smell of fat cigars and convent parlors."[70]

There was another person behind Frère Untel. Louis Grégoire was a Director of the Collège Classique at Alma. J. Claude Paquet revealed that he was more closely connected than one generally thought to the "Arrogance Affair".[71]

Who was Louis Grégoire? He had been a Director of many schools besides being Director at the Classical College at Alma at the time of the writings of Frère Untel. He followed the usual path for Teaching Brothers at that time in Quebec, "Entering the Marists at the age of 14, Grégoire admits, not without a smile, that he underwent, like all others, a period of regimentation under pressure."[72] But Louis Grégoire had passed many of his peers academically, according to his record he was the first philosophy graduate of his community. [73]

Following the publication of that book (*Les insolences de Frère Untel*) these two men were sent into exile. Frère Untel (Pierre-Jérôme) was treated lightly. In exile, he spent time in Rome with the Jesuits, and then he went to the University of Fribourg in Switzerland where he would've liked to complete a Doctorate in Philosophy. He was called home to Quebec before he could finish his studies, though. He was very popular, especially with intellectuals, but also with the population in general because his letters-to-the-editor and writing the bestselling book of its time. It was even difficult for the Catholic Church to punish him openly. Furthermore, by 1963 the Quiet Revolution was in full swing.

On the other hand, the unknown partner in the book, Frère Grégoire, was the object of the wrath of the Catholic Church. He was exiled by order of the "Sacrée Congrégation des Religieux"[74] to Rome where he was scolded mercilessly. He was exiled to the United States without permission to pass by Canada.

### The Quiet Revolution Growls

The events of 1970 that frightened Quebec and shook Canada were not an afterthought of the Quiet Revolution. The death of Duplessis in 1959, the fall of the Union National Party, and the decline in the power of the Catholic Church allowed Jean Lesage's Liberal government to carry out the "rapid political modernization of Quebec Society."[75] Quebeckers began to feel that they were freed from the domination of an exclusive religion.

Dr. W. S. Whitcombe pointed out in a 1971 article, "The Power and Rule of the Catholic Church," that a

highly respected French-Canadian Senator made a speech in the Upper House, in which he dared to utter some passing criticisms of the teaching of history in the French and Roman

Catholic schools of his native province. Within a day he learned, through the newspapers, of his summary dismissal from the honored position of Chairman of Hydro-Québec! The Cardinal-Archbishop had telephoned the Prime Minister of Quebec and ordered that the recalcitrant Senator be removed from office at one![76]

It's shocking what the Church could do to a high profile and esteemed person before the Quiet Revolution.

The failure of the Church is well explained by Gregory Baum:

In the 1840s, thanks to a new, ultramontane Catholicism – aggressive, disciplined and other-worldly, promoted by a large number of priests and religious adherents arriving from France – the Catholic Church was able to affirm itself as the spiritual and cultured force that defined, with ever-increasing intensity, the social reality of French Canada. This Catholicism was the religious cement that enabled French Canadians to resist assimilation and decline.[77]

However, the cement of the church crumbled. There was no one to protect Quebec from English Canada. Other countries were finding freedom by decolonization so that seemed to be the way to go. Separatist parties appeared on the horizon, such as "L'Alliance Laurentienne" in 1957. Then there was "Le Rassemblement pour l'indépendance nationale" (RIN) founded by Marcel Chaput in 1962, and later led by Pierre Bourgault. Bourgault, a writer and journalist, argued from his point of view of the present state of French Canadians in Canada that the hope for their future lied in separation from Canada and having their own nation.

Another party, which was notable in its day, was the "Le Rassemblement National" (RN) founded in 1965. It briefly had a member of parliament, Gilles Grégoire, elected to the House of Commons.[78]

Then,

> The Parti Québécois (PQ) had the merit, in 1968, of realizing the unification of the preceding forces and, by a mix of compromise and moderation, to give the independence movement a character of plausibility and respectability in the more hesitant middle classes.. The PQ also had an eminently popular leader, the former journalist and minister René Lévesque, who was to become premier of Quebec after the elections of November 15, 1976.[79]

René Lévesque declared, "I do not want to break but radically transform our reunion with Canada."[80] Though Lévesque seems to want to have a less radical approach to separation, his plans do not carry this out.

All these separatist parties wanted to settle the problem of separation by democratic means. But besides these groups there was also a very dangerous party with ties to International Marxists, "Le Front de Libération du Québec" (The FLQ). It was responsible for a series of violent attacks:

> The Front de Libération du Québec (Quebec Liberation Front), commonly known as the FLQ, was a nationalist and Marxist revolutionary group in Quebec, Canada with at least two terrorist cells. It was responsible for more than 200 bombings, including the bombing of the Montreal Stock Exchange in 1969 and the deaths of at least five people. These attacks culminated in 1970 with what is known as the October Crisis, in which British Trade

Commissioner James Cross was kidnapped and Quebec Labour Minister Pierre Laporte was murdered.[81]

I recall watching the news on the 17th of October 1970, when Mr. Laporte was assassinated by the Chénier cell of the FLQ. I was with a family from the church that night. We were startled and frightened to see a picture of Pierre Laporte's crumpled body left in the trunk of a car at the Canadian Military Airfield. What would happen next?

Fear set in. The sight of armed soldiers everywhere caused people to stay home at night. Missionaries at that time were also worried about what would come out of this. Would they still have an opening for the work of the gospel? No one knew. We wondered if the Evangelical churches would have to go underground.

Fear wasn't limited to ordinary citizens. Three of Quebec's most fearless politicians, Pierre Elliott Trudeau, Gérald Pelletier, and Jean Marchand, were also shaken.

Prime Minister Pierre Trudeau called out the army and applied the War Measures Act. It was the only peacetime usage of these measures in Canada's history.

Gérard Pelletier, secretary of State, recounted his feelings in a book he wrote after these events:

One of the most acute fears I experienced during this period of the crisis was that a group of extremist students, believing that the big night had arrived, would go down the street and cause disorders which, police and the army on their teeth, could have ended in shooting.[82]

Marchand shared his fears openly, even in Parliament:

In the midst of a harangue in the afternoon of the proclamation
of the War Measures Act, the Minister of Regional Economic
Expansion deeply impressed the Commons, the Anglophone
press and the Canadians by declaring that the FLQ possessed,
in his opinion, enough dynamite (2,000 pounds) to blow up the
heart of the city of Montreal. It is not known if it is regrettable,
as the broadcasting of debates did not exist in the House
of Commons at that time, that the recording of this historic
document could not be retained. Mr. Marchand estimated the
FLQ's membership at about 3,000 members, their arsenal at
2,000 pounds of explosives, not to mention the rifles and stolen
ammunition, their communication dishes and sympathizers
planted here and there. People are scared; they do not want to
go out, "he says. 'I am not the only one to be afraid because
I am no better than the others, nor more brave, but let us ask
all the members from Quebec, blue and red! And if there were
New Democrat MPs in Quebec, they would be in the same
position, 'he adds.[83]

Quebec and Canada were relieved when four key members of
the FLQ, le Chénier cell of Paul and Jacques Rose, Francis Simard,
and Bernard Lortie were captured in their hideout on a farm near St.
Luc, a small village southeast of Montreal. They had underground
caves and tunnels where they'd hid.

In the fall of 1970, Canada was shaken by what has become
known as "the October crisis." In the November 1970 edition of
The Evangelical Baptist, Leslie Tarr wrote a timely editorial, "Most
of us doubtless assumed that bombs, bullets, blackmail and blood
were part and parcel of life in faraway places."[84] In view of the
crisis in Quebec he warned readers not to have attitudes that were
unbecoming of Christians, but rather to see through the events to
"the need to reach all phases of our country's life with the gospel."[85]

### The Preparation for a Revival

With the Quiet Revolution, authoritarian political and religious control began to disintegrate. It opened the door to new freedoms, but it also left a spiritual void.

William Phillips reminds us some other aspects of the 1960s and 70s:

Québécois youth were challenging their Church and losing faith in established religion. Cults were rampant and hippies were everywhere. Drugs, sexual freedom, student revolts, and anticlericalism abounded. The Church's influence on youth was further diminished when the school system fell into the hands of the laity and became largely secularized. The middle generation was enjoying the 'good life' and with higher incomes, turned to materialism. The strong family ties of the past began to crumble and the institution of the family was threatened.[86]

However, God used this period to bring about a time of spiritual revival that is still evident today. The work of the pioneers of the gospel in Quebec prepared French Canada for a period of unprecedented growth that was about to begin in the 1970s. The Quiet Revolution brought something great, but now it would be God's turn to do something great. This is the theme of a second volume intended to follow this one.

(Endnotes)
1   Gregory Baum, *The Church in Quebec*, (Ottawa: Novalis, St. Paul's University, 1992), p. 20.
2   Gregory Baum, *The Church in Quebec*, p. 20.
3   Mason Wade, *The French Canadians 1760 – 1945* (Toronto: MacMillan, 1950), p. 15.

4   Robert Larin, *Brève Histoire des protestants en Nouvelle-France et au Québec (XVIe – XIXe siècle)*, Éditions de la paix, Saint-Alphonse-de Granby, Québec, 1998, p. 49.

5   Hélène Poulin, *La Chrétienne*, Vol. 24, nov. à déc. 1975.

6   R.P. Duclos, *Histoire du Protestantisme français au Canada et aux États-Unis*, Vol. 1, Librairie Évangélique, 68, rue Sainte-Catherine, Montréal, 1913, p. 15.

7   Robert Larin, *Brève Histoire des Protestants*, pp. 70-71.

8   Robert Larin, *Brève Histoire des Protestants*, pp. 70-71.

9   Mason Wade, *The French Canadians*, p. 3.

10  Marcel Trudel, *Histoire de la Nouvelle France*, II, Le Comptoir, 1604-1627, Montréal, Fides, 1971, p. 68.

11  François-Xavier Garneau, *Histoire du Canada Français*, Vol. 1, Montréal, François Beaver, Editor, p.92.

12  Jean Liebel, *Jean-Pierre Dugua, sieur de Mons fondateur de l'Acadie et du Québec*, Bordeau, Reprographié par les services techniques de l'Université de Bordeau III 988, p. 297

13  Marcel Trudel, *Histoire de la Nouvelle France*, p. 452.

14  Robert Wilson, *The New Dictionary of the Christian Church*, Editor: J.D. Douglas, Zondervan Publishing House, p. 828.

15  Jean-Louis Lalonde, *Des loups dans la bergerie, Les Protestants de la langue française au Québec, 1534-2000,* Fides, Montréal, 2002, p. 27.

16  Thomas Guthrie Marquis, *The Jesuit Missions*, 1915, p. 10.

17  Thomas Guthrie Marquis, *The Jesuit Missions*, p. 11.

18  Mr. Gizot and Madame Guizot de Witt, *History of France, World's Best Histories in 8 vol.*, Vol. 3, translated by Robert Black, New York and London, 1869, The Cooperative Publication Society, p. 467.

19  Mr. Gizot and Madame Guizot de Witt, *History of France*, p. 467.

20  Thomas Guthrie Marquis, *The Jesuit Missions*, p. 29.

21  Thomas Guthrie Marquis, *The Jesuit Missions*, p. 48.

22  Mason Wade, *The French Canadians*, p. 6.

23  Mason Wade, *The French Canadians*, p. 15.

24  Mason Wade, *The French Canadians*, pp. 20-21.

25  Mason Wade, *The French Canadians*, p. 15.

26  Michel Gaudette, *Guerres de religion d'ici : catholicisme et protestantisme face à l'histoire,* Trois-Rivières,: Éditions Souffle de vent, 2001, p. 11.

27  Robert Larin, *Brève Histoire des Protestants*, p. 81.

28  Robert Larin, *Brève Histoire des Protestants*, p. 81.

29  Robert Larin, *Brève Histoire des Protestants*, p. 106.30        Michel Gaudette, *Guerres de religion d'ici*, pp. 44-45.

31  R.P. Duclos, Histoire du Protestantisme au Canada, Vol. 1 p. 49.

32  Lacour-Goyet, Histoire du Canada, (Librairie Fayard, 1966), p. 221.

33  Mason Wade, *The French Canadians*, p. 50.

34  Richard Lougheed, Glenn Smith, Wesley Peach, *Histoire du Protestantisme au Québec*, La Clairière, Québec, 1999, p. 160.

35  Jean-Louis Lalonde, *Des loups dans la bergerie*, p. 160.

36  Jean-Louis Lalonde, *Des loups dans la bergerie*, p. 160.

37  Michel Gaudette, *Guerres de religion d'ici*, p. 64.

38  R.G. Letourneau, *Mover of Men and Mountains, The Autobiography of R.G. Letourneau*, (Chicago: Moody Press Edition, 1972). Quotation from the book cover.

39  R.G. Letourneau, *Mover of Men and Mountains*, p. 4, 5.

40  R.G. Letourneau, *Mover of Men and Mountains*, p.120-121.

41  http://www.letourneau-inc.com/about/RG_bio.htm (May 11, 2006)

42  Robert Larin, *Brève Histoire des Protestants ...*, p. 81.

43　Kenneth Scott Latourette, A History of Christianity, p. 1281.
44　Brian Moore and Editors of Life (The World Library of Time Incorporated, A Stonehenge Book, New York, Vol. 6. page 2).
45　Rémi Maillard. René Lévesque mot à mot : citations (colligées par Rémi Maillard), Montréal : Stanké, 1997, p. 301.
46　Rémi Maillard. René Lévesque mot à mot : citations, p. 302.
47　Rémi Maillard. René Lévesque mot à mot : citations, p. 24.
48　F.X. Garneau, Histoire du Canada, p. 102.
49　Mason Wade, The French Canadians, p. 18.
50　Mason Wade, The French Canadians, p. 47.
51　Mason Wade, The French Canadians, p. 47.
52　Anita DeMers, Mes pas sur la plage, Mon histoire, p. 34
53　Mason Wade, The French Canadians, picture facing p. 288.
54　René Lévesque, Option Québec, Édition du jour, Montréal (1968), pp. 23, 24.
55　The Conversion of Senator Nicol, in The Canadian Baptist, October 15, 1958, p. 3
56　Gregory Baum, The Church in Quebec, (Ottawa: Novalis, St. Paul's University), 1992, p. 35.
57　Gregory Baum, The Church in Quebec, p. 35.
58　Gregory Baum, The Church in Quebec, p. 18.
59　Le Mémorial du Québec, Tome VIII, 1966-1976, Montréal, Éd. du Mémorial, 1979, p.145.
60　Jean-Marie Lebel & Alain Roy, Québec 1900-2000, p. 86.
61　Wm. Phillips, Modern Miracles, p. 21.
62　Rémi Maillard. René Lévesque mot à mot : citations,, p. 301.
63　René Durocher, Paul-André Linteau, Jean-Claude Robert et Francis Ricard, Histoire du Québec Contemporain, Vol. 2. Le Québec du 1930, (Les Éditions du Boréal Express Montréal 1986), p. 279.
64　Paul Gérin-Lajoie, Pourquoi le Bill 60, (Les Éditions du Jour), Montréal, 1963, p. 7.
65　Paul Gérin-Lajoie, Pourquoi le Bill 60, p. 22.
66　Paul Gérin-Lajoie, Pourquoi le Bill 60, pp. 22-23.
67　Paul Gérin-Lajoie, Pourquoi le Bill 60, p.23.
68　Jean-Marie Lebel & Alain Roy, Québec 1900-2000, p. ?
69　Jean-Marie Lebel & Alain Roy, Québec 1900-2000, p. ?
70　Louise Côté, Le Magazine Macleans, mai, 1963, p. 31.
71　J. Claude Paquet, Le Magazine Macleans, mai, 1963, p. 30.
72　J. Claude Paquet, Le Magazine Macleans, mai, 1963, p. 30.
73　J. Claude Paquet, Le Magazine Macleans, mai, 1963, p. 30.
74　J. Claude Paquet, Le Magazine Macleans, mai, 1963, p. 31.
75　Gregory Baum, The Church in Quebec, p.16.
76　Dr. W. S. Whitcombe, Evangelical Baptist Magazine, 1971, Editorial. p. 2.
77　Gregory Baum, The Church in Quebec, p. ?
78　Germain Dion, Une Tornade de 60 jours, p. ?
79　Germain Dion, Une Tornade de 60 jours, p. ?
80　Germain Dion, Une Tornade de 60 jours, p. 18.
81　http://en.wikipedia.org/wiki/Front_de_libération_du_Québec, July 28th 2009,
82　Germain Dion, Une Tornade de 60 jours, p. ?
83　Germain Dion, Une Tornade de 60 jours, p. ?
84　Leslie Tarr, The Evangelical Baptist, October 1970, p.3.
85　Leslie Tarr, The Evangelical Baptist, October 1970, p.3.
86　Wm. L. Phillips, Modern Day Missionary Miracles, p.33.

# CONCLUSION

This brings us to the end of this book. We, as a family, came to Québec in 1954 to help with a Canadian Sunday School Mission Camp while waiting to meet with a Mission Board concerning our planned service in Africa. During that summer and fall God showed us a people who had been deprived of the Bible and the gospel for three hundred years. We came to realize that on the day in the college chapel in London Ontario, when Ernest Tétreault made a call for workers for the Canadian Sunday School Mission summer camp, God's Macedonian call was to us. It was not to minister to the English minority but rather to respond to the French majority and their spiritual need. You have read what happened from the time I was put in prison until the quiet revolution in the 1960's.

Our baby, Ernest, had his first birthday in Quebec. When we were in Trois-Rivières, he was old enough to sing a duet with his mother on our radio broadcast. Brian, our second son, is three years younger than Ernie. At ten years of age, he was our mechanic. When I was away on deputation, the electric floor polisher stopped. Brian pled with his mother to let him fix it. Finally he told her that he would put all the pieces on the table so nothing would be lost and he would likely find the problem. With this assurance, she let him work on it. Before I got back home, he had the polisher working like new. He always had that gift, and later became Boeing's representative for the Maritimes. Paul was our peacemaker. He was the baby of the family at that time. He was blessed with a good disposition and sometimes mothers would call Betty and ask her to send Paul over because, they said, "When he's here, there is no squabble among the kids." Betty was the most precious gift God gave me this side of heaven. Besides that, she played the organ and accordion, and as for the piano, as far as I'm concerned, nobody played it like Betty. She played for a male quartet when she was only fourteen years old. That was our family to date. Jeff had not yet arrived on the scene. He was born thirteen years after Paul. He was a fireball, an active boy. Before going to bed, his mother would stop at his room, and often out of the dark a little voice would call, "Hi, Mom!" He wasn't sleeping yet! As a family we were living together through these great times of change in Quebec.

The first thirty years of our time in Quebec were difficult, facing resistance and opposition and sometimes working so hard for so little fruit. But the call of God who had saved us pushed us on to reach others. There is no greater sadness than to see people live and die without ever hearing the gospel. This was our motivation. Every day, as we gave out the gospel, we wished that others would be saved that day. As we went out, we relied upon the promise of God to Paul in Acts 18:9-10: "Do not be afraid; keep on speaking, do not be silent. For I am with you, and no one is going to attack and harm you, because I have many people in this city." That was what kept us going. I knew that God could save people, even if they were few and far between. And the harder we worked, the more we rejoiced when we found a lost sheep.

When we went to Asbestos, there was only one French-Canadian believer in town. God kept the promise I had taken from Acts 18:9-10 and a few years later we had a thriving church. We rejoiced as we looked at those who had come to Christ at the price of persecution and rejection.

There was great love between the French Canadians and us. They loved us for bringing them the gospel; we loved them for making our work worthwhile because they accepted the free gift of God's Son, and they fearlessly witnessed to other people. French Canadians began to answer the call to full-time service too. And then we think of the baptisms of new believers. There were hugs and tears and joy and usually a good big lunch together afterward.

We thank God for the team of missionaries that was steadily growing. We had our times of getting together. Sometimes when seeing a whole line of Volkswagen Beetles at a pastor's home or at a church, we knew that pastors were there. We were sharing our blessings and our tears, sharing new ways of evangelism, and blessing God for the breakthroughs. We were praying for things that we almost didn't think possible, without realizing that God had a big surprise for us.

We didn't know at that time how God was going to break through in Quebec after those pioneer years. But, it would become one of Canada's greatest revivals, and it would be in French! We were privileged to witness that great era of change. Thirty years before, it was total darkness. As the prophecy of Isaiah was fulfilled in Galilee in Jesus' day (Matthew 4:15-16), we can say that the people living in darkness have also seen a great light in our day. From every corner of Quebec, the light of revival has shone through.

After reading about the first thirty years, we hope you'll be with us for the second volume, to see how God brought that revival to French Canada. You will read of things that we never thought would come to pass, and rejoice, drawing praise out of your heart to his glory.

### Those who have left us

Some of God's team who were pioneers and who have gone to be with the Lord:

Élisée Beau
Tom and Margaret Carson
Jean Flahaut
William and Betty Frey
Yvon and Marion Hurtubise
Betty Keefe
Bill Phillips
Wilfred and Edna Wellington

# APPENDIX A

## Remembering Ernest Keefe

### *1929-2011*

Ernest Keefe was looking for a great career with the National Hockey League. During a match, he was seriously injured, to the point that he began to think about his relationship with God, and he made the decision that changed his life forever—the decision to follow Christ. After his convalescence, he continued to have great success in hockey, but God called him to be somebody greater.

Ernie became one of the pioneers of the Gospel in Quebec, in the most challenging days of persecution in that province. He was arrested for having distributed Bibles in Asbestos-Danville, but he persevered and started a church in that town. Ernest went on to pastor in Trois-Rivières, Montreal and several other regions in Quebec.

There are so many ways in which Ernest Keefe served his God. The directors and students of SEMBEQ are grateful towards God for all the gifts of Mr. Keefe. He was a pastor, an evangelist, a church planter and a key player in church transition in Quebec. He was a teacher, a writer and a theologian. The churches of Quebec will miss Ernest, but they are grateful for his many contributions and the heritage left to the churches of his well-beloved province.

Thrive: The EB Online Magazine, Summer 2011

# APPENDIX B

The Viewpoint of a Fellow Christian, Referee, Student, Colleague
and History Teacher

---

**Repêché pour la mission
plutôt que pour la Ligue nationale de hockey**

«Je cours (patine) vers le but pour remporter le prix...»
(Philippiens 3.14)

Qui de mieux qu'un arbitre au hockey pour présenter un joueur de
hockey? Qui de mieux qu'un chrétien pour en admirer un autre?
Qui de mieux qu'un élève pour apprécier son professeur? Qui de
mieux qu'un collègue pour en émuler un autre? Qui de mieux qu'un
professeur d'histoire pour raconter l'autre? Un des buts de l'histoire
de l'Église est de «passer» l'inspiration d'une génération à l'autre.
Car, au-delà de l'œuvre, il y a le modèle; son efficacité peut durer
tant et aussi longtemps qu'on le rappellera. Or, la génération actuelle
a besoin de se souvenir de ces noms qui, à coups de sacrifices, de
persécutions et de passions engagées, ont permis que l'Évangile
s'installe solidement dans le paysage québécois. M. Ernest Keefe
est définitivement un de ces «bâtisseurs».

La perspective d'un arbitre de hockey, chrétien de surcroît,
est qu'il vaut vraiment mieux jouer pour le Seigneur que pour les
Rangers. Ernest Keefe aspirait à une carrière dans la Ligue nationale
de hockey. Athlète polyvalent, il excellait tant au baseball junior
qu'au hockey, comme joueur avant et gardien de but. Vedette de
l'équipe des Porcupines Combines de Timmins du hockey junior

majeur de l'Ontario, M. Keefe subit une grave blessure à la tête lors d'un match. Déjà, sa mère lui avait dit «si tu mets quelque chose avant le Seigneur, il va te l'enlever». C'est alors qu'il prit une décision qui transforma sa vie. Alors qu'il était si près de son but, ayant signé une entente avec les Rangers de New York, Dieu l'appela à quelque chose de plus grand encore. Ernie Keefe devint l'un des pionniers de l'Évangile au Québec, à une époque difficile.

La perspective d'un chrétien est qu'il vaut mieux être sauvé que... repêché. C'est au cours de sa carrière de hockey que M. Keefe fut touché par le Seigneur. Le livre de Paul aux Romains, principalement les versets 3.23 et 5.8, pénétra son cœur l'année même où il se blessa, en décembre 1948. Dès lors, son intérêt pour la mission grandit tandis que son désir d'être repêché s'estompa. En effet, c'est le Seigneur qui le repêcha pour une carrière infiniment plus glorieuse : devenir pêcheur d'hommes. M. Keefe commença ses études au London Bible Institute en 1950. Au début, il croyait devenir missionnaire en Afrique. En effet, le premier livre chrétien qu'il lut parlait du courage des missionnaires en Chine lorsque le pays bascula dans le communisme . Mais lorsqu'Ernest Tétreault (mon pasteur dans les années '70) présenta les opportunités de service dans un camp d'été chrétien, M. Keefe se sentit interpellé par le Québec. Dès lors, il y servit le Seigneur, et ce jusqu'à sa mort. Sauvé par la foi, repêché pour la mission.

Très aimé de tous, Ernest Keefe était un homme de paix. La qualité de son caractère chrétien ne faisait pas de doute. M Keefe était, comme Bill Philips, un médiateur qui savait quoi faire dans des situations de crises d'Église pour toucher le problème sans attaquer directement les personnes. Il avait un cœur de berger, doux et tendre. Ce pionnier n'était pas pour autant mou! Lorsqu'une de ses brebis était en danger, M. Keefe intervenait vigoureusement auprès des autorités catholiques. Il sut défendre plusieurs familles québécoises opprimées. Il était un fonceur, tant dans la mission qu'au hockey. Par exemple, M. Keefe défendit avec brio la cause de Lionel Gosselin, victime de discrimination religieuse à Asbestos. Il savait trouver les bons mots pour résoudre les dilemmes.

La perspective d'un élève est qu'il vaut mieux avoir un professeur fondé dans la Parole que dans ses paroles. Ernest Keefe était un homme de parole, de la Parole. Pour régler les problèmes des Églises où il était envoyé, il ouvrait la Parole. Pour former les étudiants dans la vérité, il ouvrait la Parole. Pour réfléchir aux enjeux modernes du mouvement évangélique, il ouvrait la Parole. Pour encourager les frères, il ouvrait la Parole. Pour nourrir son âme, il ouvrait la Parole. Les différentes bibles qu'il a laissées derrière lui témoignent d'une interaction certaine, fréquente, et multilinguistique avec la Bible.

Le contexte québécois du début de son ministère était difficile. L'Église catholique avait main mise sur toutes les dimensions de la vie québécoise. La persécution était vive et l'opposition constante. C'est probablement ce qui a mené M. Keefe à étudier le catholicisme dans ses études supérieures. En effet, à cette époque, Sembeq ne comptait aucun professeur qualifié dans ses rangs et devait inviter des enseignants de l'extérieur. Voulant répondre à ce besoin, il décida de partir à Grand-Rapids pour parfaire son don d'enseignant, voulant ajouter à Sembeq une profondeur théologique. Ainsi, il vendit tous ses biens pour aller se faire former. M Keefe fut enseignant, écrivain et théologien. Le cours du livre de l'épitre aux Romains fut son « dada » principal. Il rédigea de la littérature pour l'évangélisation, ainsi qu'un populaire cahier de formation pour disciples, « Le maître et son disciple ».

La perspective d'un collègue est qu'il vaut mieux servir le Seigneur que de se servir de lui. Ernest Keefe fut un homme totalement engagé dans la mission, comme en témoigne son parcours. Plus qu'un enseignant, il était un évangéliste. Passionné d'évangélisation, il avait toujours des traités dans ses poches. Ainsi, il avait constamment dans sa veste de la littérature évangélique, même à son mariage. Son implication pour l'Évangile rencontrait cependant beaucoup d'opposition. Par exemple, à Coaticook en 1957, M. Keefe et d'autres pasteurs baptistes furent « baptisés » dans une fontaine publique alors qu'ils tentaient de prêcher l'Évangile.

Il va sans dire que l'eau ne les empêcha pas de poursuivre la proclamation de la Parole! Plus tard, M. Keefe fut arrêté pour avoir distribué des bibles à Asbestos-Danville. Malgré tout, il persévéra pendant douze ans et y implanta même une Église. M. Keefe visita personnellement toute la région d'Asbestos, une maison à la fois. Partant de chez lui avec son lunch, comme un ouvrier, il visitait du matin au soir les foyers de la région. Il avait une mémoire incroyable pour se souvenir des détails de ses visites (le nom des gens, les caractéristiques des maisons, etc.) Ernest et son épouse Betty œuvrèrent également à Trois-Rivières, à Montréal, et dans plusieurs autres régions au Canada français. Le détail et l'étendue de son ministère se trouvent dans les pages de ce livre.

«Notre Église ne nous enseigne pas le chemin vers le ciel, mais ce jeune homme semble avoir la réponse. J'ai peur qu'il soit déjà parti dans une autre ville pour donner ses bibles et que nous mourions sans connaitre le chemin vers le ciel.» — Octave Tellier, Québécois non converti de 72 ans, au sujet de M. Keefe.

«Combien d'Octave Tellier au Québec attendent que quelqu'un leur montre le chemin vers le ciel?»

– Ernest Keefe

La perspective d'un professeur d'histoire est qu'il vaut mieux laisser à Dieu le soin de déterminer quel sera notre impact dans l'histoire. Ernest Keefe ne cherchait pas les honneurs. À plus d'une reprise, il a travaillé dans l'ombre, dans la pauvreté, dans l'opposition. Cependant, dans l'équipe du Seigneur pour le Québec, M. Keefe a été un jouer qui a pris position, et qui a tenu sa position. C'est par son témoignage que Jacques Alexanian, qui cherchait la direction du Seigneur pour sa vie, a été repêché pour le Québec. Ce dernier entendit à la radio le message de M. Keefe, qui plaidait pour le Québec. Les deux hommes allèrent manger ensemble et M. Keefe invita Jacques à venir passer quelque temps au Québec. L'histoire se poursuivit. Dans son ministère à Asbestos, M. Keefe prit M. Lionel Gosselin afin de le former pour l'aider dans son ministère. Il utilisa l'Épitre de Tite comme fondement. Le coaching d'alors était différent, mais l'Intention de former y était déjà une valeur de notre association d'Églises. M. Keefe a laissé un impact dans de nombreux étudiants fondés dans la Parole, de nombreux disciples ayant établi leurs bases grâce à son guide de formation, de nombreux collègues ayant vu son zèle, de nombreuses Églises devant leur santé ou leur restauration à cet homme, de nombreux canadiens ou américains ayant été sensibilisés à la cause du Québec, de nombreuses personnes ayant connu le salut par la foi en Jésus-Christ. Gloire à Dieu d'avoir envoyé ce joueur de premier trio, un compteur naturel qui respectait le livre de jeu, qui travaillait en équipe, et qui était sur la glace pour défendre le Québec en désavantage numérique.

La perspective de Stéphane est qu'il vaut mieux lire la biographie de M. Keefe que n'importe quel livre de sport, d'histoire, de cuisine ou de voyage. Car dans un tel ouvrage se trouve l'expression de la sagesse de Dieu, sa bonté et sa miséricorde au travers d'un simple homme, dans une simple province, avec de simples québécois. Cette carrière nous permet de constater ce que peut faire le divin coach dans la vie d'un jouer qui suit le plan de Dieu.

L'écriture de ce livre était d'une grande importance pour M. Keefe. Il y a travaillé pendant plusieurs années. J'ai vu les nombreux documents, les coupures de journaux, les annotations personnelles dans des livres spécialisés, tout cela dans un souci de rigueur et de précision. En fait, cet ouvrage ne représente qu'une portion de la rédaction totale que M. Keefe a effectuée, une œuvre littéraire de près de 1000 pages. M. Keefe était tellement préoccupé par l'avenir de l'Évangile au Québec qu'il ne voulait pas que nous oubliions d'où nous venons, et quels avaient été les combats de ces pionniers de l'Évangile. Il était si détaché de lui-même que ce qui devait être la rédaction de sa biographie s'est développé en histoire du contexte social et religieux du Québec dans la mouvance du concile catholique de Vatican II. La présente biographie est donc tirée de ses propres écrits. Elle a été retravaillée pour faciliter la lecture de la vie de cet homme courageux et généreux. C'est notre façon, à tous ceux qui ont travaillé sur ce livre et à tous ceux qui ont côtoyé M. Keefe, de rendre grâce à Dieu en l'honorant.

«Aucun trophée et honneur dans le sport ne peut se comparer avec la joie d'amener une âme à Christ, spécialement quand on le voit entrer dans l'Éternité.»

– Ernest Keefe, suite au décès de M. Octave Tellier.

*Pasteur Stéphane Gagné*

# APPENDIX C

Commande de DVDs
## Les pionniers de l'Évangile
## au Québec

| Nom : | |
|---|---|
| Adresse postale : | |
| | |
| | |
| | |

| DVD | Quantité | Coût (poste et manutention inclus) | Total |
|---|---|---|---|
| Survol de l'œuvre des pionniers (Compilation) | | 20$ | |
| Jacques Alexanian | | 20$ | |
| Élisée Beau | | 20$ | |
| Gabriel Cotnoir | | 20$ | |
| Lionel Gosselin | | 20$ | |
| Ernest Keefe | | 20$ | |
| Leçons d'objets qui touchent le cœur, par Murray Heron | | 20$ | |
| Jan Gazdik (à venir) | | (à venir) | |
| Murray Heron (à venir) | | (à venir) | |
| Lorne Heron (à venir) | | (à venir) | |
| Newton McKenzie (à venir) | | (à venir) | |
| Bill Phillips (à venir) | | (à venir) | |
| William Frey (à venir) | | (à venir) | |
| Yvon Hurtubise (à venir) | | (à venir) | |
| Don au comité historique | | | |
| | **Grand total** | | |

Veuillez rédiger votre chèque à l'ordre de

## A.E.B.E.Q

et poster à

**AEBEQ / Littérature**

9780 rue Sherbrooke Est, Montréal, QC   H1L 1N6

**Paiement par carte de crédit**      MasterCard \_\_\_\_      VISA\_\_\_\_

Nom (tel qu'il se trouve sur la carte de crédit) :

Numéro de carte :

Date d'expiration :

Signature: